Microprocessors in
Instruments and Control

Microprocessors in Instruments and Control

Robert J. Bibbero

Process Control Division
Honeywell Inc.

A Wiley-Interscience Publication

JOHN WILEY & SONS, New York / London / Sydney / Toronto

Library of Congress Cataloging in Publication Data:

Bibbero, Robert J.
    Microprocessors in instruments and control.

    "A Wiley-Interscience publication."
    Includes bibliographical references and index.
    1. Microprocessors.   2. Electronic instruments.
3. Automatic control.   I. Title.

TK7895.M5B5   001.6′4   77-9929
ISBN 0-471-01595-4

Printed in the United States of America

10 9 8 7 6 5 4 3

To Lillian,
sine qua non

Preface

Microprocessors are the newest and most rapidly ascending stars in the computer galaxy. With annual growth rates above 100% since their introduction in 1971, microprocessor and microcomputer shipments have long exceeded those of their larger and more costly counterparts combined—general purpose computers and minicomputers.

But the main thrust of the microprocessor is not felt in its rivalry with traditional computers and tasks, but in its ubiquitous applications. As many as 70% of the more recent models will be used in new applications. The microprocessor's miniature size—it occupies no more space than one or two conventional components—and its low cost permit it to infiltrate all manner of host devices, instruments, and machines, like a benign virus, giving them entirely new dimensions of sophisticated capability. For many of these advanced applications, the incorporation of larger computers would be so complex as to be absurd. For others, cost restrictions have up to now been too stringent to permit their general use.

Even a random sampling of applications for the microprocessor reveals its protean utility:

Automobiles
Atomic absorption spectrometers
Batching systems
Chromatographs
Games
Machine tools
Medical equipment
Microwave ovens
Process controllers
Point-of-sales terminals
Robot arms
Word processors

What new capabilities justify the design and development effort of the incorporation of a microprocessor into a system? One example, an automotive microprocessor, can regulate the fuel-air mixture and ignition timing with unprecedented precision and speed, so as to optimize gasoline consumption dynamically over the entire driving range while remaining within the rigorous constraints of air pollution control requirements. The same microprocessor, time shared, may have enough capacity to control antiskid braking, and even the logic of door locks and theft prevention devices. For this capability the carmaker will pay less than $100, including the sensors.

In a simpler application, the microprocessor acts as a controller for a microwave oven. It adapts the control parameters to the sequential functions of defrosting, browning, and cooking, functioning as a conventional timer in the last stage. Even video games, the modern equivalents of pinball or Japan's pachinko machines, use the microprocessor to implement the logic, eliminating mechanical and discrete electronic parts. The logic can then be made far more complex, as suited to home games which will be used again and again by the same people. As an added bonus, the entire game can be changed by reprogramming, accomplished merely by exchanging a plug-in read-only memory (ROM) or tape cassette memory.

There is a dearth of authentic definitions in this field, but let us try to define a few terms, or at least bound them, in order to describe the scope of this book. A *microprocessor* includes all the elements of a conventional computer central processing unit, specifically arithmetic, logic, and control, but contains them all on a single large scale integrated (LSI) chip, or at most two or three chips. There are *discrete microprocessors* in use employing individual logic elements, but these are either special purpose devices or interim stages toward an LSI design, so we will in general disregard them. As a consequence of their LSI character, microprocessors are small, cheap, and complex. The active portion of a typical one-chip processor (Texas Instrument TMS-1000) is 0.2 in. square; prices range from a few hundred to less than $100 each (and are heading below the $10 level); complexity is in the tens of thousands of transistors per chip—over 100,000 for a board-mounted microcomputer complete with memory and an input/output interface.

We use the term "microprocessor" to refer to the chip level components, even though they may contain most of the elements of a complete computer. The word "microcomputer" is taken here to mean an entire computer, capable of interfacing with peripherals such as a teletypewriter and disk or tape storage and using a microprocessor element. Thus a microcomputer is generally a board-mounted collection of LSI chips, from several up to a hundred, including memory and interface components.

Most microprocessors are controlled through a stored program kept within a ROM. The ROM is a regular LSI component, mounted on the board, which gives the microprocessor its individual functional capability. In large scale usage the ROM is programmed for the particular task and produced in that configuration by the same mass production techniques used in making other LSI components. On a smaller scale, programmable ROMs (PROMS) are employed. They can be individually programmed after manufacture, usually by means of a tape produced by a larger computer, but from then on act in a read-only capacity. In distinction, general purpose computers are programmed through a keyboard or cards—the program is then read into a volatile core memory or transferred between disk and core until the processing task is complete. It is then erased or stored off-line on disk, cards, or tape.

If the microprocessor program is a built-in component, the entire assembly becomes a dedicated and special purpose device (albeit a great deal of flexibility and adaptation can be incorporated into the program). Although some microcomputers can be programmed through conventional keyboards and tape or card readers, they then become a species of general purpose computer, in effect, minicomputers.

We are not concerned with the general-purpose programmed data processing uses of microcomputers in this book. What we investigate is the dedicated special-purpose uses of the microprocessor in combination with a *host*. The host may be a machine, an analytic laboratory instrument, or a process controller. We are concerned with the *real time* control of the host, not only in the production of printed data, although data (reports) may be a valuable if not the only valuable output of the combination. By real time operation we mean that the computation and control tasks of the processor occur rapidly enough to permit or even improve the normal dynamic operation of the host device. Generally, the microprocessor as controller replaces an electronic analog or mechanical function which defines the scale of real time.

It is also clear that the dedicated microprocessor, using a ROM, is not *user programmed*. The ROM is either manufactured for the original equipment manufacturer (OEM) or created by him from a PROM. The user has operating options and choices but is not concerned with software. The OEM must create the programs that encompass all logical functions desired by the end user and convert them to ROM. Thus, if the user wishes to convert to a new program, the OEM must create a new ROM and retrofit it to the user's processor (which may involve merely exchanging a plug-in component).

However, the options offered to the user (and allowed by the ROM program) may be so extensive that a form of user programming is called for. These programs can be entered into a random access memory (RAM) by dedicated switches or pushbuttons, all of which are defined by the original ROM program. Thus user control of a microprocessor device may be made as simple or as complex as needed. The RAM chips, being usually semiconductor (transistor flip-flop) storage, are "volatile"; that is, the user program will be lost if power is shut down. If this is critical, special provisions (such as cassette tape storage) can be used to preserve the user program.

With regard to this book, its *raison d'etre* is the interdisciplinary nature of the instrument-control microprocessor field. This is not a book about microcomputers or their fabrication and design—many excellent works have already been published on these subjects. It is about the microprocessor-host relationship—how they should be mated and interfaced and what must be known and employed to launch the combination successfully.

In particular, we are concerned with the broad field of instruments and industrial control systems incorporating microcomputers—fields involving moderate to high volume usage of a particular dedicated ROM or PROM program. Extremely large consumer applications, such as automobiles, ovens, and appliances, may require special techniques for device fabrication and programming, which are not covered here.

This book is intended for both users and designers of instruments and controls and those who seek such new applications or markets for microprocessors. It will be useful to medical, chemical, and biological laboratory instrument users and manufacturers, process control engineers and those who develop control systems, those responsible for new markets and applications of microprocessors and semiconductor products, research scientists, students, technicians, and laboratory workers.

The book first introduces the elements of instrumentation and control, with particular regard to the dynamics and computational instrumentation required to accomplish real-time data processing tasks. Next, it demonstrates the tools for digital computation and shows the capability of microprocessors to perform the necessary functions. Since dynamic control is an important feature of the applications with which we are concerned, the development of control algorithms and programs is discussed.

This background is intended to be self-contained and tutorial, leading into the applications of subsequent chapters. These contain specific examples, including the mating of microprocessors with simple analytical instruments, a more complex laboratory analytic instrument, an industrial process controller, and a complete multiprocessor control system equipped with data communication and interface equipment. The examples are supported by a coverage of microprocessor hardware architecture and technology, and of the all-important software aspects, to help the reader understand the logic behind the application architecture.

This book should be of help to all those who must work in and contribute to the industrial, scientific, and technical world that will be dominated by a yearly production of millions of microprocessors.

ROBERT J. BIBBERO

Fort Washington, Pennsylvania
May 1977

Acknowledgments

I am indebted to Renzo Dallimonti of the Fort Washington, Pa., Process Control Division of Honeywell, Inc. (PCD/FW) for permission to use much of his excellent tutorial material on process control fundamentals and for his patient explanations, to Alan Kegg of PCD/FW for encouraging me to learn microprocessor software programming and for his contributions to Chapters 7 and 8, and to Ed Rang of the Honeywell Corporate Research Center for his assistance and permission to use his original work in the development of difficult algorithms. I appreciate the time spent by Eugene Manno and his associates in the PCD/FW engineering department, especially A. Demark, M. Sklaroff, R. Metarko, and C. Farmer, for patiently checking these chapters, although I retain full responsibility for any errors or omissions that may remain. I thank George Reed and his excellent art crew and Veronica Saboe, all of Honeywell, for their unstinting cooperation in producing the illustrations and typing the manuscript, respectively. And I am of course grateful to the management of Honeywell and PCD/FW for permission to publish this work and to use material developed at Fort Washington for microprocessor applications. Finally, I wish to thank my chapter contributors, Alexander B. Sidline and Stanley T. Zawadowicz (president of Datalab, Inc.) for their excellent work.

R. J. B.

Contents

Microprocessors in
Instruments and Control

One

Static and Dynamic Calculations for Instruments

The object of this chapter is to survey the range of static and dynamic computational tasks encountered in measurement and control instrumentation that can employ a microprocessor for their solution.

Nearly all instruments and controller systems are basically continuous (analog) in nature; therefore we first consider the manipulations of quantities in analog form. Later we consider their translation into digital quantities and operations.

Basically, we are concerned with three entities, each of which can be represented mathematically as a group of static and dynamic properties. These are the *process* (any physical quantity that can vary, such as the level of fluid in a tank), the *measuring instrument*, and, if the system is controlled, the *controller*. They can be represented by three blocks, comprising a *block diagram* of the system (Fig. 1.1).

Each block represents in abstract form the static and dynamic quantities with which we are concerned, approximated to some degree appropriate to the problem. If the instrumentation is considered ideal, that is, having perfect dynamic properties, it is often omitted from the block diagram. The arrows represent signals or information interconnecting the blocks and determining the *configuration* of the system, which may be open loop (solid lines) or fed back into a closed loop (dashed lines).

The kinds of instrumentation employed in laboratories and in industry have an almost infinite variety, and we make no attempt to enumerate

1

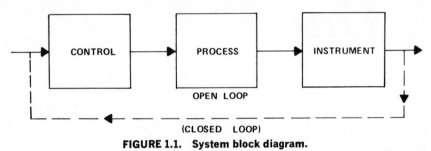

FIGURE 1.1. System block diagram.

them here. (In later chapters, we describe some specific instrumentation in detail, so as to show how they can utilize a microprocessor.) Quantities commonly measured and controlled in industrial or laboratory situations include physical properties such as the following:

Temperature
Pressure
Level of liquid
Flow rate
Density
Weight or mass
Viscosity
Humidity or moisture control
Vibrational frequency and amplitude
Speed
Proximity or displacement

Also included are physicochemical properties relating to analysis or chemical composition:

Heat of combustion
Thermal conductivity
pH
Electrical conductivity
Magnetic properties
Infrared or ultraviolet absorption and emission
Mass spectrum (mass spectroscopy)
Diffusion coefficient (chromatography)

The numbers and kinds of these instruments, especially laboratory types, are being constantly added to, although those accepted in industry

for control purposes are relatively fewer and more static. Most of them
have been well described in the literature.[1,2]

In any event, we are not so much concerned in this chapter with the
measuring device (*transducer*) as we are with the signal it produces. In all
cases of interest to us this must ultimately become an electrical signal so
that it can be digitized and entered into a digital computer. Therefore we
consider only the electrical signal and how it relates to or differs from the
physical quantities it represents. Most often in modern instrumentation
the signal is electrical to begin with, such as the output of a thermocouple
or electrical bridge circuit. In cases where it is not, a pneumatic or hydraulic
quantity, for example, the signal to be processed by a computer must be
converted by means of a transmitter to an electrical quantity. The P/I or
pressure-to-current transmitter is a case in point—it can convert an absolute
of differential pressure to a current signal by some means such as a strain
gage bridge or force balance (servo) system.

Signal Conditioning

Several static operations are normally performed on signals before they
are suitable for further processing—these are generally lumped under
the heading "signal conditioning," although there is not universal agreement on the meaning of this term. We take it to mean those operations
involving static manipulation of the signal. (In this we vary from the common practice of including *noise filtering* as signal conditioning, since
filtering, or separation by frequency content, is essentially a dynamic
operation.)

The initial conditioning operation (excluding filtering) is then *signal
conversion*, that is, the standardization of all signals to fit a common format.
To accommodate subsequent signal processing equipment, this is generally
a standard voltage range, such as 1 to 5 or 0 to 10 V dc. That is, zero
signal is represented by 1 V (or 0) and a maximum by 5 V (or 10).

Many industrial instruments and transmitters, such as the P/I just
mentioned, output a current signal of 4 to 20 mA dc. A precision dropping
resistor and appropriate offset or zero adjustment where needed can convert
this current to the desired voltage format.

Linearization is required for many kinds of signals. A most common
need is to linearize thermocouple signals. A limited variety of thermocouples
is used in industry and can be calibrated to a standard conversion formula
(millivolts output versus temperature) against primary standards originating
at the U. S. National Bureau of Standards. Extracts from such a typical
conversion for a type-T (copper-constantan) thermocouple are given in

TABLE 1.1.   Type-T Copper-Constantan Thermocouple*

°F	Millivolts	Slope, millivolts/°F
750	20.805	
		0.03384
650	17.421	
		0.03264
550	14.157	
		0.03127
450	11.030	
		0.02966
350	8.064	
		0.02784
250	5.280	
		0.02569
150	2.711	
		0.02180
50	0.389	
		0.02043
−50	−1.654	
		0.01726
−150	−3.380	
		0.01367
−250	−4.747	
		0.01074
−300	−5.284	

* Reference temperature, 32°F.

Table 1.1. Note that the output in millivolts (second column) is highly nonlinear, especially at the lower end, with respect to temperature. If a voltage output linear with temperature is wanted to display or for digital conversion, a compensating function of the form shown in Fig. 1.2 is required. This can be constructed of several short segments, as shown, each segment obeying a linear law:

$$Y = MX + C \qquad (1.1)$$

where Y = linearized input or process variable (PV)
M = gradient or slope of linearizing curve
X = raw PV
C = offset

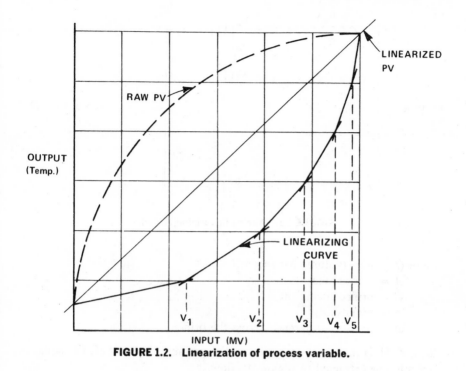

FIGURE 1.2. Linearization of process variable.

The resultant of the raw *PV* and the compensation curve is a straight line.

Again with reference to Table 1.1, the slopes *M* in (1.1) can be obtained from column 3, which is merely the average slope between temperatures.

One way of constructing such a compensating function using analog electronic components is shown in Fig. 1.3. The bias voltages V_n are adjusted so that the diodes become conductive in proper sequence as the input rises, adding their resistances to the parallel circuit. Any monotonic curve can be approximated this way, the accuracy depending primarily on how many segments (diode-resistor branches) are included. Each thermocouple type requires a separate linearizer. There are several other linearizing methods having advantages in precision or cost, but we do not describe them here because our interest is in the function, not the analog implementation.

Another important linearization device is the square root extractor. This task is necessary because many, if not most, industrial flow measuring instruments incorporate an orifice. The fluid flow through a submerged orifice is measured by the differential pressure between the two sides:

$$Q = CA \sqrt{2g\,\Delta h} \tag{1.2}$$

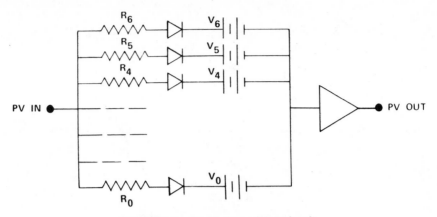

FIGURE 1.3.   Analog linearizing circuit.

where Q = flow (volume per second)
      A = orifice area
      C = orifice coefficient
      g = gravity
     Δh = pressure difference across the orifice

Thus, if Δh is measured by a differential pressure transmitter, the square root must be extracted to obtain the flow.

This can be accomplished with the same kind of analog circuit shown in Fig. 1.3. With three segments (diodes) the accuracy is $\pm 2\%$, it is about $\pm 1\%$ with five segments, and about $\pm 0.5\%$ with 15.[3]

Often better accuracy than this is wanted and, with increasing accuracy, the number of components and cost rise rapidly. As can be seen from (1.1), this task can be readily accomplished by numerical methods. Slope values such as those of Table 1.1 need only be stored and substituted into (1.1), switching from one to another as the input changes. A digital computer can perform this task to any reasonable degree of accuracy—tables of 64 segments are commonly stored, resulting in accuracies substantially better than 0.1%.

Once a signal has been linearized, it is necessary to establish the *span* and *zero*. The span is merely the range of the process variable, minimum to maximum, that is equivalent to the range of the normal standardized system input. For example, we could say that the PV range 150 to 650°F for a type-T thermocouple is equivalent to the standard range of 1 to 5 V for a particular instrumentation system. This means that the gain of the TC linearizer must be adjusted to give 1 V at a 2.711 mV input and 5 V for 17.421 mV, and produce an output linear with temperature between these values. The span is then 500°F (650 − 150), and the zero is offset to 150°F.

When the signal has been normalized and the span and zero established, *limits* can be established to trigger *alarms*. That is, the normalized *PV* can be compared with a preset voltage equivalent to the alarm *PV* value and set to close a relay when this is reached.

Both high and low limits are employed—these can be used to turn on and off apparatus, alarm lights, horns, and the like.

Many other algebraic functions are commonly performed on analog instrument signals for industrial or control purposes. Devices accomplishing these functions are often called *auxiliaries*, a term which is also applied to some of the signal conditioning functions already described. Before turning to these, an important thermocouple correction term should be mentioned—the *isothermal correction*. It is needed since the thermocouple millivolt output represents only the difference between the measuring and reading ends. For tables like Table 1.1 to be applied, the reading (reference) end temperature should be at the ice point (32°F). Since it usually is not, a correction can be made by algebraically adding the millivolts corresponding to the reference function temperature.

In industrial practice, thermocouples are commonly referenced to an isothermal (metal) block whose temperature is monitored by a precise, independent device, for example, a platinum resistance thermometer bulb (see Fig. 1.4). The corrected temperature is then computed by an expression of the form

$$T_{corr} = A + \frac{E_o}{E_1}\left(B + C\,\frac{E_o}{E_1}\right) \tag{1.3}$$

where A, B, and C = parameters of the particular instrumentation

E_o and E_1 = bridge output and reference voltages, respectively

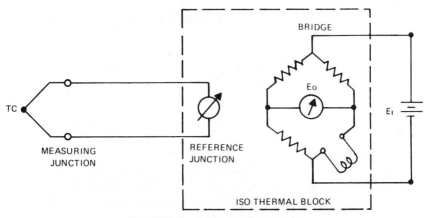

FIGURE 1.4. Isothermal correction.

Auxiliaries

Typical analog computing auxiliaries required in conventional industrial control and measurement systems can be understood with reference to the above-mentioned functions. In addition, there are many algebraic expressions that must be computed from measured variables in order to derive new quantities, such as Btu, efficiency, and other generally unmeasurable states of the process. These are known as *derived quantities,* and the expressions from which they are computed can often be considered *static mathematical models* of the process or portions of it. Mathematical models of this type are considered at greater length later on. At this time, the point is merely made that to effect them we often require multiplication, division, square root, and similar elementary operations of algebra.

Typical analog auxiliaries function as follows:

1. *Low Range MV/I*

    INPUT: millivolt or thermocouple signals, types J, K, T, E, Y, R, S, and B

    SPAN: 2 to 100 mV adjustment

    ZERO: −55 to +25 mV

    OUTPUT: 4 to 20 mA

    SPECIAL: cold junction compensation; burnout protection

Note: Burnout protection ensures that a thermocouple in a control circuit will "fail safe," that is, go off scale on the high end if the thermocouple burns out, rather than give a false low signal (0 mV) calling for more heat. Refer to Fig. 1.5. Assume a thermocouple and leads having a resistance AB of 1 ohm and a measuring circuit G with a shunt resistance R_1 of 500 ohms. The burnout circuit is voltage source V of 1 V and R_2 of 5000 ohms in series across the TC. When the TC is operating, the bucking voltage caused by V is $1/(5000 + 1) = 0.0002$ or 0.2 mV. This is equivalent

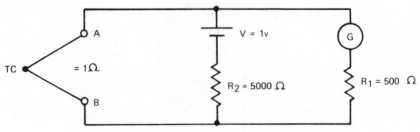

FIGURE 1.5.   Thermocouple burnout protection.

to a 0.7°F shift of copper-constantan at 200°F and can be compensated for by adjusting the zero. Now assume that *TC* opens. The voltage appearing at *G* is then 500/(5000 + 500) = 0.091 or 91 mV. This is off-scale for a type-T thermocouple (over 750°F).

2. *High Range MV/I*
INPUT: millivolt or J, K, T, E, R, S thermocouples
SPAN: 10 to 50 mV
ZERO: −10 to +10 mV

3. *R/I*
INPUT: resistance bulb or RTD
SPAN: 5 to 600 ohms
ZERO: 0 to 400 ohms
OUTPUT: 4 to 20 mA
SPECIAL: leadwire resistance compensation

Note: The temperature coefficient of a platinum resistance bulb is 0.00392 ohm/ohm°C.

4. *Square Root Extractor*
INPUT: 1 to 5 V dc
OUTPUT: 1 to 5 V dc
EQUATION: $V_o = 2\sqrt{V_i - 1} + 1$

5. *Multiplier-Divider*
INPUT: two or three signals, 1 to 5 V dc (V_A, V_B, V_C)
OUTPUT: one signal, 1 to 5 V dc (V_o)
EQUATION:
$$(a)\ V_o = \frac{K_o (K_A V_A + a)(K_B V_B + b)}{K_C V_C + c} + 1$$

Note: K_o, K_A, K_B, K_C; a, b, and c are adjustable parameters.

$$(b)\ V_o = \frac{K_o}{4}(K_A V_A + a)^2 + 1$$

$$(c)\ V_o = \frac{K_o}{4}(K_A V_A + a)(K_B V_B + b) + 1$$

$$(d)\ V_o = 4K_o \frac{(K_A V_A + a)}{K_C V_C + c} + 1$$

$$(e) \quad V_o = K_o \frac{(K_A V_A + a)^2}{K_C C + c} + 1$$

$$(f) \quad V_o = 2K_o \sqrt{K_A V_A + a} + 1$$

$$(g) \quad V_o = K_o \sqrt{(K_A V_A + a)(K_B V_B + b)} + 1$$

6. *Signal Isolator*

INPUT: 1 to 5 V dc

OUTPUT: 4 to 20 mA (isolated)

7. *Signal Selector, Scale, and Bias*

INPUT: two, three, or four inputs, 1 to 5 V dc. Each has variable scale K_1 and bias K_2.

OUTPUT: 1 to 5 V dc each input or 4 to 20 mA (one input only)

EQUATION: $V_o - 1 = K_1(V_i - 1) + K_2$; K_1 variable 0 to 4 V and K_2 variable -4 to $+4$ V

SIGNAL SELECT

OUTPUT: set to highest or lowest of each unit

SCALE AND

BIAS OUTPUT: same as in above equation for each input

8. *Signal Limiter*

INPUT: 1 to 5 V dc

OUTPUT: 1 to 5 V dc or 4 to 20 mA.

Output is limited at high or low preset values variable between 0 and 100% of full scale

9. *Single Alarm*

INPUT: 1 to 5 V dc

OUTPUT: alarm (solid state closed circuit for relay) if input greater (or less) than adjustable set point

SET POINT: 0 to 100% full scale

DEADBAND: A deadband around the set point of a 0 to 10% span may be set without affecting the set point.

10. *Dual Alarm*

Same as item 9 but has two outputs; either may be set as a high or low alarm. Two separate set points are provided.

11. *Adder-Subtractor*

   INPUT: four inputs, 1 to 5 V dc

   OUTPUT: 1 to 5 V dc

EQUATION: $V_o - 1 = \pm K_1(V_1 - 1) \pm K_2(V_2 - 1) \pm K_3(V_3 - 1) \pm K_4(V_4 - 1)$; K_1 to K_4 may vary from 0 to 2; K_5 varies from -0.5 to 8 V. Maximum output $= 16$ V

12. *Linear Integrator*

   INPUT: 1 to 5 V dc

   OUTPUT: count rate; adjustable full scale 60 to 50,000 counts/hr

INTEGRATOR

   OUTPUT: transistor closure to 0 V capable of driving external 25 V dc counter

13. *Square Root Integrator*

   INPUT: same as item 12

   OUTPUT: count rate proportional to $\sqrt{E_i - 1}$; also $E_o - 1 = 2\sqrt{E_i - 1}$ (1 to 5 V dc)

Table 1.2, extracted from the Scientific Apparatus Makers Association (SAMA) standard[4] on functional diagraming of instrument and control systems, is a summary and definition of the kinds of signal processing recognized by industry.

Signal Dynamics

Important as they are, algebraic and other static calculations are only one portion of the total computational tasks demanded of microprocessors used in instrumentation and industrial control. Nearly all processes and measurements have associated with them time delays and lags as a result of inertial effects and the finite velocity of signals or transportation of process materials. Delays associated with signal velocity are independent of the nature of the signal (its waveshape or frequency content); these are known as *transportation delays* or *dead time*. Inertial effects—those associated with energy storage, including thermal and electrical as well as mechanical energy—give rise to time lags dependent on signal or process variable frequency. The variation of signal lag with frequency is termed *phase shift*. For a regular periodic signal, such as a sine wave, a delay time equal to one complete period of the wave equals a phase shift of 360°; a delay equal to a half period, equivalent to a reversal in sign of the

TABLE 1.2. Signal Processing Systems

FUNCTION SYMBOL	MATH EQUATION *	GRAPHIC REPRESENTATION *	DEFINITION
SUMMING Σ	$m = X_1 + X_2 + \; + X_n$		The output equals the algebraic sum of the inputs.
AVERAGING Σ/n	$m = \dfrac{X_1 + X_2 + \; + X_n}{n}$		The output equals the algebraic sum of the inputs divided by the number of inputs.
DIFFERENCE Δ	$m = X_1 - X_2$		The output equals the algebraic difference between the two inputs.
PROPORTIONAL K OR P	$m = Kx$		The output is directly proportional to the input.
INTEGRAL $\int$ OR I	$m = \dfrac{1}{T_I} \int x\,dt$		The output varies in accordance with both magnitude and duration of the input. The output is proportional to the time integral of the input.

Function	Equation		Description
DERIVATIVE d/dt or D	$m = T_0 \dfrac{dX}{dt}$		The output is proportional to the rate of change (derivative) of the input.
MULTIPLYING ×	$m = X_1 X_2$		The output equals the product of the two inputs.
DIVIDING ÷	$m = \dfrac{X_1}{X_2}$		The output equals the quotient of the two inputs.
ROOT EXTRACTION √	$m = \sqrt{X}$		The output equals the root (i.e., square root, fourth root, 3/2 root, etc.) of the input.
EXPONENTIAL X^n	$m = X^n$		The output equals the input raised to a power (i.e., second, third, fourth, etc.).
NONLINEAR OR UNSPECIFIED FUNCTION f (X)	$m = f(X)$		The output equals some nonlinear function of the input.

TABLE 1.2. (*Continued*)

FUNCTION SYMBOL	MATH EQUATION	GRAPHIC REPRESENTATION	DEFINITION
TIME FUNCTION $f(t)$	$m = X\,f(t)$ $m = f(t)$		The output equals the input times some function of time or equals some function of time alone.
HIGH SELECTING $>$	$m = \begin{cases} x_1 \text{ FOR } x_1 \geq x_2 \\ x_2 \text{ FOR } x_1 \leq x_2 \end{cases}$		The output is equal to that input which is the greatest of the inputs.
LOW SELECTING $<$	$m = \begin{cases} x_1 \text{ FOR } x_1 \leq x_2 \\ x_2 \text{ FOR } x_1 \geq x_2 \end{cases}$		The output is equal to that input which is the least of the inputs.
HIGH LIMITING $\curlywedge$	$m = \begin{cases} x \text{ FOR } x \leq H \\ H \text{ FOR } x \geq H \end{cases}$		The output equals the input or the high limit value whichever is lower.

Function	Equation	Graph	Description
LOW LIMITING ⋏	$m = \begin{cases} X & \text{FOR } X \geq L \\ L & \text{FOR } X \leq L \end{cases}$		The output equals the input or the low limit value whichever is higher.
REVERSE PROPORTIONAL $-K$ OR $-P$	$m = -KX$		The output is reversely proportional to the input.
VELOCITY LIMITER V⋗	$\dfrac{dm}{dt} = \dfrac{dx}{dt} \begin{cases} \dfrac{dx}{dt} \leq H \text{ AND} \\ m = x \end{cases}$ $\dfrac{dm}{dt} = H \begin{cases} \dfrac{dx}{dt} \geq H \text{ OR} \\ m \neq x \end{cases}$		The output equals the input as long as the rate of change of the input does not exceed a limit value. The output will change at the rate established by this limit until the output again equals the input.
BIAS $+,\ -,$ OR $\pm$	$m = x \pm b$		The output equals the input plus (or minus) some arbitrary value (bias).

TABLE 1.2. (Continued)

FUNCTION SYMBOL	MATH EQUATION	GRAPHIC REPRESENTATION	DEFINITION
ANALOG SIGNAL GENERATOR A	$m = A$	DOES NOT APPLY	The output is an analog signal developed within the generator.
TRANSFER T	$m = \begin{cases} X_1 \text{ FOR STATE 1} \\ X_2 \text{ FOR STATE 2} \end{cases}$		The output equals the input which has been selected by transfer. The state of the transfer is established by external means.
SIGNAL MONITOR H/	STATE 1 $X \leq H$ STATE 2 (ENERGIZED OR ALARM STATE) $X > H$		The output has discrete states which are dependent on the value of the input. When the input exceeds (or becomes less than) an arbitrary limit value the output changes state.
/L	STATE 1 (ENERGIZED OR ALARM STATE) $X < L$ STATE 2 $X \geq L$		
H/L	STATE 1 (FIRST OUTPUT m_1 ENERGIZED OR ALARM STATE) $X < H.L$ STATE 2 (SECOND OUTPUT m_2 ENERGIZED OR ALARM STATE) $X > H.L$		

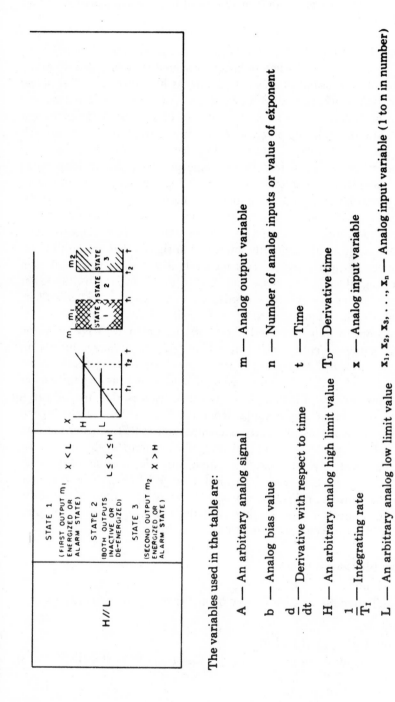

H//L	STATE 1 (FIRST OUTPUT m_1 ENERGIZED OR ALARM STATE)	$X < L$
	STATE 2 (BOTH OUTPUTS INACTIVE OR DE-ENERGIZED)	$L \leq X \leq H$
	STATE 3 (SECOND OUTPUT m_2 ENERGIZED OR ALARM STATE)	$X > H$

The variables used in the table are:

A — An arbitrary analog signal

b — Analog bias value

$\dfrac{d}{dt}$ — Derivative with respect to time

H — An arbitrary analog high limit value

$\dfrac{1}{T_I}$ — Integrating rate

L — An arbitrary analog low limit value

m — Analog output variable

n — Number of analog inputs or value of exponent

t — Time

T_D — Derivative time

x — Analog input variable

$x_1, x_2, x_3, \ldots, x_n$ — Analog input variable (1 to n in number)

signal amplitude, is a phase shift of 180°; and so proportionally for greater or smaller lags.

Noise and Filtering. A dynamic signal disturbance independent of the true or desired value of what is being measured or controlled is called *noise*. But noise is not always easy to define, as it involves a philosophical determination of what is "true" or "desired." In an academic sense noise can only be defined in terms of the statistics of signals measured over a long period of time. In the practical view it is relatively easy to distinguish conceptually between signal and noise in the control and measurement of industrial processes, compared to the same problem, say, in long range radar or satellite communications, although this certainly does not mean that industrial noise is not troublesome and hard to separate from signals. Because our ability to control most industrial processes is limited dynamically (and the processes themselves change state slowly because of time lags and delays), we are primarily interested in signals that are meaningful in the lower frequency range. This means that we can usually call high frequency signal variations noise and discard them, and act on the lower frequency variations—in other words, we can apply a *low pass filter*.

Specifically, most noise picked up by electrical signal wires in an industrial environment is in the band above 50 Hz, up to 10 MHz or more. The noise power is concentrated at 60 and 120 Hz (where fluorescent lighting is present). Measuring instruments themselves generate noise in the range 0.5 to 100 Hz as a result of causes such as the turbulence around flow sensors. Finally, there are disturbances due to industrial processes themselves—these range from 0.005 to 1 Hz, rarely higher.

The *amplitude* of noise of course is as important as its frequency content, since it is the signal/noise *ratio* that is significant, not the absolute values (which may be freely attenuated or amplified). We have stated that we generally work with high level signals in the range 1 to 5 or 10 V generated by industrial sensors or their transmitters. Thermocouple outputs, however, are in the millivolt range. Liptak[5] cites the following noise amplitudes (electrical pickup) typical of certain industrial environments:

Chemical process industries
    Normal mode   1 to 10 mV
    Common mode   4 to 5 V (may be higher on lighting circuits)
Steel industry
    Normal mode   2 to 7 mV
    Common mode   4 to 5 V (may be 220 or 440 V on electric furnaces)

(Normal mode noise is noise measured between the signal leads of a sensor at the input to a high level transmitter or data processing amplifier. Common mode noise is the noise measured between both leads together and the signal cable shield or ground.)

It can be seen from these values that a high frequency noise filter effective for 10 to 100 mV thermocouple signals, for instance, must have a rejection ratio of 10^3 for normal mode noise and 10^6 for common mode noise.

Generally, this can be accomplished satisfactorily in the usual laboratory or industrial environment with a simple first order, single resistance-capacitance element (*RC*) filter having a cutoff below 60 Hz, such as that shown in Fig. 1.6a. ("First order" is defined more generally further on.)

If greater speed of response is needed in the thermocouple (i.e., less time lag caused by the filter), the more expensive inductance-capacitance (*LC*) combination shown in Fig. 1.6(*b*) can be used.

The subject of noise reduction by analog filters for industrial and laboratory signals is a very complex one—largely empirical and ad hoc for a particular installation. Therefore it does not pay to pursue this important subject here at much greater length. Suffice it to note that these signals are generally filtered by a first order low pass analog filter cutting off at about 1 Hz, consistant with the noise ferquencies noted above, in addition to electrical noise filters like those shown in 1.6. Additional filtering (in microprocessor systems) is best accomplished by digital means, which we consider at the proper time. Furthermore, most digital processing of these signals requires analog prefiltering, eliminating signals above 5 Hz to prevent *aliasing*, which we also discuss subsequently.

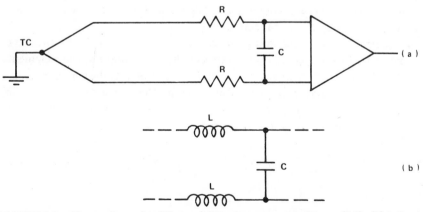

FIGURE 1.6.   First order noise filters. (a) Resistance-capacitance (RC). (b) Inductance-capacitance (LC).

Signal Transmission Lines. Before leaving the subject of analog noise elimination, the role of the signal transmission line should be mentioned. It is clear that means to prevent external noise from entering the signal lines will be even more effective than means to reject them after they are present. Therefore the design of transmission lines is of great importance. They should be routed away from power lines and equipment emitting switching transients and radiofrequency radiation. Twisted pairs reduce the pickup of normal mode noise. Signal pairs should be run individually and individually shielded where possible; shielding is particularly effective against high frequency signals and transients. Signals and power should never be run in the same multiconductor cable. In general, signal lines should be balanced as shown in Fig. 1.6—any leakage impedance causing unbalance increases noise pickup. Signals should be grounded at one point to prevent ground loops; however, it is beyond our scope to discuss all the ramifications of grounding here.

First Order Measurement and Process Lags. We examine the dynamic behavior of processes and sensors because it is necessary for the microprocessor or any other device operating on the signal to interpret, and often, as in the case of a controller, to compensate for it. The dynamics of the process also establish the minimum performance in real time—that is, the processing speed required of a microprocessor.

The simplest form of dynamic process behavior is the first order lag which we have already introduced in terms of a simple RC filter. The physical reason for the time lag is easy to see. The capacitor represents an energy storage element, a place where the electrical charge making up the current flow accumulates. Since the current flow (amperes, or coulombs per second) is at a finite rate, it takes time for the charge (coulombs) to flow in and out of the capacitor.

In general, any process that involves energy storage involves a time lag. A first order time lag results from a process having a single storage element.

Consider the arrangement of electrical components shown in Fig. 1.7 that comprise a first order RC filter. Assume that an input voltage e_i is applied to the input terminals, giving rise to a current I in the circuit. The voltage drops across R and C are then

$$e_i = RI + \frac{1}{C}\int I\,dt \tag{1.4}$$

and

$$e_o = \frac{1}{C}\int I\,dt$$

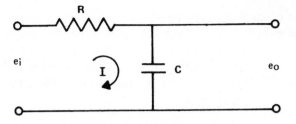

FIGURE 1.7.   First order *RC* filter.

or

$$I = C \frac{de_o}{dt} \tag{1.5}$$

Eliminating I from (1.4) and (1.5) yields

$$RC \frac{de_o}{dt} + e_o = e_i \tag{1.6}$$

The solution to this equation depends on the nature of e_i as a function of time. If, in the simplest case, both e_i and e_o are equal to some constant value E (since de_o/dt is euqal to zero under these conditions), and if e is then suddenly dropped to zero at some time $t = 0$, then it has been shown in many places that the solution to (1.6) is

$$e_o = E\epsilon^{-t/RC} \tag{1.7}$$

A plot of this function is given in Fig. 1.8 (solid line). It is seen that the value of e_o drops to 0.368 of its initial value in the time RC, which is the

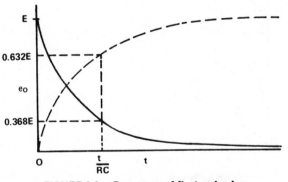

FIGURE 1.8.   Response of first order lag.

time constant of the first order lag. After several time constants, the value of e_o is virtually zero, which is its *steady state* value.

Now let us suppose that e_i in (1.6) has been zero for a long time and, after e_o has also reached zero, the value of e_i is suddenly raised back to E. (Again we call this time $t = 0$.) The solution to (1.6) becomes

$$e_o = E(1 - \epsilon^{-t/RC}) \tag{1.8}$$

and e_o follows the dashed curve in Fig. 1.8. After one time constant (RC), e_o has risen exponentially to $0.632E$. The steady state value of e_o is then E, achieved substantially after four or five time constants. What does this mean with respect to instrument and process dynamics? Look at Fig. 1.9, which is an actual plot of the response of an industrial thermometer bulb. This is a *filled system* thermometer consisting of a cylindrical element containing a gas or liquid that expands with temperature and thereby actuates an indicator or mechanical control. The two curves, A and B, show the response of the thermometer to sudden immersion in a bath at some constant elevated temperature. The curves are identical in shape to the exponential rise in Fig. 1.8 and in (1.8). The bath temperature is equivalent to the applied voltage E of (1.8), and the time constant or *lag coefficient*, 0.1 min, is independent of the bath temperature and equivalent to RC in the electrical case. Clearly, the thermometer exhibits a first order time lag. It could be assumed, then, that the thermometer system

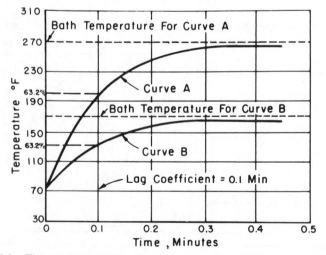

FIGURE 1.9. Thermometer bulb response. (Copyright Honeywell Inc., 1955–1957. By permission.)

contains a single energy storage element and a thermal resistance, as does the *RC* filter. Let us now try to define the thermal analogs of the electrical parameters that cause identical first order lag dynamic behavior in the two systems.

We start with the basic equation of heat transfer:

$$q = UA \, \Delta\theta \qquad (1.9)$$

where q = rate of heat transfer (Btu/min)
U = overall heat transfer coefficient [Btu/(min)(°F)(ft²)]
A = area
$\Delta\theta$ = temperature difference

In terms of the filled bulb thermometer the area can be taken as that of the bulb, the temperature difference that between the bulb fluid and bath; q and U refer to the heat flow through the resistance of the wall of the bulb and a fluid film, which depends on the velocity of process fluid flow past the bulb.

Note that this equation can be expressed in the same form as Ohm's law if we assume that heat flow q is analogous to current, $\Delta\theta$ is the potential, and UA is the overall thermal conductance [Btu/(min)(°F)] or the inverse of *thermal resistance*. In other words,

$$q = \frac{\Delta\theta}{1/UA} \qquad (1.10)$$

identifies the quantity $1/UA$ as the resistance component of the thermal circuit.

Now let us rewrite (1.9) once again in differential form:

$$q = \frac{dQ}{dt} = UA(\theta_i - \theta_o) \qquad (1.11)$$

where Q in Btu is now the quantity of heat (equivalent to the charge in coulombs of the electrical case) and we have replaced $\Delta\theta$ with the instantaneous temperatures θ_i and θ_o on either side of the thermal resistance. We can now introduce the *thermal capacitance* C_p, which is the heat capacity of the thermometer bulb assembly in Btu/°F, and make use of the relationship

$$dQ = C_p \, d\theta \qquad (1.12)$$

which follows from the definition of *Cp*. Now combining (1.12) and (1.11) and rearranging,

$$\frac{C_p}{UA} \frac{d\theta}{dt} + \theta_o = \theta_i \qquad (1.13)$$

It can be seen that (1.13) has exactly the same form as (1.6) and that the product of the thermal resistance and thermal capacity Cp/UA has the same role as the time constant RC in (1.6). This is to be expected as the units

$$\frac{C_p}{UA} = \frac{°F}{Btu/minute} \times \frac{Btu}{°F} = minutes$$

are those of time.

If this is the case, we can expect that the bulb temperature will rise exponentially when subject to a sudden rise in ambient temperature T, in a manner equivalent to (1.8) [the solution to (1.6)] or

$$\theta_o = T(1 - \epsilon^{-tUA/C_p}) \tag{1.14}$$

which is precisely the form of Fig. 1.9.

We can also expect that the thermal time constant varies inversely as U, that is, it decreases with a decrease in thermal resistance $1/UA$.

Figure 1.10 shows the thermometer bulb time constant (lag) decreasing rapidly as the velocity of the fluid in which it is immersed increases. Heat transfer theory of course tells us that the film resistance decreases (U rises) in rapidly flowing fluids and is highest in stagnant liquids.

Dynamic Error of a First Order System.   Assume that the area of the bulb is 0.01 ft², its heat capacity is 0.005 Btu/°F, and the coefficient of heat transfer in a moving stream of fluid is 1 Btu/(min)(°F)(ft²). If the process fluid changes temperature at 25°F/min, is there a dynamic measurement error?

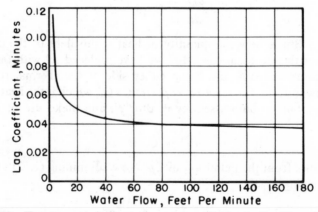

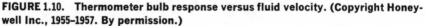

FIGURE 1.10. Thermometer bulb response versus fluid velocity. (Copyright Honeywell Inc., 1955–1957. By permission.)

The rate of heat transfer change q must be equal to the bulb heat capacity times the temperature change in the steady state:

$$q = (25)\,(0.005) = 0.125 \text{ Btu/min}$$

From (1.9):

$$\theta = \frac{q}{UA} = \frac{0.125}{(1)(.01)}$$
$$= 12.5°F$$

This is the dynamic error of the system.

The time lag is:

$$\frac{12.5}{25}\,\frac{°F}{°F/min} = 0.5 \text{ min}$$

We should obtain the same answer if we calculate the time constant directly:

$$\text{Time constant} = \frac{C_p}{UA} = \frac{0.005}{(1)(0.01)} = 0.5 \text{ min}$$

Figure 1.11 is an illustration of the actual dynamic error resulting from a steady increase in the process variable (bath temperature) on an instrument that has no static error. It is seen that there is indeed a constant time lag and dynamic measurement error that results from these conditions, as we would expect from the calculations. The condition of steady increase

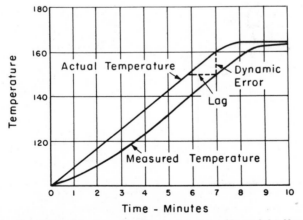

FIGURE 1.11.   Example of instrument dynamic error. (Copyright Honeywell Inc., 1955–1957. By permission.)

or ramp change in process variable is more commonly encountered in practice than the mathematically simple step change we first considered.

Dynamic Flow System.   We consider one more example of a first-order system. A cylindrical tank (Fig. 1.12) is being filled with fluid at some variable rate Q_i cubic feet per second and is simultaneously being drained through a valve at a rate Q_o (Fig. 1.12). If it is desired to keep the level in the tank h between certain limits by manipulating the valve, it is necessary to be able to calculate the effect of changes in Q_i on h for any given valve setting. This is accomplished by the construction of a mathematical model.

The two basic physical principles applied are those of conservation of mass and conservation of energy. The first tells us that the accumulation of fluid, proportional to the height of fluid in the tank, is equal to the net flow into the tank:

$$A_T \frac{dh}{dt} = Q_i - Q_o \qquad (115)$$

The accumulation is the rate of change in level times the tank area A_T. The second principle tells us that, for the flowing fluid, the sum of kinetic and potential energies

$$\frac{1}{2}(mv)^2 + mgh$$

is a constant (v is the fluid velocity).

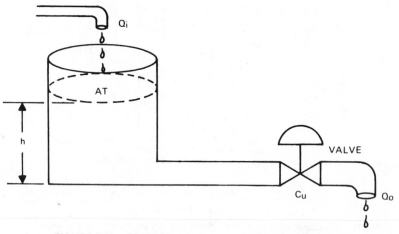

FIGURE 1.12.   First order system example (dynamic flow).

It follows that

$$v = K\sqrt{2gh}$$

or

$$Q_o = C_u\sqrt{h} \tag{1.16}$$

where C_u is a constant for a given valve opening.

Now we can write

$$A_T\frac{dh}{dt} + C_u\sqrt{h} = Q_i \tag{1.17}$$

but, comparing this with (1.16), we can see that they are not of the same form, because (1.17) is not a *linear* equation in h. That is, an exponent of h other than one enters the equation. In order to arrive at the first order lag form, the dynamic equation must be linear.

So let us assume linearity, by changing (1.16) to read:

$$Q_o = C_u h \tag{1.18}$$

which will be approximately true for small changes in h. This is a common means of approximating mathematical models. Substituting (1.18) into (1.17) we obtain

$$\frac{A_T}{C_u}\frac{dh}{dt} + h = \frac{Q_i}{C_u} = h_i \tag{1.19}$$

which meets the criterion.

Now, for a *small* step change in input Q_i, equal to H_i, the level will rise or fall in accordance with the equation

$$h = H_i\,\epsilon^{-t/(At/Cu)}$$

or

$$h = H_i(1 - \epsilon^{-t/(At/Cu)})$$

where the dimensions of the time constant At/C_u are again

$$\frac{\text{area}^2}{\text{area}^2/\text{time}} = \text{time}$$

The above relationships for the three common physical processes are summarized in Table 1.3.

TABLE 1.3   First Order Lag Process Models

	Electrical	Heat Flow	Fluid Flow
Quantity	Q, charge (C)	Q (Btu)	Volume (ft³)
Flow	i (A, or C/sec)	q (Btu/min)	Q (ft³/sec)
Potential	E (V)	$\Delta\theta$ (°F)	h, head (ft) or p, pressure (psi)
Resistance	R (ohms) ($= E/i$)	$1/UA$ (°F/Btu)	h/Q or p/Q ($\doteq 1/C_u$ for small Δh)
Capacitance	C (F, or C/V)	C_p (Btu/°F) ($= q/\Delta\theta$)	Volume/$h = A$ (ft²) for constant cross section
Time constant	RC	C_p/UA	$\doteq A/C_u$ for small Δh

Second Order System

So far we have considered only the dynamics of systems that store energy in one element—a capacitor, a tank of liquid, or heat stored in a mass—these are first order systems. As we have seen, these systems, even with a step input, the most violent form of excitation, respond merely with a gradual, delayed output. These systems are stable; they cannot oscillate or produce an output greater than input.

If a system has more than one place to store energy, its behavior can become oscillatory and even destructive when excited by certain inputs. Its response is much more complex than the simple exponential behavior we have seen. These are many kinds of higher order systems, but it suffices here to note the behavior of second order types—those with two major storage locations. These are typical of a great many (but by no means all) systems to be controlled.

One such system is a pneumatically actuated valve; the force operating the valve can be derived from a controller. The simplified representation of Fig. 1.13 is the familiar spring-mass system. The restoring force is given by the spring k, the applied (pneumatic) force is F, the mass of the valve moving parts is m, and viscous friction forces opposing motion are represented by the damper c. Newton's law, $F = ma$, states that the sum of the forces acting equals mass times acceleration, or

$$F - kx - c\dot{x} = m\ddot{x} \tag{1.20}$$

where $\dot{x} = dx/dt$
  $\ddot{x} = dx^2/dt^2$
  x = spring displacement
  k = spring constant
  c = damping force

We note that energy is stored in two places in the system; in the moving mass m as kinetic energy, and in the compressed spring as potential energy.

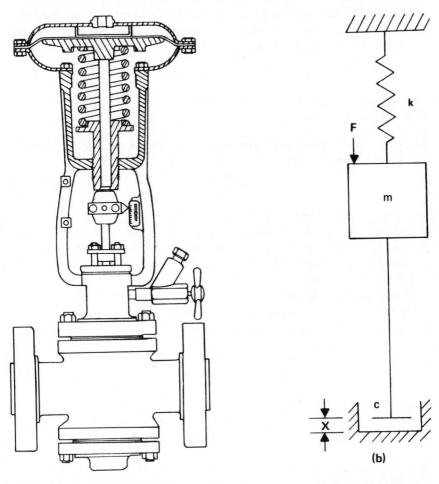

(a)

(b)

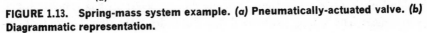

FIGURE 1.13.   Spring-mass system example. *(a)* **Pneumatically-actuated valve.** *(b)* **Diagrammatic representation.**

If the applied force F is oscillating sinusoidally, $F = F_0 \sin wt$; then

$$-kx - c\dot{x} - M\ddot{x} = F_0 \sin wt \qquad (1.21)$$

If the system is electrical rather than mechanical, the analogous expression will be (see Fig. 1.14)

$$L\ddot{Q} + R\dot{Q} - \frac{1}{C} Q = E_o \sin wt \qquad (1.22)$$

The solutions to these equations can take many forms, depending on the relative values of the damping, mass, and spring constant. (See, for example, Den Hartog[6]). If there is no damping, even in the absence of an applied force, the system exhibits continued oscillation according to the expression

$$X = C_1 \sin tw_n + C_2 \cos tw_n \qquad (1.23)$$

where $w_n = \sqrt{k/m}$ = *natural frequency*
C_1 and C_2 = constants

In other words, the system will be *unstable* and may oscillate without bounds if undamped. When damping exists, the solution is

$$X = C_1 e^{S_1 t} + C_2 e^{S_2 t} \qquad (1.24)$$

where $S_{1,2} = -(C/2m) \pm \sqrt{(C/2m)^2 - k/m}$.

The system will be *overdamped, critically damped,* or *underdamped* depending on whether the expression under the radical is positive, zero, or negative. In the last case, the system will oscillate, but the vibrations will die out with time.

Finally, for a sinusoidal applied force, the response of the system exhibits a phase shift and a gain (attenuation or magnification of the applied force amplitude), which is a function of the applied frequency. The solution

$$X = e^{-c/2mt} (C_1 \sin qt + C_2 qt)$$

+ a "particular solution" depending on the applied force   (1.25)

has both exponential and oscillatory terms.

The phase and amplitude (gain) characteristics of a second order system subject to an applied sinusoidal force are given in Fig. 1.15. The possibility of amplification, or resonance of the applied signal at certain frequencies, is shown. Since a step function has components of all frequencies up to infinity, and since each component acts independently on a linear system, a second order system less than critically damped (C_c) always exhibits some resonance. The phase shift resulting from the time delays inherent in

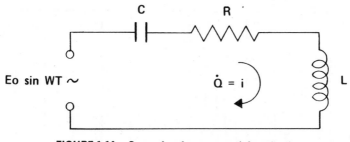

FIGURE 1.14.   Second order system (electrical).

energy storage approaches 180°, unlike the situation in the first order system, where it cannot exceed 90°. If an additional delay, such as another lag or dead time (see below), causes the phase shift to reach or exceed 180°, the system will become unstable, like an undamped system. This is because a 180° phase shift is equivalent to a reversal of the sign of the output relative to the input, so that the applied force and response work together in increasing the amplitude of motion.

Figure 1.16 summarizes the transient or step response and the responses to varying input frequencies for both first and second order systems. The gain and phase curves together are known as Bode plots.

The results just shown can be obtained in a different way which is much more convenient when higher order systems are involved. By using operational or Laplace notation, the differential terms $\dot{x}$ and $\ddot{x}$ are replaced by an operator S:

$$SX = \dot{x}$$

$$S^2X = \ddot{x}$$

and so on. Equation (1.20) can then be written:

$$(mS^2 + CS + k)\,X = F \tag{1.26}$$

The advantage of this notation is that the functions of S can now be manipulated like ordinary algebraic terms rather than differential quantities, and solutions to the equations can be obtained by the use of special tables of *Laplace transforms*. These convert them from the *complex domain* (since the S functions are actually complex variables) to ordinary equations in the time domain, such as (1.25). Many of these solutions have been listed and are found in standard references.[7] The Laplace transform method is utilized in the next chapter.

Before leaving the second order system, we note the results of some actual tests shown in Figs. 1.17 and 1.18. Figure 1.17 demonstrates the

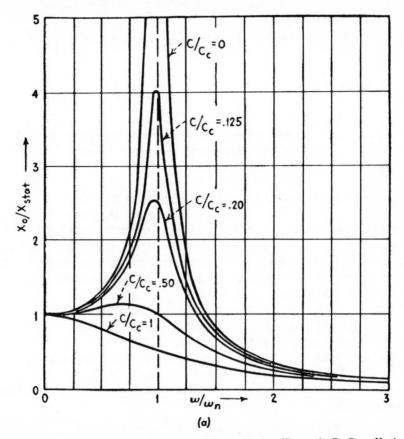

FIGURE 1.15. Response of a second order system. (From J. P. Den Hartog, *Mechanical Vibrations*, 2nd ed. Copyright 1940. By permission of McGraw-Hill Book Co.) (a) Amplitude versus frequency. (x_{stat} = static deflection). (b) Phase versus frequency.

conversion of a first order lag, the bare thermometer bulb, to a second order system as a result of the addition of another heat storage element in the form of a thermometer well. The effective lag is increased by about 16 times. In Fig. 1.18, the first order response of the thermocouple, which has a lag of 0.58 min, is successively increased to 1.1, 1.7, and 2.0 as different wells, thermal elements of greater capacity, are added. When the bare element is compared to Fig. 1.16, it is seen to have the exponential shape of a first order lag, while the instrument-well combinations clearly show the ogival characteristic of damped second order systems.

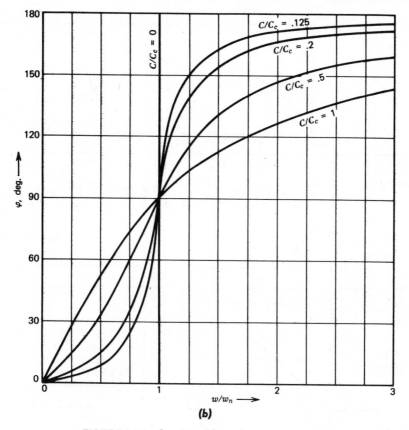

FIGURE 1.15. *(continued from the previous page)*

Dead Time

The characteristic of pure delay, independent of frequency control of the applied signal (or what is the same thing, waveshape) was mentioned earlier in this chapter. It is also called *transportation lag*, because the transportation of material (such as fluid in a pipe) is a most likely cause of this behavior. If, for example, the temperature of a heat exchanger is being controlled by signals from a thermocouple downstream from a valve (Fig. 1.19), the time required for the valve action to be sensed by the thermocouple (distance times velocity) will be a constant, the dead time. This delay does not depend at all on the frequency content of the valve signal but only on the time it takes for the fluid to reach the measuring element

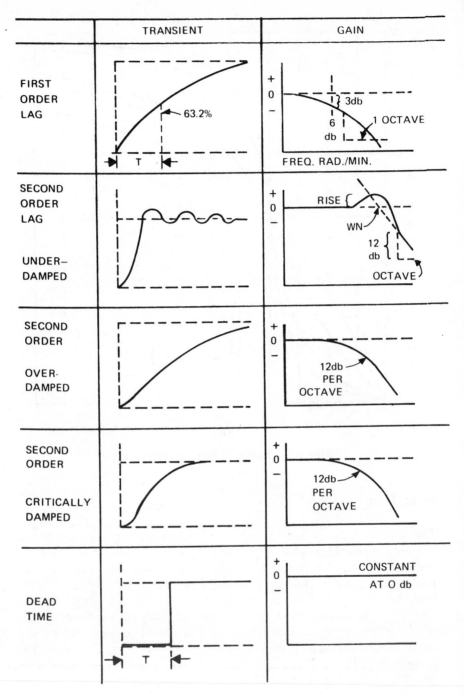

	TRANSIENT	GAIN
FIRST ORDER LAG	63.2% — T	+ 0 − 3db 6 db 1 OCTAVE FREQ. RAD./MIN.
SECOND ORDER LAG **UNDER– DAMPED**		+ 0 − RISE WN 12 db OCTAVE
SECOND ORDER **OVER-DAMPED**		+ 0 − 12db PER OCTAVE
SECOND ORDER **CRITICALLY DAMPED**		+ 0 − 12db PER OCTAVE
DEAD TIME	T	+ 0 − CONSTANT AT O db

FIGURE 1.16.

34

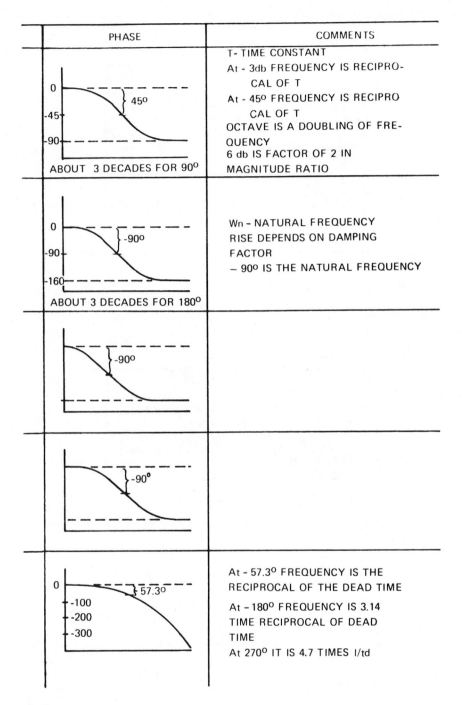

PHASE	COMMENTS
0 / -45 / -90 / 45° / ABOUT 3 DECADES FOR 90°	T- TIME CONSTANT At - 3db FREQUENCY IS RECIPRO- CAL OF T At - 45° FREQUENCY IS RECIPRO CAL OF T OCTAVE IS A DOUBLING OF FRE- QUENCY 6 db IS FACTOR OF 2 IN MAGNITUDE RATIO
0 / -90 / -160 / -90° / ABOUT 3 DECADES FOR 180°	Wn - NATURAL FREQUENCY RISE DEPENDS ON DAMPING FACTOR − 90° IS THE NATURAL FREQUENCY
-90°	
-90°	
0 / -100 / -200 / -300 / 57.3°	At - 57.3° FREQUENCY IS THE RECIPROCAL OF THE DEAD TIME At − 180° FREQUENCY IS 3.14 TIME RECIPROCAL OF DEAD TIME At 270° IT IS 4.7 TIMES l/td

System responses.

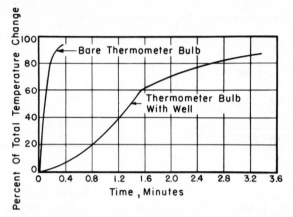

FIGURE 1.17. First and second order instrument lags. (Copyright Honeywell Inc., 1955–1957. By permission.)

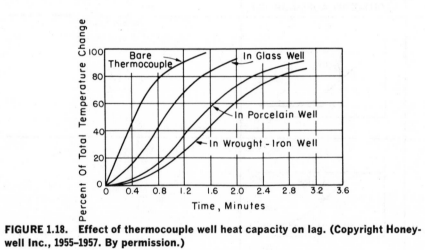

FIGURE 1.18. Effect of thermocouple well heat capacity on lag. (Copyright Honeywell Inc., 1955–1957. By permission.)

after leaving the heat exchanger. Schematically, this reaction is shown in Fig. 1.20, assuming a first order lag system.

The phase shift resulting from dead time is a function of the frequency f:

$$\phi = -360ft_d$$
$$= -57.3wt_d \tag{1.27}$$

where w = circular frequency $(2\pi f)$
t_d = dead time

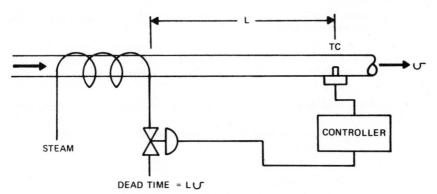

FIGURE 1.19. Transportation lag or dead time.

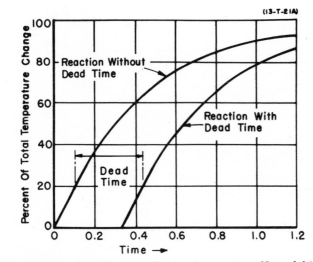

FIGURE 1.20. Effect of dead time on first order system. (Copyright Honeywell Inc., 1955–1957. By permission.)

The amplitude response of a pure dead time system is always unity, regardless of frequency, These relationships are shown in Fig. 1.16.

References

1. W. G. Holzbock, *Instruments for Measurement and Control*, Reinhold, New York, 1955.

2. B. G. Liptak, Ed., *Instrument Engineers' Handbook*, Vol. 1, Chilton, Philadelphia, 1969.

3. W. J. Karplus, in *System Engineering Handbook* (R. E. Machol, Ed.), McGraw-Hill, New York, 1965, pp. 10–11.

4. Extracted from SAMA Standard RC22-11-1966, Functional Diagramming of Instrument and Control Systems—Analog and Digital Systems, with the permission of the publisher, Recorder-Controller Section, SAMA, 370 Lexington, Ave. New York, N.Y.

5. Liptak, *op. cit.*, Vol. II, p. 941.

6. J. P. Den Hartog, *Mechanical Vibrations*, 2nd ed., McGraw-Hill, New York, 1940, pp. 61–65.

7. F. Nixon, *Principles of Automatic Controls*, Prentice-Hall, New York, 1953.

Two

Process Control Fundamentals

As in the last chapter, it is not intended to delve deeply into the theory or practice of automatic process control but merely to present enough of the background and fundamentals to define the task of the microprocessor in this duty. The task of a controller is to adjust the state of a process as measured by some variable—the *process variable* (*PV*)—to conform to a particular standard value called the *set point* (*SP*). The difference between them is termed the *error E*. Usually we define

$$E = PV - SP \qquad (2.1)$$

although it is sometimes defined oppositely as $SP - PV$.

Some means must be provided to measure the PV using an instrument such as one of those described in Chapter 1; the output of the instrument (measured variable) is related to the PV in the same units as the set point, and the difference then measured. The controller acts on the error and, through the agency of yet another component, the *final control element*, acts on the process to change the PV in the desired direction (toward the SP) and so reduce the error. These relationships are shown schematically in the block diagram in Fig. 2.1, which is an elaboration of Fig. 1.1.

As a concrete example of what the block diagram represents, Fig. 2.2 shows a process—a heat exchanger— in which a product is being heated by some medium, such as steam, controlled by a valve (final element) which in turn is opened or closed under the direction of a controller commanded by the error signal.

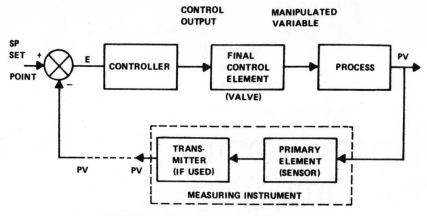

FIGURE 2.1.   Control system block diagram.

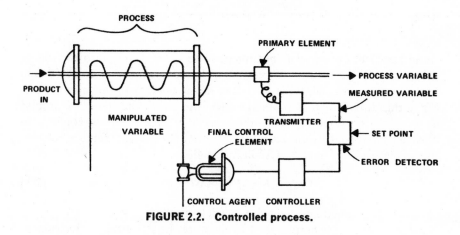

FIGURE 2.2.   Controlled process.

Note that there are at least three dynamic elements other than the controller in Fig. 2.1; any one or all of them can exhibit dynamic characteristics like those described in Chapter 1 and be significant in the overall task of controlling the *PV*. These elements and their characteristics are usually determined by factors that must be accepted by the controller designer as facts of life—either they are inherent in the process and the hardware or represent the best components that can be obtained for the purpose, or their performance is constrained by economics. This means that the ideal controller should be able to compensate for excessively undesirable dynamic characteristics, for example, lags, that may be introduced by the other elements. The way the controller operates—its response to an error signal—is called its *control mode* or *control law*. Another term, more appropriate for digital computer implementation, is *control algorithm*, meaning in this instance a calculation method that produces a control output by operating on an error signal or a time series of error signals.

It is often important to remember that the state of a process can be described by several process variables and that they frequently interact with each other. An example is the control of relative humidity, in which both temperature and moisture variables must be controlled but are not independent. This type of control is termed *multivariable* and, though much more complex than the usual case of independent process variable control, is particularly suited to digital processing.

The number of independent variables such as temperature, pressure, concentration, and so on, that can be controlled independently in a given process is not unlimited but is a function of the total number of possible variables and the equations relating them. The difference is termed *degrees of freedom* of the system. Examples are given later.

We now proceed to a description of the elements of a one-dimensional controlled system—the control of a single independent process variable. Our objective is to arrive at the algorithms normally inplemented in a process controller and to describe the dynamic behavior of the controlled process. Our descriptions are in analog form, that is, in continuous functions of the variables. Subsequently, we translate these into digital algorithms and then show how they can be implemented in a particular microprocessor.

In this descriptive process there is no attempt to achieve mathematical rigor or to carry out the analytic process far enough to arrive at theoretically optimum control systems. This is not possible in the space alotted; scores of excellent texts have been written on these subjects, some of which are listed at the end of this chapter.[1,4–6,8] Furthermore, today's practice is generally not to optimize controls but to rely largely on a few relatively simple and familiar algorithms known to give a reliable and stable performance in the majority of cases when they are properly implemented and adjusted.[3,7] In the past, there was little clear-cut economic incentive to use complex forms of control, especially if they did not have a long history of reliable operation. Furthermore, in many cases the dynamic parameters of the process are not known precisely enough to justify theoretical improvement of a few percent. With the advent of digital computers and the inherent flexibility they have brought to process control, some of these arguments have weakened, since it is only a little more costly to implement a sophisticated algorithm than a simpler one. The economic pressures to improve energy utilization and exploit feedstocks more efficiently—particularly petroleum-based raw materials—are also growing. It is expected that the use of advanced control theory and optimization techniques will become more common in the future and that the introduction of microprocessors at the basic control level will greatly enhance the rate of this evolution. Hence we take note of these developments, although perhaps not at the length they deserve.

Open and Closed Loop Control

In Fig. 2.1, the dashed signal flow line denotes an *open loop* system. If an operator monitoring the process were to insert a setting for the valve and if there were no *PV* input to the comparison device, that is, if the dashed line were left open, the valve stem would travel to some point and remain there regardless of what happened to the process and to the value of *PV*. If the instrument sensor and an appropriate display were in place, the operator could note the *PV* reading on occasion and, mentally predicting the response of the process, reset the valve according to an estimate of process behavior.

Classic manual open loop control, in many cases of slow and elementary process behavior, may be quite sufficient. The control law, then, is limited to a mere repeating of the valve position commanded by the operator at the remote valve location. Thus there is no automatic control mode, and no algorithms other than those mentally stored by the operator. But if we connect the two points marked *PV*, the system becomes *closed loop*, and we have a basic automatic feedback control system.

It is possible and quite desirable in many instances to use open loop or combine both open and closed loop modes in a very sophisticated way, termed *feedforward* control. This is described later, but it can be seen at once that a feedforward system must be capable of predicting the response of the process, just as the operator does in manual control. Therefore an automatic open loop (feedforward) system must incorporate some kind of "predictor" or model of the process behavior.

On-Off Control

Assume that the final control element in Fig. 2.1 has only two states, full on and full off. An example is a home furnace which is either operating or not, depending on the state—open or closed—of a switch operated by the thermostat. When the temperature at the thermostat falls, the switch is closed, the furnace operates, and the temperature rises. When a higher temperature is sensed at the thermostat, the switch is opened, shutting down the furnace. This up-and-down cycling continues indefinitely. To prevent cycles from repeating too rapidly and becoming destructive to the equipment, a gap (also called a differential, neutral, or dead zone) is built into the thermostat control so that nothing happens until the temperature overshoots the set point and passes the gap boundaries, going in either direction (Fig. 2.3).

If this concept is applied to Fig. 2.2, the valve could be solenoid-operated so as to be limited to the full on (open) or off (closed) state. Then the characteristic of the valve-controller combination would be that shown in Fig. 2.3. With the *PV* (temperature of the process fluid) at the upper end of its span (100%) the valve is closed, and at the lower end (toward 0%) the valve is open and steam is admitted to the heat exchanger. Between, the valve characteristic exhibits hysteresis—it must travel past the *SP* by half the total gap before it can change its condition.

The control law of the on-off mode can then be stated:

$$E = PV - SP \tag{2.1}$$

$$V = \text{sign } E \tag{2.2}$$

if $|E| - \frac{1}{2}$ gap ≥ 0 (assuming the gap is symmetric about the *SP*). $V+$ means the valve is closed (steam is shut off), and $V-$ that it is open. E is defined in (2.1), and $|E|$ is the absolute value of E (disregarding the sign).

The effect of this control law—the on-off mode—on the behavior of the process is seen in Fig. 2.4. When the temperature drops past the lower bound of the gap, the valve is turned on, but inertia determines some delay

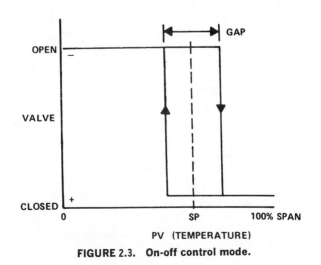

FIGURE 2.3. On-off control mode.

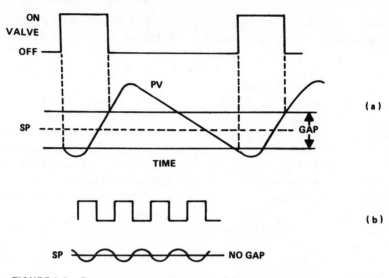

FIGURE 2.4.   Response to on-off control. *(a)* **With gap.** *(b)* **Without gap.**

before the temperature PV starts to rise again. Again, when the PV reaches the upper gap limit and the controller shuts off the valve, the temperature overshoots. It can be seen that, even if there is no deliberate gap (Fig. 2.4*b*), the thermal inertia demands continual overshoot and cycling of the PV at some higher frequency.[2] Thus cycling and overshoot are characteristics of the on-off control mode, regardless of the system.

Proportional Control

To avoid cycling and its attendent wear and energy problems, it should be possible to find an intermediate valve opening that will maintain the process variable at a steady value relative to the set point. In the example pictured in Fig. 2.2, the rate of energy input corresponding to the steam flow at that valve setting must equal the energy leaving the system by heating the product flowing through the heat exchanger plus losses to the surroundings. It is clear that the valve setting is different for every condition of product flow or loss factor.

The desired mode of control then consists of manually setting a valve position corresponding to zero error under average process conditions and instructing the controller to close the valve proportional to a positive error $(PV > SP)$ and open it proportional to a negative error $(PV < SP)$. In other words, the control law for the *proportional mode is*

$$V = KE + M \qquad (2.3)$$

where $E = PV - SP$

K = a proportionality constant

M = constant valve setting at $E = 0$

Equation (2.3) is the equation of a straight line and, as defined, is shown in Fig. 2.5a. K, the proportionality constant, is usually termed the *gain* of the controller. As seen in Fig. 2.5b and c, the gain or slope of the line determines the change in valve opening corresponding to a given error. The percent change in error needed to move the valve full scale is often called the *proportional band* (PB) by process engineers. In Fig. 2.5c a small error is required to open or close the valve fully—this is a high gain system. In Fig. 2.5b the opposite is true. Hence the relationship between gain and proportional band is inverse:

$$K = \frac{100}{PB} \qquad (2.4)$$

where PB is in percent.

The steady state term M in (2.3) is called the *manual reset* by process control engineers for reasons that will shortly become obvious.

Figure 2.6 demonstrates the action of the proportional controller in time. If for some reason, say the injection of a slug of cold product or an increase in product flow, the error jumps quickly to a fixed value, the valve will move instantly (or try to) by a porportional amount in the direction necessary to reduce the error to zero. If the error is kept constant, the new valve position will stay the same. The disadvantages of the proportional mode of control can be determined by following the consequences of this kind of disturbance (a *load disturbance*) in a closed loop system.

Assume that the system is placed in open loop and that there is no control. If a step load disturbance then takes place as shown in Fig. 2.7, the valve position will not change and the temperature will drop to some new steady state value with a constant error. Now let us restore the close loop condition with proportional control. The valve will respond as in Fig. 2.6 to reduce this error, but the control law [see (2.3)] states that V can change only if E does, since M is a constant. That is, for any new valve position not M, which corresponds to the average load from which we have deviated, there must be a definite value of E, the error. This residual error, shown in Fig. 2.7, is called the *offset*. Proportional mode control, then, with less

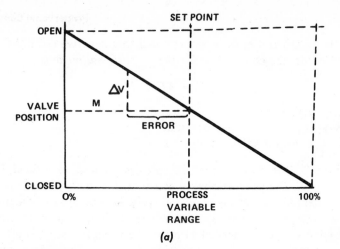

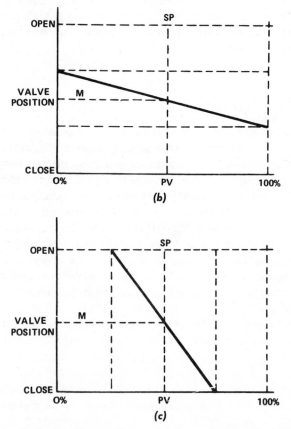

FIGURE 2.5. Proportional control law. (a) Proportional gain (ΔV/error). (b) Low gain. (c) High gain.

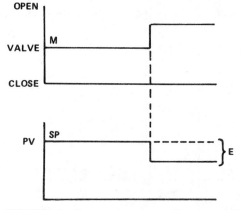

FIGURE 2.6.   Response to proportional control.

than infinite gain, results in zero error only for one load condition, that established by the value of M, the manual reset. To eliminate the error when load changes occur, the value of M must be manually reset. Thus the origin of the name becomes clear. For frequently changing loads it is necessary to somehow automate the reset function. This is the next task of the controller.

Gain, Offset, and Stability.   Before digressing from the proportional controller let us examine the gain term K in (2.3). First, if the controller is actually represented by the equations, there are no time dependent (dynamic) terms in the algorithm representing its behavior. If we assume for the moment that none of the other components in Fig. 2.1 have time lags, we can redraw the block diagram of the system as in Fig. 2.8, where each component is represented by a transfer function in its block.[1] The transfer function is merely a mathematical relationship between the single output and input of each block, and, since none of them are dependent on time, they are all simple gain terms K_i. Since the signals flow only in the direction shown by the arrows, the basic algebra of transfer functions allows us to combine them simply by multiplication. Thus the total forward gain of the system is obtained by multiplying all the gain terms in the forward branch of the loop. In this process, care must be taken to establish the correct value of the units for each K. When an electronic controller is assumed, the input and output are electrical signals and

$$K_c = \frac{\text{volts output}}{\text{volts input}} = \frac{V}{V}$$

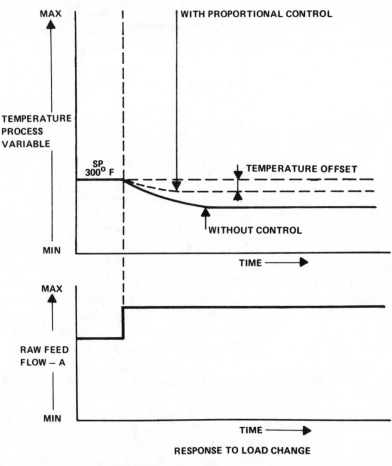

FIGURE 2.7.   **Load step response.**

The valve can be assumed to yield steam flow proportional to the controller output signal, or

$$K_v = \frac{\text{flow}}{\text{volts}} = \frac{F}{V}$$

The process responds to increased steam flow by a linear rise in temperature of PV, or

$$K_p = \frac{°\text{F}}{F} = \frac{T}{F}$$

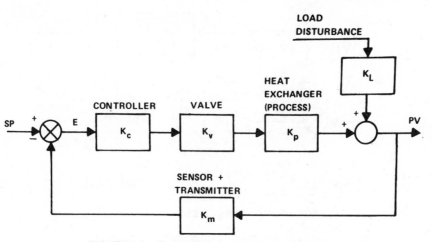

FIGURE 2.8.   Proportional control block diagram.

Multiplying these together,

$$K = K_c K_v K_p = \frac{V}{V}\frac{V}{F}\frac{T}{F} = \frac{T}{V}\frac{°F}{\text{volt}}$$

Since the sensor must convert temperature into an electrical signal for E to be in volts,

$$K_m = \frac{\text{volts}}{°F} = \frac{V}{T}$$

and $K K_m$, going all around the loop, is a dimensionless gain, as it should be.

If it is assumed for simplicity that the value of K_m is unity, the block diagram Fig. 2.9 using K is also valid. The dimensions of K_L depend on the kind of disturbance but, for example, let the disturbance be the initial temperature of the product feeding the heat exchanger, so that $K_L = 1°F/°F$. Then, if ΔPV is the change in the process variable (temperature of the outgoing product) and ΔT_F is the disturbance (change in the feed temperature), redefining ΔE as $SP - PV$,

$$\Delta PV = K \Delta E + K_L \Delta T_F$$

and, as SP remains constant,

$$\Delta E = -\Delta PV$$

$$\Delta PV = -K \Delta PV + K_L \Delta T_F$$

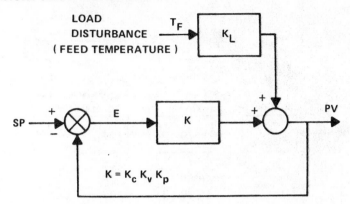

FIGURE 2.9.   Simplified block diagram.

or

$$\Delta PV = \frac{K_L}{1 + K} \Delta T_F = \frac{1}{1 + K} \Delta T_F$$

We can now quantify the temperature offset resulting from the utilization of the proportional mode controller sketched in Fig. 2.7. The steady state offset error can be made as small as desired, but never reaches zero, by increasing the overall gain of the forward loop, since the magnitude of the load disturbance is reduced by a factor of $1/(1 + K)$.

But this is true only if there are no delay terms in the transfer functions, as we assumed, unrealistically. Whenever there is a time delay, no matter how small, an increase in gain will ultimately lead to instability.

For example, let the primary element in Fig. 2.2 be located so that it introduces a 1 min dead time (transportation delay) in sensing the product temperature change brought about by the heat exchanger, and let all the other delays in the system be inconsiderable. Then assume the feed temperature drops by 1°F. We set the controller initially so that the overall gain of the forward loop K is 0.5. At the end of 1 min, the temperature at the sensor has dropped by 1°F and the controller manipulates the valve to raise it back by $\frac{1}{2}$°F. This temperature rise is not detected for 1 min. When it is, the controller operates to reduce the temperature by one-half times the rise, or $\frac{1}{4}$°, and so on indefinitely. The sequence of temperature changes followed is

$$\text{Initial } PV - (1 - \tfrac{1}{2} + \tfrac{1}{4} - \tfrac{1}{8} + \cdots)$$

The portion in the parentheses is a geometric series which has the limit $\frac{2}{3}$, so that the final PV stabilizes at (initial $PV - \frac{2}{3}$)°F.

With the same logic, it can be seen that, if the gain is just one, the series for a 1°F disturbance will be

$$\text{Initial } PV - 1 + 1 - 1 + 1 - \cdots$$

and the system will cycle indefinitely at 1 min intervals. If K is allowed to become larger than one, the oscillations will increase in magnitude and the error will become ever larger. If K is only 1.1, and therefore $\Delta PV = -1.1 \, \Delta E$, the following sequence will be obtained with increasing time periods:

t (min)	0	1	2	3	4
ΔE	-1	$+1.1$	-1.21	$+1.331$	-1.4641
ΔPV	0	$+1.1$	-1.21	$+1.331$	-1.4641
E	-1	$+0.1$	-1.11	$+0.221$	-1.243

The consequence of dead time lag therefore is instability when the overall gain is one or more. It should be understood that gain and stability as used here are properties of the entire closed loop system, including the process, and not of the controller alone. Therefore they are the province, correctly speaking, of the process control engineer rather than the controller designer, with the proviso that the controller is sufficiently flexible and does not inadvertently introduce instability into the loop.

The techniques of calculating stability and stability margins occupy much of the controls systems application literature, and the reader is referred to the numerous texts on the subject.[5,6,8]

Integral Control

We have noted that the proportional controller algorithm leads to a steady state error whenever the load exceeds that initially set by the value of M in (2.3); this value must be reset if the error is to be reduced to zero. One way of doing this automatically is merely to instruct the controller to drive the valve in the direction to reduce the error so long as any error persists. For example, the valve may be driven by a constant speed motor—this type of automatic reset is known as a *single speed floating control*, where the word "floating" refers to the dependence of the rate of change in the controller on the error. A more common reset mode is the *proportional speed floating control*, in which the rate of valve motion is proportional to the derivative of error:

$$\frac{dV}{dt} = K_I E \qquad (2.5)$$

Integrating this equation we obtain

$$V = K_I \int E \, dt \qquad (2.6)$$

(if initial conditions are zero) which justifies the more modern term *integral control* for this mode. It is both intuitively and mathematically correct to conclude that integral control will completely null the error and correct the offset, given enough time, since the controller continues to drive the valve so long as any error exists.

If both proportional and integral control are combined, the control equation will be

$$V = KE + K_I \int E \, dt + M \qquad (2.7)$$

This is known as the *two-mode* or *PI* controller.

The behavior of the PI controller when subject to an error step is seen in Fig. 2.10. The controller output (valve position) rises almost instantly by an amount KE as a result of the proportional term. But since the error persists (an open loop system is assumed in the figure), the integral term continues to move the valve at a constant rate [see (2.5)], where the slope of the rise is given by the reset gain K_I. After a time T_I, called the *reset time*, the valve movement due to the slope of the integral term becomes equal to the original proportional contribution KE. The controller reset adjustment can thus be expressed in terms of T_I, the reset time, or its reciprocal, repeats per minute (RPM), since the latter expresses how many times per minute the integral adjustment repeats the proportional correction KE.

The PI algorithm in terms of reset time is

$$V = KE + \frac{K}{T_I} \int E \, dt + M$$
$$= K \left(E + \frac{1}{T_I} \int E \, dt \right) + M \qquad (2.8)$$

The relationship between K_I, T_I, and K, the proportional gain, is then

$$K_I = \frac{K}{T_I} \qquad (2.9)$$

Figure 2.11 shows, in terms of a closed loop system, the improvement resulting from the addition of this reset or integral mode. The response of a stable system to a step load change is thus eventually a nulling of the error.

PROPORTIONAL PLUS RESET CONTROL

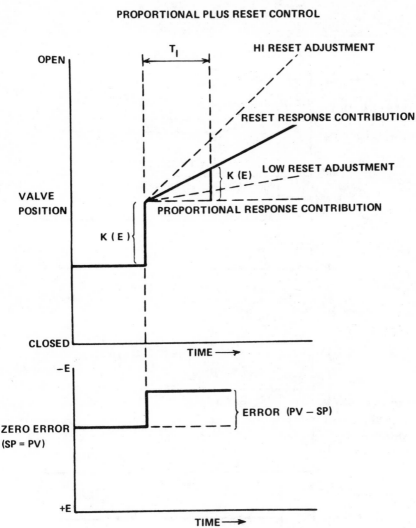

FIGURE 2.10.   Response to PI control.

Derivative (Rate) Control and the PID Algorithm

Consideration of Fig. 2.11 leads to the conclusion that a substantial amount of time could elapse before a fairly slow process returns to zero error. If a product sensitive to variation in the controlled variable, temperature, for instance, were being processed, a large amount of off-standard product

PROPORTIONAL PLUS RESET CONTROL

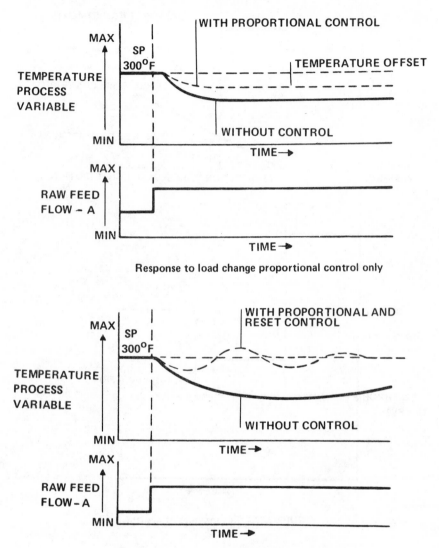

Response to load change proportional control only

Response to load change proportional plus reset control

FIGURE 2.11. Improvement in closed loop performance due to PI control.

might result before the system returned to normal. Intuitively, it seems that a means of improving the controller would be to have it "anticipate" the error by sensing when, and how fast, it begins to move. That is, we can sense the rate of change or derivative of the error and add a term proportional to this factor as a correction to the controller. Expressing this concept mathematically,

$$V = K_D \frac{dE}{dt} \tag{2.10}$$

where K_D is the *derivative* or *rate constant*.

It is clear that this rate term affects the controller only during a change in the magnitude of the error. A steady state value of E can be corrected only by the proportional, integral, or PI algorithms. Although the derivative term can also be used with the proportional mode to form another two-mode (PD) controller, a much more common type is the *PID* or *three-mode* controller. The algorithm for the PID controller is a combination of (2.10) and (2.8):

$$V = K \left(E + \frac{1}{T_I} \int E \, dt + T_D \frac{dE}{dt} \right) + M \tag{2.11}$$

The term T_D is the *rate* or *derivative time* and is related to K_D, the rate gain constant in (2.10), just as T_I and K_I are related, thus

$$K_D = KT_D \tag{2.12}$$

Figure 2.12 demonstrates the performance of a PD two-mode controller. If the set point is moved linearly (ramped) so that the open loop error is a function of time $E = ct$, the rate action will produce an immediate step in valve position proportional to the error slope c. It takes a time T_D for the proportional factor KE to equal this anticipated rate correction, thus leading to (2.12). As shown in Fig. 2.12*a*, this controller, when actuated by rising and falling ramps as *SP* inputs, has a complex response composed of both rate and proportional components, the net effect being to accelerate the valve action. If the linear ramp expression $E = ct$ is substituted into the equation

$$V - M = KE + KT_D \frac{dE}{dt}$$

[from (2.3), (2.10), and (2.12)], the result will be

$$V - M = Kc(t + T_D)$$

demonstrating that the valve response is advanced in time by the amount T_D. The response of the PID (three-mode) controller, combining the actions of Figs. 2.10 and 2.12, is illustrated in Figs. 2.14 to 2.19.

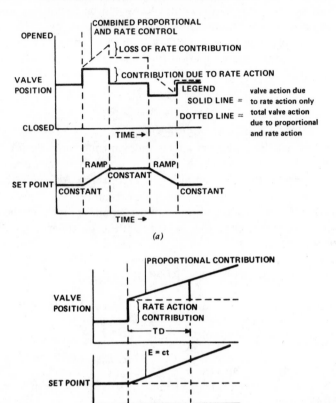

FIGURE 2.12. PD controller action. *(a)* **Rate action only.** *(b)* **Rate plus proportional action.**

It should not be assumed that the PID algorithm and its components are the only control modes in use. Many variants are possible, especially where the added flexibility of digital computers is available. Some of these include nonlinear gain terms, such as slope changes and dead zones (gap), powers of E such as E^2, and families of "optimum" algorithms such as the sampled data minimal prototype forms that may be particularly appropriate to digital microprocessors. Nevertheless, most currently used controllers are of the PI or PID type—90% of all controllers are said to be the former. From the standpoint of universality and stability they represent a standard by which all other control forms are measured.

It follows that any new applicants for the process control task, such as the microprocessor, must be able to demonstrate at least the equivalent of PID performance.

Modifications of the PID Algorithm.   Using Table 2.1 we can write (2.11) in the Laplace form (neglecting the manual reset term M), obtaining:

$$\frac{V}{E} = K\left(1 + \frac{1}{T_I S} + T_D S\right) \tag{2.13}$$

as the transfer function of the controller. (We note from the table that multiplication by $1/S$ represents the Laplace equivalent of the operation of integration, just as multiplication by S represents the first derivative.) This transfer function is pictured in Fig. 2.13. Another name for this form is *ideal* or *noninteractive* three-term controller, since each of the three terms is additive and the gain of each block can be set independently. Most analog controllers, however, have a transfer function more nearly represented by

$$\frac{V}{E} = \frac{K_1(1 + T_1 S)(1 + T_2 S)}{(T_1 S)(1 + \gamma T_2 S)} \tag{2.14}$$

where T_1 = equivalent of the integral time
$\quad\;\; T_2$ = rate time constant of an ideal controller

The latter form comes about historically as a result of physical construction features of analog mechanisms, in particular the pneumatic controller. (See Ref. 1, Chapter 6, for example.) Equation 2.14 is thus called the *real* or *interactive PID* algorithm.

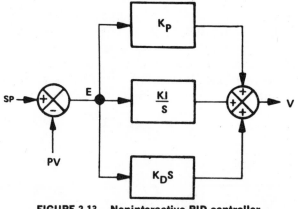

FIGURE 2.13.   Noninteractive PID controller.

TABLE 2.1.   Short List of Laplace Transform Pairs

$f(t)$	$F(S)$	
$\delta(t)$	1	(unit impulse)
$u(t)$	$\dfrac{1}{S}$	(unit step)
e^{-at}	$\dfrac{1}{S + a}$	
$\cos \omega t$	$\dfrac{S}{S^2 + \omega^2}$	
$\sin \omega t$	$\dfrac{\omega}{S^2 + \omega^2}$	
$f(t - T)$	$e^{-Ts} F(S)$	(time delay)
$1 - e^{-t/T}$	$\dfrac{1}{S(TS + 1)}$	
$\dfrac{1}{T} e^{-t/T}$	$\dfrac{1}{TS + 1}$	
$\displaystyle\int f(t)$	$\dfrac{F(S)}{S}$	[if $f(0) = 0$]
$\dfrac{df(t)}{dt}$	$SF(S)$	[if $f(0) = 0$]
$\dfrac{d^2f(t)}{dt^2}$	$S^2F(S)$	$\left[f(0) \text{ and } \dfrac{df(0)}{dt} = 0 \right]$

In actual practice, the ideal form is further modified by a low pass filter [the first order transfer function $1/(1 + T_F S)$] which multiplies (2.13) in order to limit high frequency gain and phase. When this is the case, it can be shown that the form of the two expressions is the same if the high frequency limits are identical, that is, if $\gamma T_2 = T_F$. With some algebraic manipulation we can readily obtain the equivalents;

$$K = K_1 \frac{T_1 + T_2}{T_1}$$

$$T_I = T_1 + T_2 \qquad\qquad (2.15)$$

$$T_D = \frac{T_1 T_2}{T_1}$$

These expressions demonstrate that T_1 is not identical to the true integral time T_I, nor T_2 the same as T_D, the rate constant, nor K_1 the same as K. The interaction between the real controller adjustments for rate and integral times is apparent; however, in the usual case, where $T_2 \ll T_1$, the the two sets of parameters become nearly equal.

There are arguments on both sides of the question as to which algorithm is better. It is alleged that the real controller is less sensitive to shifts in process parameters, and this may compensate in some measure for interactive tuning difficulties. In digital controllers, interaction may be more obvious, since adjustments can be made more precisely and are more stable, hence it appears advisable to make provision for either to be used.

The algorithms discussed so far are of the *whole value* type, so called because they compute the absolute value of the valve position continuously. A valuable variation is the *incremental value* equation. In this modification only the difference between the currently computed whole value and that of a prior time interval is transmitted to the valve; that is, only a position change is sent. If regular sampling time intervals are assumed, the incremental algorithm is better suited to digital systems that "update" the ouptut regularly. Advantages of the incremental algorithm include freedom from *windup* or saturation of the integral term.

Control Criteria

To compare the controllability of systems, objective criteria are needed. Obviously, a system must remain stable so that it will not engage in destructive oscillations. Further than that, we wish to keep product characteristics, as measured by the chosen *PV*, within stated limits. That is, we want to keep error at a minimum, but, in all the modes we have so far considered, the control algorithms require the error to assume some value before corrective action takes place. Therefore we are concerned with the time history of the error after a disturbance.

Disturbances that cause error are of four general types:

Changes in set point
Changes in supply
Demand changes
Environmental changes

A change in set point such as that shown in Fig. 2.12*a* requires the *PV* to follow it, and, as it fails to follow identically, error is generated. A drop in steam pressure in the system pictured in Fig. 2.2 is a supply change.

If the demand for hot product rose and the rate of product flow were increased, this would be a demand change. An environmental change would be a drop in ambient temperature, increasing the heat loss and requiring more steam to keep the same heat flow to product. Each type of disturbance requires a different kind of controller response—algorithms that behave well for one do not necessarily do so for another type. Supply changes are considered easier to correct than demand changes, because more time is available to correct them. In the worst case, a demand change occurring identically at the measuring element cannot be corrected.

The criterion for goodness of control, we stated, is least error, but even this is subject to varying interpretation. One criterion is the *quarter amplitude decay*. After a complete cycle of oscillation following disturbance, the amplitude of the error is reduced by one quarter (see Fig. 2.14). Such heavy damping ensures stability. Another is minimum peak deviation or *overshoot*. This also can be related to damping in second order systems (Chapter 1). For very sensitive products, zero overshoot may be demanded which could be accomplished by critical damping of a second order system or a first order system with proportional control. Other special requirements may be minimum time to return to set point (zero error), minimum offset in the steady state, or minimum cycling.

A more quantitative measure of goodness is the minimum error integral $\int |E| dt$ which essentially averages the product of error magnitude and its duration. Related criteria are $\int E^2 dt$ (error integral squared) and $\int t |E| dt$. The first of these exaggerates the role of error magnitude, and the second emphasizes the persistence of errors.

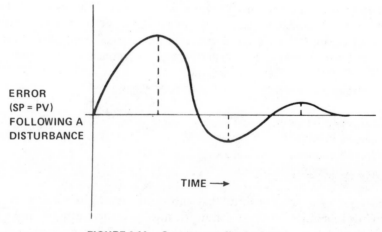

ERROR
(SP = PV)
FOLLOWING A
DISTURBANCE

TIME ⟶

FIGURE 2.14.   Quarter amplitude decay.

The gain and phase margin criteria refer to the open loop response of a system (amplitude and gain) when excited by a sinusoidal forcing function, usually at the valve. They can be determined from the graphs of gain and phase versus frequency or Bode plots (see Fig. 1.16). *Gain margin* is the amount by which the system gain is less than unity at the critical (resonant) frequency where the phase shift is 180°. This frequency is also called the *ultimate frequency*. *Phase margin*, similarly, is the amount by which the phase shift of the system is less than 180° where the gain is one. As we have already noted, 180° phase shift and unity gain are criteria for instability, so these margins quantitatively relate how far the system is from instability and govern such factors as overshoot and damping. For further information on this topic the reader is referred to numerous texts that discuss the frequency analysis of closed loop systems.[5,6,8]

Cascade Control

So far we have looked only at the simple case of a single controller operating on a single process variable, as in our example, Fig. 2.2. The situation shown in Fig. 2.15 is similar, but here we have a furnace fed by gas (which may be a by-product of some other part of the plant), also with the objective of heating a fluid feed to the process. To control the feed temperature we measure it at the outlet with an instrument T_2 and use this as feedback to a PID (or PI) controller, *TC*, operating the fuel valve. Combustion air for the furnace is set manually by means of the damper shown. Certainly this gives an improvement over the uncontrolled temperature variation (shown in the sketch) that would obtain if the feed valve were left in one position, since the by-product gas may be subject to variations in pressure as a result of fluctuations in its own process. However, even with the controller, the feed temperature may often exceed desired limits after a disturbance. One reason for this may be the limitations on upstream fuel gas supply pressure which could therefore drop when the controller calls for a higher temperature and opens the valve. Severe upstream pressure drop could reduce the flow of gas so that the temperature falls even further.

It becomes clear on reflection that the controller should adjust the flow of gas, not the valve position, so that in a sense we are concerned with two process variables, flow and temperature, not just temperature.

To remedy this fault, we can add another loop which will control gas *flow* and adjust the set point of the flow loop with the *temperature* controller. This kind of system, diagramed in Fig. 2.16, is called *cascade control*. The output of controller *TC*, still determined by the temperature error (and controller dynamics) is interpreted by *FC*, the flow controller, as a demand

SIMPLE CONTROL LOOP

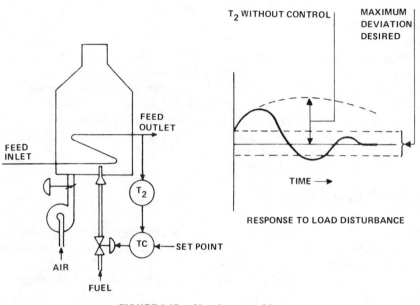

FIGURE 2.15.   Simple control loop.

for change in gas flow, which *FC* accomplishes irrespective of the current upstream pressure. If the pressure should now fluctuate, *FC* will correct the flow *even before the temperature* begins to change, since its flow sensor feedback will generate an error signal even though its set point (resulting from temperature error) remains constant. It can be readily seen that the cascaded secondary or "inner" loop responds much more quickly to supply variations than if these were required to go through the thermal inertia of the process and act through the primary loop.

These advantages require a duplicate set of controller hardware if implemented in analog form, and here the microprocessor may have an advantage because of its time sharing capability.

Feedforward Control

We have repeatedly shown that it is necessary to measure an error in a PV before control action can be initiated; thus some error is bound to

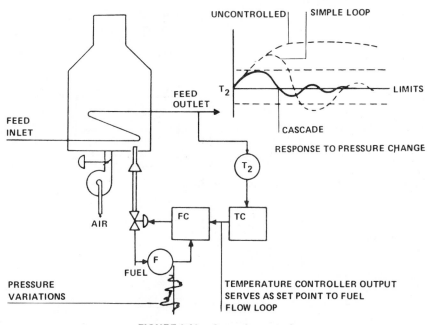

FIGURE 2.16. Cascade control.

occur in the event of disturbances in the process. Actually this is true only of feedback systems. As suggested earlier, it should be possible to anticipate certain errors and correct for them in advance.

Suppose, for instance, the demand for hot feed changes at random times in the system we are considering. Every large change in feed flow through the furnace demands a change in heat input, which now must work itself around the loop from the temperature sensor and through *TC*, and the process lags. Thus we would expect a continuation of large fluctuations such as in Fig. 2.15, at intervals, even though the gas flow variations are straightened out by the cascade loop. But we can obtain advance warning of the demand change by measuring flow at the feed inlet. Whenever the flow changes, we will know of it before it enters the furnace, hence the fuel gas flow can be adjusted upward to compensate. With proper adjustment, it may be possible to just balance the change in feed flow rate with the fuel increment so that a temperature error will never occur. This is what is meant by *feedforward control*, and it is pictured in Fig. 2.17. We have added an inlet feed flow measuring device *F* and two additional boxes—one merely a gain adjustment to obtain the correct ratio of feed to fuel increase, and the other a summing box to add the feed change increment

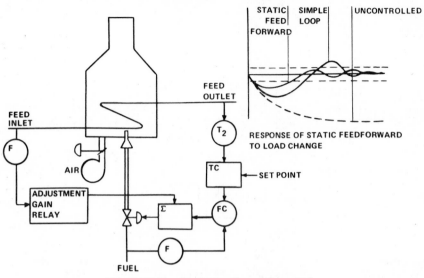

FIGURE 2.17.   Static feedforward control.

directly to the valve signal. Thus there is no time delay between the feed change and the fuel change. If the correct setting of the gain box (called a *relay* in process control practice) can be found, a greatly improved response such as that shown in the diagram will be obtained.

As we hinted earlier, the feedforward element represented by the gain relay represents a model of the process. It should represent the process to the extent that, when it is subject to the same input, the feed flow change, it responds in such a way as to cancel out the response the process itself would have made. But a simple gain is not a very good model of real process, because it has no dynamic terms and takes into account only one variable. In general, a feedforward arrangement with no dynamic terms is called a *static feedforward* system. A simple adjustment term like that in Fig. 2.17 may be extremely effective for a limited range of demand changes but should not be expected to compensate for all disturbances.

It is necessary to pay some attention to the dynamics of a system if another order of magnitude of improvement is needed.

Lead-Lag Networks and Dynamic Feedforward.   We have seen that the first order system represented by a series resistance and shunt capacitor and having transfer function $1/(RCS + 1)$ represents a phase lag. The inverse of this network introduces a phase lead, as shown in Fig. 2.18.

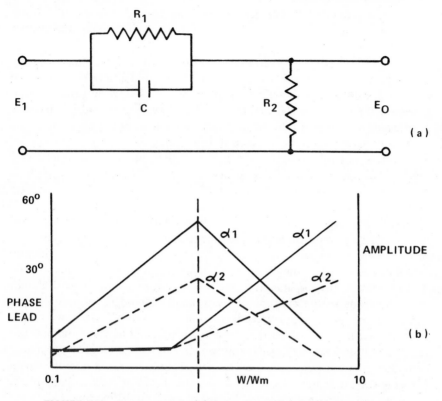

FIGURE 2.18.   Lead network. (a) Network schematic. (b) Bode plots.

The transfer function of the network is

$$\frac{E_o}{E_1} = \frac{R_2(1 + R_1CS)}{R_1 + R_2 + R_1R_2CS} = K_1 \frac{(1 + \alpha T_1 S)}{1 + T_1 S} \qquad (2.16)$$

where $\alpha = 1/K_1 = (R_1 + R_2)/R_2$
$\alpha T_1 = R_1 C$
$\omega_m = \sqrt{\alpha}/R_1 C$

Lead and lag networks can perform many useful tasks by altering the dynamics of systems—*compensation* as it is termed in servomechanisms practice. For example, if a first order lag process is compensated for by a cascaded lead network, the overall transfer function is

$$\frac{K_o}{TS + 1} \; \frac{K_1(1 + \alpha T_1 S)}{1 + T_1 S} = \frac{K_o K_1}{1 + T_1 S}$$

Process   Lead network

if α is made equal to T. This leaves the compensated system with a time constant T_1 which may be much smaller than T, improving the system response speed.

With respect to the feedforward problem, a combination lead-lag network, usually less expensive than two individual modules,[9] can be employed to alter the dynamics of any system widely; the results in the time domain are shown schematically in Fig. 2.19a. If the lead-lag network is cascaded with the gain block of the static feedforward system, the result is *dynamic feedforward*, as pictured in Fig. 2.19b.

It is now possible to adjust the gain and two time constants, lead and lag, of the "model" used for feedforward, and a further improvement in control performance would be expected.

Computer Process Models.   The process of improving control described above is largely empirical and in practice reduces to cut-and-try adjustment of the various gain and dynamic adjustments, either on-stream with the actual process or in conjunction with a computer simulation of the process. The increasing use of analytic methods in process and control design naturally leads to the concept of using analytic models for feedforward compensation. A completely accurate model of even a reasonably simple situation, such as a jacketed batch reactor kettle, can be very complex and tax the real time modeling capabilities of even larger digital or analog computers. In most cases, however, even a models approximation, which nevertheless takes into account all the significant variables, can justify its use by improved performance. The art of good model making is knowing what to leave out and what to retain—generally this can result only from specific process experience, leaving the controller designer with the obligation to include sufficient flexibility for the user to practice his art.

As an example, let us model the product heater we have been considering. This will be a simple static model but will include all the variables of interest. Clearly, a static model can be converted later to a dynamic one if need be.

The model is based on two primary physical principles:

Heat balance (conservation of energy)
Material balance (conservation of mass)

1. *Heat Balance*

$$\text{Heat in} = \text{heat out}$$

Heat in inlet feed + heat from fuel combustion = heat in outlet feed + losses

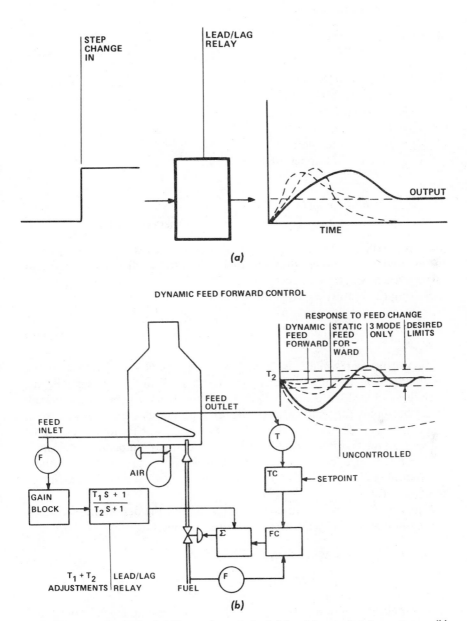

FIGURE 2.19. Dynamic feedforward control. *(a)* Lead-lag network response. *(b)* Feedforward control using lead-lag.

2.   *Material Balance*

Feed in = feed out

Let F = fuel flow (1b/min)
  F_1 = feed flow (1b/min)
  h = fuel heat content (Btu/1b)
  C = feed specific heat Btu/(1b)(°F)
  T_1 = inlet feed temperature
  T_2 = outlet feed temperature

Then,

$$Fh = F_1 C(T_2 - T_1)$$
$$= \text{Btu supplied to feed from fuel combustion} \qquad (2.17)$$

We have assumed that heat losses are negligible, that there are no material losses, and furthermore, that the fuel combustion efficiency is constant at the critical value assumed by h.

Solving (2.17) for the controlled variable,

$$T_2 = T_1 + \frac{F}{F_1}\frac{h}{C} \qquad (2.17a)$$

demonstrates that, while T_2 is a function of five variables, we have attempted to compensate for only two of them, the flows F and F_1. Meanwhile the variations in feed temperature T_1 and in h and C have gone on unnoticed. It has been only the temperature feedback loop that has enabled the system to compensate for fluctuations in these variables, but to do so, they must traverse all the lags in the system prior to the point of temperature measurement and connection. While feedback is essential to correct for these (up to now) unknown errors, dependence on feedback implies the existence of some error.

Equation 2.17 can be further rearranged to give the desired model which can be implemented by a simple algebraic computer.

$$F = F_1 \frac{C}{h}(T_2 - T_1) \qquad (2.18)$$

This equation gives the fuel flow required to maintain the desired value of T_2 for each condition of fuel and feed. A common implementation found in many furnace systems is shown in Fig. 2.20. An analog computer may be employed. The feed input parameters F_1 and T_1 are measured and automatically inserted into the "black box," while the set point T and the more esoteric quantities C and h are inserted manually (the latter probably as a result of laboratory analysis).

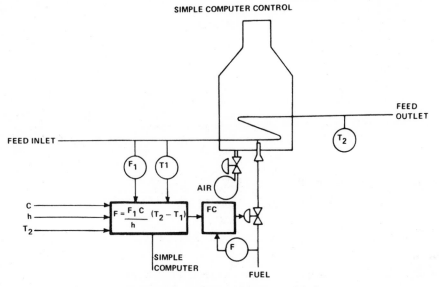

FIGURE 2.20. Simple computer control.

If the dynamics of the system are to be included, the computer will be required to solve differential equations in real time, not merely static algebraic representations. Today, this would most likely mean a general purpose mini- or microcomputer. Where general purpose computers are used in control, either the entire computation including the controller algorithm is done by the computer and a valve signal outputted (*direct digital control*, DDC), or the desired set point is calculated and transmitted to another microprocessor or a conventional controller that performs the algorithm (*set point control*, SPC).

In practice, the system in Fig. 2.20 is employed in many industrial combustion control systems. Most often, the imperfections in (2.18) (such as ambient variations not considered) are compensated for by "closing the loop" with the temperature feedback control shown in Fig. 2.21.

Ratio Control.   The feed heater example can be used to demonstrate one further common mode, that of *ratio control*. In this case, the set point of a controller is held to a ratio of some other variable. This could be the output of another controller if, for example, the flows of two streams are to be kept in constant proportion, or the primary variable could be an uncontrolled "wild" flow which is simply measured.

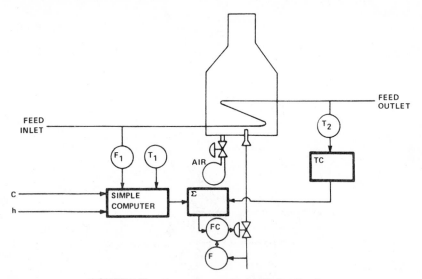

FIGURE 2.21.   **Computer control with feedback.**

In our example we need to keep the amount of combustion air in fixed ratio to the fuel gas flow. This is necessary to maintain fuel combustion efficiency and, in many places, to comply with air pollution smoke ordinances. A ratio controller is employed which also permits the value of the ratio to be adjusted. Figure 2.22 shows such a system in which the furnace damper (air flow) is controlled in direct ratio to the fuel flow which is the output of the fuel flow controller on the right.

A real criterion of combustion efficiency is the oxygen content of the stack gases, which is a measure of excess air. As a feedback around the ratio control (which is seen to be really a feedforward with the air/fuel ratio as the combustion "model"), an oxygen analyzer is used. In Fig. 2.22, the excess oxygen signal is added to the ratio before moving the damper. In other systems, the signal can be used to vary the ratio instead of being added.

How Much Control Is Possible?

Before concluding this discussion, we should recognize the limits placed on any controlled system. It is not possible to constrain all the variables that can be named in a process, but only a number equal to the *degrees of freedom* in the system.[10] This is a perfectly familiar concept which can be

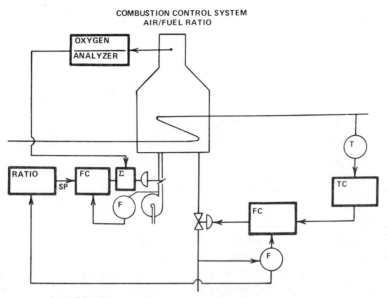

FIGURE 2.22. Combustion control system. Air/fuel ratio.

compared to the motion of a point in space. The position of the point, its "state," can be described by three independently variable coordinates, X, Y, and Z, so that is has 3 degrees of freedom. If the point is confined to a plane, $Z =$ constant, it will have only two independent coordinates left—the number of degrees of freedom will be 2. If we add another constraint, say, that the point must travel on a curve $X = f(Y)$, only 1 degree of freedom will be left, since, if we specify Y, X is fixed so that the state of the point X, Y, Z is completely determined. Generalizing, it is true that the number of degrees of freedom equals the number of variables minus the number of equations that relate them.

Returning to our feed heater example, we have assumed the following variables:

Feed flow in,	F_1
Feed flow out,	F_2
Feed temperature in,	T_1
Feed temperature out,	T_2
Feed specific heat,	C
Fuel flow,	F
Fuel heat content,	h
Total variables,	7

and the following relationships:

$$F_1 = F_2 \quad \text{(material balance)}$$
$$h = \text{constant}$$
$$C = \text{constant}$$
$$\text{Heat balance } Fh = F_1 C(T_2 - T_1)$$
$$\text{Total equations} = 4 \tag{2.17}$$
$$\text{Degrees of freedom} = 7 - 4 = 3$$

Therefore the maximum number of variables that can be independently controlled is 3.

For example, these three variables could be fuel flow, feed flow, and feed-in temperature. If the last two were held constant by some control means, the feed-out temperature would be a function of fuel flow, leaving only 1 degree of freedom. We could constrain that by keeping fuel flow constant, fixing the system state completely. Now if we should attempt to add another controller, say, a feed-out temperature feedback control on the fuel flow, we will have redundant control of the latter and a conflict, resulting in an overspecified (overcontrolled) system.

Note that the variables chosen are somewhat arbitrary and can be specified in most cases to result in more or fewer variables. When this is done, however, it is found that the number of equations relating them increase or decrease correspondingly, so that the calculated degrees of freedom come out the same.

Interacting Control Loops

Throughout this chapter we have assumed that the process variable can be independently controlled (within the limitations just stated), but in fact, many chemical and physical processes are multivariable so that each control loop affects all the other control loops. Distillation columns provide a classic example—if the temperatures at the top and bottom of the column are used to control two different manipulated variables, say, overhead reflux and the boiler, the two process variables will interact and may cause oscillation. Interaction should be avoided wherever possible, and, if not, means to decouple the two variables should be employed.

The method of analysis for decoupling is beyond the scope of this chapter, but a single result is shown here.[11] Figure 2.23 represents the control of relative humidity in a conditioning chamber by controllers manipulating moisture content and temperature. These two PVs interact in the manner shown by psychometric charts. Four controllers must be used to decouple the two variables. The interactive effects of the valve

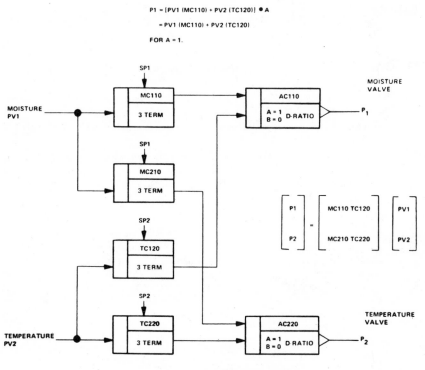

P1 = [PV1 (MC110) + PV2 (TC120)] • A

= PV1 (MC110) + PV2 (TC120)

FOR A = 1.

MULTIVARIABLE CONTROL

FIGURE 2.23.   Multivariable control.

outputs (P_1 and P_2) on the measured variables (PV_1 and PV_2) are given
by the equations

$$P_1 = PV_1(MC110) + PV_2(TC120)$$

$$P_2 = PV_2(MC210) + PV_2(TC220)$$

where the MC's and TC's represent the cross-coupling effects of the three-
term controllers. (This can be also expressed in matrix notations, as shown
in the figure.)

The additional controllers can be thought of as compensating for the
coupling coefficients of the process by feedforward interaction. The direct
and compensating inputs are summed in the blocks labeled AC (actually
ratio controllers with a ratio of unity and an offset bias of zero).

In general, it is necessary to provide N^2 controllers to decouple the
effects of N interactive variables. Interactive processes therefore offer
an advantage to a time sharing controller based on digital techniques.

References

1. P. Harriott, *Process Control*, McGraw-Hill, New York, 1964.

2. *Ibid.*, pp. 10–11.

3. G. K. Tucker and D. M. Wills, *A Simplified Technique of Control Systems Engineering*, Honeywell Inc., Ft. Washington, Pa., 1962.

4. W. L. Lubyen, *Process Modeling, Simulation, and Control for Chemical Engineers*, McGraw-Hill, New York, 1973.

5. H. Chestnut and R. W. Mayer, *Servomechanisms and Regulating System Design*, Vol. I, John Wiley, New York, 1951.

6. V. W. Everleigh, *Introduction to Control Systems Design*, McGraw-Hill, New York, 1972.

7. M. H. La Joy, *Industrial Automatic Controls*, Prentice-Hall, New York, 1954.

8. G. S. Brown and D. P. Campbell, *Principles of Servomechanisms*, John Wiley, New York, 1948.

9. C. H. Cho and K. P. Schwarz, *Electronics* **48**(26) 78–82 (Dec. 25, 1975).

10. B. Liptak, *Instrument Engineers' Handbook*, Vol. II, Chilton, Philadelphia, 1970.

11. Honeywell Inc., Vupak III Systems Manual, Honeywell Process Control Div., Phoenix, Ariz., 1970, p. 63.

Three

Digital Computation and Systems

Fundamentals of Digital Systems

So far we have discussed the workings of control systems and control equations as if the variables treated were analog quantities and always remained so. Of course, the real world of the control engineer is an analog world (but not necessarily linear), and variables such as pressure, temperature, and flow appear to vary continuously as long as we are measuring quantities above the level of quantum physics. Why, then, should we concern ourselves with discrete, digital representation of process data while continuing to measure and control with analog instruments such as transmitters and valves?

There are many good answers to the question, but the most important advantages are:

Lower cost per function
Flexibility
Security—accuracy and stability
Human factors
Advanced control capability

Enormous advances in the electronic manufacturing art during the last few years have made it possible to reduce both the size and cost of digital circuits by many orders of magnitude. It is now possible to fabricate over 30,000 transistors on a silicon chip less than 0.01 in.^{2} in area, and over

10^9 per chip is predicted for the future.[15] In comparison, the transistors and diodes in a modern electronic controller number less than 20. An entire microprocessor, the basic arithmetic and control elements of a digital computer can be placed on a single chip. With the addition of a few more chips (less than 10) to supply memory and perhaps timing, it becomes a complete microcomputer, comparable in most ways with minicomputers costing over $10,000. The microprocessor computer, on the other hand, now costs only a few hundred dollars and is expected to drop to as low as $10. The similar and ubiquitous electronic calculator can already be bought for well under $100 including its displays, keyboard, and so on.

All this implies that tens or hundreds of functions, judged by the electronic complexity of the new digital devices, can be accomplished in less space and at a cost (for the electronic hardware) comparable to that of a single analog controller; consequently, the cost per function is certain to be lower. Or, looking at another aspect, it is now feasible from the standpoint of cost and control room space to conduct multiple and complex tasks where only a single analog function was performed before.

Once the digital path is chosen, the protean flexibility of the digital computer becomes available. Since the basic computer hardware (the processor) performs many arithmetic tasks sequentially and with extreme rapidity, measured in microseconds, and because the sequence of operations is governed by an alterable series of instructions or software program, rather than by hard wiring, it is possible to perform many different functions so quickly that they appear (to the process and to the operator) to be done simultaneously. Because the software program governs the job, the functions can be readily altered to suit changes or additions made to the process.

Security, which means accuracy, stability, and reliable signal transmission; is another hallmark of digital systems. They can exceed with ease the high standards achieved by analog hardware only with great care and at some cost.

For example, a high-quality analog controller has a drift rate of typically less than 0.1 % per hour, or 5 mV for a 0 to 5 V signal. Measurements made on shielded, twisted pair cables running a few hundred feet through typical industrial environments show noise levels of ± 0.1 V, reducible with special precautions to about 10 mV.[1] In other words, the electrical noise level, even in a favorable situation, limits the accuracy of analog control signals to about 0.1 to 0.2 %.

There is no such limit on digital control. Digital signals are transmitted as bits, or binary digits, and the receiver need only distinguish between the binary numbers 1 (presence of a signal) and 0 (absence of a signal).

If the signal level is 5 V, it is 500 times the noise level in the cable described above, and the probability of confusing the 0 and 1 states becomes vanishingly small. Consequently, the accuracy of signal transmission depends only on the number of binary digits used to describe the signal. Since digital signals can be processed readily at rates exceeding 10^5/sec, a large number of bits can be used to describe the signal amplitude at any given time, even if they are sent down the line sequentially. For example, any decimal number from 0 to 1,048,575 can be sent using only 20 bits, which exceeds an accuracy of 1 part in 10^6. If the bit transmission rate is only 200,000/sec, 10,000 such numbers can be transmitted each second. If some of the bits are used as labels, many different kinds of digital signals can be sent on the same line, or *multiplexed*. The number of signal types, the accuracy, and the speed of transmission (in samples per second) can all be traded off in a digital system to achieve the desired results.

Since the binary signal bits start off far above noise level, the transmitted signal is not subject to drift or error so long as the bits are not greatly attenuated by long lines. Even attenuated bits can be restored to their original waveshape by simple amplifiers or "repeaters." Furthermore, some bits can be devoted to a code which checks each "word" (number) received for errors and even requests a retransmittal if one is found. Consequently, the reliability and stability of digital signals are far greater than that of their analog counterparts.

Digital representation also possesses some well-recognized advantages as an operator interface. Errors in inserting or reading numbers are largely eliminated. And where human factors favor analog presentations, as when observing trends, the digital form can readily be converted to the analog, while the reverse interchange is not so easy.

Finally, the digital format makes for compatibility with other computers of the same or different hierarchical level. This feature alone makes it easier to implement advanced control capability. Because a digital controller can take on a wider variety and greater number of functions than its analog counterpart, the assignment of tasks between it and a supervisory computer can more closely approach optimum; furthermore, the latter can devote all its capability to advanced control and need not be concerned with A/D or other interface tasks.

Digital Representation and Codes

Now that we have seen the "why" of digital representation and, more particularly, the advantages of binary signals, it is necessary to convince ourselves that the fundamental computational operations, both of static arithmetic and in the time domain, can be performed equally well or better than with analog circuitry.

First, as those who have struggled through the "new math" are aware, there are many ways of representing number, of which our decimal system is but one example. In modern arithmetical systems, the concept of positional notation is used. A restricted number of symbols, called the *base* or *radix*, is permitted, and the position of these symbols relative to a dot or a *point* (.) determines the value of a multiplier attached to the symbol.[2] For example, 10 is the radix of our decimal system, and the number

$$N = 7980.42$$

can be expressed in the form

$$N = 7 \times 10^3 + 9 \times 10^2 + 8 \times 10^1 + 0 \times 10_0 + 4 \times 10^{-1} + 2 \times 10^{-2}$$

since the decimal point separates the zero exponent from the negative exponents.

In general, any number

$$N = \cdots + a_3 R^3 + a_2 R^2 + a_1 R^1 + a_0 R^0 + a_{-1} R^{-1} + a_{-2} R^{-2} + \cdots$$

where R is the radix. In the *normal binary* system, the radix is 2 and the number

$$N = \cdots + a_3 2^3 + a_2 2^2 + a_2 2^1 + a_0 2^0 + a_{-1} 2^{-1} + \cdots$$

can be represented in positional notation by

$$\cdots a_3 a_2 a_1 a_0 . a_{-1} \cdots$$

where the a's are either 1 or 0 and each is multiplied by a power of 2 equal to its position relative to the *binary point;* again, the dot between a_0 and a_{-1} signifies the beginning of the negative exponents.

The number binary 11011.1 can be converted to decimal form by evaluating its digits according to their position using the rule, thus

$$1 \times 16 + 1 \times 8 + 0 \times 4 + 1 \times 2 + 1 \times 1 + 1 \times \tfrac{1}{2} = 27.5$$

A decimal integer can be converted to binary by (*a*) dividing by 2, (*b*) calling the remainder a_0 (least significant digit), (*c*) dividing the integral remainder again by 2, (*d*) setting the remainder equal to a_1; the process is repeated until the division produces only a remainder. For 27

$$\frac{27}{2} = 13 + \tfrac{1}{2} \qquad a_0 = 1$$
$$\frac{13}{2} = 6 + \tfrac{1}{2} \qquad a_1 = 1$$
$$\frac{6}{2} = 3 + \tfrac{0}{2} \qquad a_2 = 0$$
$$\frac{3}{2} = 1 + \tfrac{1}{2} \qquad a_3 = 1$$
$$\frac{1}{2} = 0 + \tfrac{1}{2} \qquad a_5 = 1 \qquad \text{or} \qquad 27_{10} = 11011_2$$

where the subscript indicates the base.

Likewise, in the *octal* or radix 8 system, the permitted symbols are 0 to 7, and a number such as

$$716.3_8$$

can be interpreted as

$$N = 7 \times 8^2 + 1 \times 8^1 + 6 \times 8^0 + 3 \times 8^{-1}$$
$$= 7 \times 64 + 1 \times 8 \times 6 \times 1 + 3 \times \tfrac{1}{8}$$

or 462.375_{10} in decimal form.

In many cases, such as that of electromechanical shaft encoders which convert analog position to digital, it is desirable that no more than one digit at a time be changed when counting in sequence; for example, the transition 999 to 1000 involves four transistions and the same number of chances for error. Codes that avoid this difficulty are called *reflecting* codes; in the binary system it is the *Gray* code (see below).

One more useful binary representation is the *binary coded decimal* (BCD) type. Ten combinations of four binary digits are used to represent the decimal numbers 0 to 9. In the weighted BCD codes, each column, a_3, a_2, a_1, and a_0 is multiplied (weighted) by an arbitrary factor; the decimal value of each tetred can be found by adding up the weights of columns in which 1's appear.

A large number of BCD weighted codes has been devised; Richards[3] lists over 70. If the weights are 8, 4, 2, and 1, the BCD code is identical to the normal binary system for the numbers 0 to 9.

Table 3.1 lists the various kinds of codes just mentioned.

Error Detecting Codes.   If more than four bits are used to represent decimal information, the redundancy provided by the extra bits can provide error detecting, or even error correcting capability. A message known to be in error can be discarded, corrected, or repeated. One common method uti-

TABLE 3.1. Digital Codes

Decimal	Octal	Normal Binary	Reflected Binary (Gray)	8-4-2-1 BCD
0	0	0	0	0000 0000
1	1	1	1	0000 0001
2	2	10	11	0000 0010
3	3	11	10	0000 0011
4	4	100	110	0000 0100
5	5	101	111	0000 0101
6	6	110	101	0000 0110
7	7	111	100	0000 0111
8	10	1000	1100	0000 1000
9	11	1001	1101	0000 1001
10	12	1010	1111	0001 0000
11	13	1011	1110	0001 0001
12	14	1100	1010	0001 0010
13	15	1101	1011	0001 0011
14	16	1110	1001	0001 0100
15	17	1111	1000	0001 0101
16	20	10000	11000	0001 0110

lizes a fifth bit added to any four-bit BCD code; it is chosen as 0 or 1 to make the total number of 1's in the group even (or odd). A *parity check* of the received code then consists of a count of 1's—if not even or odd, as prescribed, the group is in error. An odd parity bit check code is shown in Table 3.2. This code can detect any single bit error (including the parity bit), but will fail if two errors occur in the same digit. Hence it is called a single error detecting code. Many more elaborate schemes have been devised. For example, three redundant bits can be added to an 8-4-2-1 code to provide a complete check on all digits.

BCD Bits				Check Bits		
8	4	2	1	*A*	*B*	*C*
	A	*A*	*A*	*A*		
B		*B*	*B*		*B*	
C	*C*		*C*			*C*

In the above scheme, bit *A* is used to provide odd parity with the combination of 4, 2, and 1 bits; *B* provides odd parity with 8, 2, 1, and *C* with 8, 4, and 2. The resultant code is shown in Table 3.3.

TABLE 3.2. Odd Parity Check 8-4-2-1 BCD Code

Decimal	8, 4, 2, 1	8, 4, 2, 1 with Odd Parity Bit
0	0000	10000
1	0001	00001
2	0010	00010
3	0011	10011
4	0100	00100
5	0101	10101
6	0110	10110
7	0111	00111
8	1000	01000
9	1001	11001

A test of the redundancy bits locates any single error and, as a consequence, permits it to be corrected. For example, if B and C fail in an odd parity check, the error is in the 8 bit; if A and C fail, it is in the 4 bit; and if all three fail, it is in the 1 bit. If only one check fails, the error is in the redundancy bit itself. However, if two errors occur in one digit representation, the system will fail.

Note that the coded representation of each decimal number in Table 3.3 differs from that of any other number by at least three bits. The number of changes required in going from digit to digit determines the error detecting or correcting property of the code; the two properties can be traded off as shown in Table 3.4.

TABLE 3.3. Three–Redundant Bit 8-4-2-1 Code

Decimal	8	4	2	1	A	B	C
0	0	0	0	0	1	1	1
1	0	0	0	1	0	0	0
2	0	0	1	0	0	0	1
3	0	0	1	1	1	1	0
4	0	1	0	0	0	1	0
5	0	1	0	1	1	0	1
6	0	1	1	0	1	0	0
7	0	1	1	1	0	1	1
8	1	0	0	0	1	0	0
9	1	0	0	1	0	1	1

TABLE 3.4.   Error Correcting or Detecting Codes

Bits Changed in Coded Digits		Property		
		Error Correcting		Error Detecting
1			None	
2		0	or	1
3		1	or	2
4		2	and	1
	or	0	and	3
5		2	and	0
	or	1	and	3
	or	0	and	4

Multiple error detection is important, since serious noise disturbances, when they occur, tend to appear in "bursts," each lasting long enough to destroy several bits in a sequence. Such impulse or burst noise is especially noticeable in common carrier–switched communication networks, such as the telephone system, where it tends to be associated with switching transients during peak traffic hours. Error detection (in control systems) is more important than automatic error correction, because the process dynamics usually allow time to repeat an erroneous message after the noise burst has subsided. Hence a practical coding system uses the multiple error detecting alternatives suggested in Table 3.4.

Many mathematicians have devoted their time to this subject because of the promise and importance of error free information handling. Some of the more sophisticated work has been done by R. C. Bose and D. K. R. Chaudhuri and their associates.[14] Many systems utilize a five-bit security code known as the 31, 26 BCH devised by them. This has the error detection properties described in Chapter 8.

Digital Machine Arithmetic

The concepts of analog computation are well known to anyone working with process controllers. The static operations of algebraic summing, multiplication, and division all can be accomplished by sufficiently clever arrangements of operational amplifiers and are basic to the more significant dynamic operations—integration and differentiation—required to solve the differential equations making up control algorithms. Although the rote operations of digital arithmetic in the decimal system were familiar to us at an early age, it is necessary to reexamine these arithmetic algorithms in order to understand the special requirements of machines, especially binary computers.

Negative Numbers. The concept of negative number must be defined before we can describe the process of algebraic (+ or −) summing. Any negative quantity can be considered positive from a different point of view; for example, − 10°C is positive on the Fahrenheit scale, and a debit is a credit on someone else's books. In digital calculating machines, negative numbers are a bother, since a counting device must sense zero and also be able to operate in both directions; thus

$$3$$
$$2$$
$$1$$
$$0$$
$$-1$$
$$-2$$

If a counter is so arranged that some positive numbers substitute for the negatives, the complexity of zero sensing and direction changing can be avoided. For example,

+2	is represented by	0002
1	by	0001
0	by	0000
−1	by	9999
−2	by	9998
	and so on	

This notation is known as *10's complement*—actually only the least significant digit is 10's complemented (subtracted from 10) to obtain the value of the negative number; the remaining digits are really 9's complemented. If we restrict the capacity of the counter to the range +8999 to − 1000, the digit 9 in the most significant place can be used to indicate the sign of the balance, for example, 9 acts as the minus sign.

In binary machine arithmetic it is equally useful to employ complements. If the 2's complement is chosen to represent negative numbers, they need no special manipulation and the same equipment can be used both for addition and subtraction. Deferring an explanation (until subtraction is described), we simply note the following rules for putting binary numbers into 2's complement form.[4]

2's Complement Form

Positive number: Append a binary 0 above the highest order magnitude bit as a + sign and keep the magnitude bits unchanged.

Example: Binary 5 $= 0101$
              2's complement form $= 00101$

Negative number: Append a binary 1 above the highest order magnitude bit as a − sign and replace the magnitude bits as follows (2's complement): (*a*) Replace all 1's by 0's, and vice versa (1's complement). (*b*) Add 1.

Example: Binary minus 7 $= -0111$
           1's complement 1000
           Add 1 $+\quad 1$
           _____
                                   1001
           Add minus sign bit 11001

Binary Logic and Addition

The rules for adding single bits are very simple:

Augend		Addend		Sum	
0	+	0	=	0	
0	+	1	=	1	
1	+	0	=	1	
1	+	1	=	0	("carry" neglected)

The complication arises when more than one bit is used, that is when the carry is considered. The carry of course is the 1 which must be carried to the next higher order of bits when we add $1 + 1$.

If we imagine a logical black box which accounts for both sum and carry, it will look like the following:

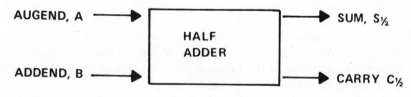

TABLE 3.5. Half Adder Truth Table

Augend, A	Addend, B	Sum, $S_{1/2}$	Carry, $C_{1/2}$
0	0	0	0
1	0	1	0
0	1	1	0
1	1	0	1

The reason for the term "half adder" is that only the outgoing carry is accounted for, not one that could enter from a lower order black box. As we will see, two half adders are needed to complete the additional task.

The rules for specifying the output of the half adder as a function of its inputs can be put in the form shown in Table 3.5.[5] Such a table is known as a *truth table* in binary logic. Note that all four of the possible combinations of A and B (where either can be 0 or 1) are specified as inputs. The sum output is the same as for single bit addition, and the carry to the next higher order of bits occurs only when both inputs are 1's.

Logic Elements. In order to see how such a black box can be constructed we must first define the elements of binary logic. These are the basic building blocks of binary arithmetic. Actually, there are a great many possible logic elements we can use as basic ones. For all combinations of two inputs, such as A and B in the above table, there are 16 different possible output combinations, including those shown in the half adder sum and carry

columns. Some of these 16 are trivial; for example, the output can always be 0 regardless of the value of A and B (an open circuit), or it can always be 1 (a short circuit). Two of these elementary logic functions are intuitively considered basic, and all other functions can be built up from these. They are AND and OR (nonexclusive). The AND function can be symbolized with a multiplication sign (dot):

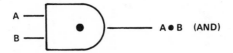

Its truth table is

A	B	A · B (AND)
0	0	0
1	0	0
0	1	0
1	1	1

In accordance with its name, the AND function is true (1) only when *A and B* are 1. Otherwise it is false, or 0.

The AND function can be easily envisioned as two switches in series:

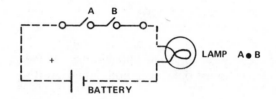

The lamp, $A \cdot B$ will light only if both *A* and *B* switches are closed. You can readily convince yourself that the circuit will obey the truth table for AND, assuming a closed switch or a lighted lamp means 1 and the converse means 0.

Obviously, semiconductor switches are substituted in the logic elements of the integrated circuits, but the principle is the same.

The nonexclusive OR is also intuitively logical. Its symbol is the + sign:

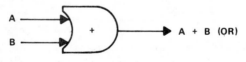

and its truth table is

A	B	A + B (OR)
0	0	0
1	0	1
0	1	1
1	1	1

The OR function is true if either *A or B* is true, and is 0 (false) only if neither is true. An embodiment of an OR element consists of two parallel switches:

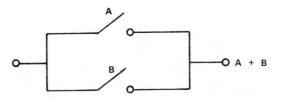

By connecting this assembly of switches to the lamp and battery circuit, you can assure yourself that it obeys the logical or truth table as well as the analogous circuit in the AND case.

With the addition of one more logical concept, that of NOT, or complementation, we can build up any of the 16 logic functions. NOT is merely the negation or inversion of a single variable. It is symbolized by an overbar such as $\overline{A}$, or by a circle in a block diagram, and can be envisioned as a one-stage (inverting) amplifier or a normally open relay closed by means of an external circuit:

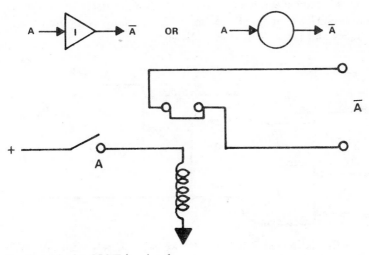

The truth table for NOT is, simply

A	$\overline{A}$
0	1
1	0

With these three logic elements, AND, OR, and NOT, we can achieve all the possible two-input logic functions including the half adder sum and carry. (Actually, there are two even more fundamental functions, the NOR or not-OR, called the Pierce function, and the NAND or not-AND, also known as the Sheffer stroke. The NOR

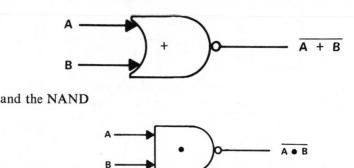

and the NAND

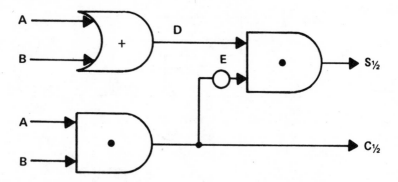

are most commonly used in practical integrated circuitry, but are more complex to show as examples of implementation.

Half Adder Implementation. Even restricting ourselves to the AND, OR, and NOT elements, there are a great many embodiments of the half adder truth table. Only one is shown here:

To prove this is indeed a half adder, we need merely construct its truth table. Note that the inputs to the $S_{1/2}$ AND element are D, the output of the OR and E, the negation of the input AND (thus E is really a NAND of A and B). Thus we can construct Table 3.6 from the possible A and B inputs. Now, comparing the $S_{1/2}$ and $C_{1/2}$ columns of Table 3.6 with those of Table 3.5, we see they are identical; therefore the circuit shown is a half adder.

TABLE 3.6. Proof of Half Adder Logic

A	B	D	$C_{1/2}$	E	$S_{1/2}$
		$A + B$	$A \cdot B$	$\overline{A \cdot B}$	$D \cdot E$
0	0	0	0	1	0
1	0	1	0	1	1
0	1	1	0	1	1
1	1	1	1	0	0

We could also show the properties of the circuit by manipulating the logical equations (Boolean algebra).[6] From the diagram,

$$S_{1/2} = D \cdot E$$

but

$$D = A + B$$

and

$$E = A \cdot B$$

Two basic theorems of Boolean algebra (which you can prove by constructing truth tables) are

$$\overline{A \cdot B} = \overline{A} + \overline{B} \qquad \text{(deMorgan's theorem)}$$

and

$$X \cdot \overline{X} = 0$$

From deMorgan's theorem,

$$E = \overline{A} + \overline{B}$$

and

$$S_{1/2} = (A + B) \cdot (\overline{A} + \overline{B})$$

Multiplying out the terms (omitting the dots), we obtain

$$S_{1/2} = A\overline{A} + A\overline{B} + B\overline{B} + B\overline{A}$$

and, dropping zero terms, $A\overline{A}$ and $B\overline{B} = 0$,

$$S_{1/2} = A\overline{B} + B\overline{A}$$

This function is call the *exclusive OR* and has the truth table:

A	B	$A\overline{B} + B\overline{A}$
0	0	0
1	0	1
0	1	1
1	1	0

which is identical to the sum $S_{1/2}$. The carry $C_{1/2}$ is merely the AND function of the inputs $C_{1/2} = A \cdot B$ as shown in the diagram.

Full Adder. Having developed the logic circuitry for the half adder, we go to the full adder which will permit us to perform all the required digital arithmetic operations. The full adder has three inputs, the augend and addend bits, as in the half adder, plus a carry bit from the *previous* stage of the adder. The outputs are a sum bit which is obtained by applying the rules for adding single bits (with no carry) to all three inputs, and a carry bit to the next stage. There is a carry bit C, if at least two of the input bits are 1's. Therefore the full adder can be cascaded for any number of stages to achieve any desired accuracy in terms of binary digit representation of a number.

The truth table for a full adder is shown in Table 3.7.

TABLE 3.7. Full Adder Truth Table

A	B	C	S	C_1
0	0	0	0	0
1	0	0	1	0
0	1	0	1	0
1	1	0	0	1
0	0	1	1	0
1	0	1	0	1
0	1	1	0	1
1	1	1	1	1

The sum S is equal to 1 if there are an odd number of 1's in the input, that is, if only one of A, B, or C is 1 or if each of A, B, and C is 1. In equation form, the logic is

$$S = \overline{A}\overline{B}C + \overline{A}B\overline{C} + A\overline{B}\overline{C} + ABC$$

Likewise, the logic equation for carry C_1 is

$$C_1 = AB\overline{C} + A\overline{B}C + \overline{A}BC + ABC$$

$$= 1 \text{ if any two or more inputs} = 1$$

The S equation can be rewritten after some manipulation as

$$S = (A\overline{B} + \overline{A}B)\overline{C} + \overline{(A\overline{B} + \overline{A}B)}C$$

which, recalling the equivalence of $S_{1/2}$ and the exclusive OR $(A\overline{B} + \overline{A}B)$, demonstrates that it is possible to make a full adder with two half adders.

This circuit is shown below, but it is only one of many ways to design an adder. For example, the original form of the logic equations can be instrumented directly.

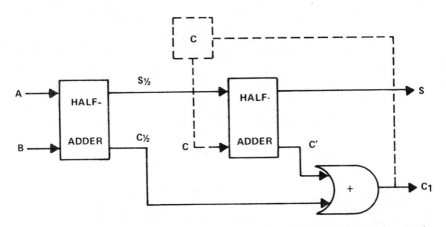

Using Table 3.5 we can construct a truth table for the above logic diagram.

A	B	C	$S_{1/2}$	$C_{1/2}$	S	C'	C_1
0	0	0	0	0	0	0	0
1	0	0	1	0	1	0	0
0	1	0	1	0	1	0	0
1	1	0	0	1	0	0	1
0	0	1	0	0	1	0	0
1	0	1	1	0	0	1	1
0	1	1	1	0	0	1	1
1	1	1	0	1	1	0	1

Note that the S and C_1 columns are identical to those of Table 3.7, proving that this is truly a full adder.

From a practical view, it is not always necessary to have one set of full adder hardware for each bit. If the carry C_1 is held in a memory (dashed box labeled C), the bits can be added serially in a single adder. Clearly, there is a trade-off between addition time and hardware; the latter constraint being much less severe with microcircuitry than has been the case heretofore.

Subtraction.   Half and full subtractors, both serial and parallel, can be designed like adders. But rather than build special hardware for subtraction, it is easier to add, using the 2's complement, as we noted earlier in this chapter. For example, the binary number 0.0110000 would normally be subtracted from binary number 0.1001001, using a subtractor:

		Decimal equivalent
A +	0.1001001	0.57013125_{10}
B −	0.0110000	0.375_{10}
+	0.0011001_2	0.1953125_{10}

Using the rules specified for 2's complement, we can convert B to that form and add, obtaining the same result:

0.0110000	$+B$ (subtrahend)
0.1001111	1's complement of B
1	Add initial carry (1)
0.1010000	2's complement of B
1.1010000	Add minus sign bit for $-B$
0.1001001	Add $+A$
10.0011001	$A - B$
0.0011001	Throw away extra carry

The answer is the same as before, and neither the hardware nor the rules must be changed, other than to 2's complement the subtrahend.

In the event that the subtrahend is larger than the minuend, the sum will be negative and the result N will be in 2's complement form $(2^n - N)$. Although this is satisfactory for the machine, for external representation, if magnitude and sign are displayed separately, the result must be again complemented, since $2^n - (2^n - N) = N$.

To subtract 8 from 3 in complement form we proceed as follows:

1000	Binary 8
0111	1's complement
1	Initial carry
11000	Add sign bit (binary -8)
00011	Binary $+3$
11011	Result, 2's complement
0100	
1	
1 0101	Recomplemented result

$-$ Sign   Magnitude 5

Practical Arithmetic Unit. In a practical microcomputer, all these functions are carried out in the form of one or a few large scale integrated (LSI) or medium scale integrated (MSI) circuit chips. A typical LSI arithmetic and logic unit (ALU) has the equivalent of 75 gates (AND, OR, or similar logics) and can perform 16 binary arithmetic or logical operations on two four-bit words. An LSI unit of this type employing some types of multichip microprocessors can do any one of the following jobs within a typical switching time of less than 50 nsec.

1. Any of the 16 possible logic functions, including AND, OR, NOR, NAND, and so on
2. 16 arithmetic operations on two four-bit words, including add, subtract, and multiply
3. Comparison—generate an $A = B$ signal if the inputs are identical
4. Decrement or increment (adding or subtracting 1)
5. Relative magnitude ($A > B$ or $A < B$)

Table 3.8 lists the possible functions, and a diagram of this black box is given below[7]:

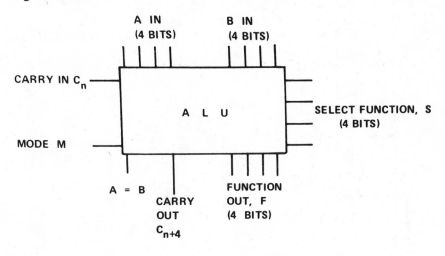

Higher Arithmetic Functions

We have spent a great deal of time on the addition function because it is fundamental to all other binary arithmetic. Once we are able to add and to handle negative numbers (subtract), all other operations can be per-

TABLE 3.8. ALU Functions

Select, S Input	Logic Function, $M=1$	Arithmetic Function, $M=0$	
		$C_n = 1$	$C_n = 0$
0000	$F = \overline{A}$ (NOT)	$F = A$	$F = A$ plus 1
0001	$F = \overline{A+B}$ (NOR)	$F = A + B$	$F = (A+B)$ plus 1
0010	$F = \overline{A}B$	$F = A + \overline{B}$	$F = (A+\overline{B})$ plus 1
0011	$F = 0$	$F =$ minus 1(2's complement)	$F = 0$
0100	$F = \overline{AB}$ (NAND)	$F = A + A\overline{B}$	$F = (A + A\overline{B})$ plus 1
0101	$F = \overline{B}$ (NOT)	$F = (A+B)$ plus $A\overline{B}$	$F = (A+B)$ plus $A\overline{B} + 1$
0110	$F = A\overline{B} + B\overline{A}$ (exclusive OR)	$F = (A - B)$ minus 1	$F = A$ minus B
0111	$F = A\overline{B}$	$F = A\overline{B}$ minus 1	$F = A\overline{B}$
1000	$F = \overline{A} + B$ (implication)	$F = A + AB$	$F = (A + AB)$ plus 1
1001	$F = \overline{AB} + AB$ (NOT exclusive OR)	$F = A + B$	$F = (A + B)$ plus 1
1010	$F = B$	$F = (A + \overline{B})$ plus AB	$F = (A + \overline{B})$ plus $A + 1$
1011	$F = AB$ (AND)	$F = AB$ minus 1	$F = AB$
1100	$F = 1$	$F = A$ plus A*	$F = (A + A)$ plus 1
1101	$F = A + \overline{B}$	$F = (A + B)$ plus A	$F = (A + B)$ plus $A + 1$
1110	$F = A + B$ (OR)	$F = (A + B)$ plus A	$F = (A + \overline{B})$ plus $A + 1$
1111	$F = A$	$F = A$ minus 1	$F = A$

* Each bit is shifted to the next more significant position.

formed with only a few minor embellishments. For example, the act of multiplication is merely repeated addition, and that of division merely subtraction.

In a microcomputer, most or all of the higher functions are performed by instructions, or programs, which are orders to control the sequence of basic operations. In older computers, these instructions were called *software routines* and were selected by the programmer as part of the overall process of setting up a particular job on the computer. In a microcomputer, these instructions are usually put into *firmware*, which amounts to a permanent memory (read only memory, ROM) which becomes an integral part of the computer.

Although we could multiply by repeated addition of the multiplicand controller by a *counter*, together with some means to detect when the count reached the value of the multiplier, in practice this would be quite slow and there are easier ways to accomplish it. The basic binary multiplication table is quite simple, and there are no carries to complicate things.

Multiplicand digit

		0	1
Multiplier digit	0	0	0
	1	0	1

Therefore it pays to use the logic in the table and to multiply by the rote method taught to schoolchildren.

Multiplicand	0.11101	
Multiplier	0.11110	Multiplier digit
	00000	0
	11101	1
	11101	1
	11101	1
	11101	1
	0.1101100110	

We have introduced one new concept here, and that is *shift*. As each higher order multiplier digit is utilized, the partial product is shifted one binary place to the left. A shift of the partial product to the left, or of the binary point to the right, is equivalent to multiplication by 2, just as shifting the decimal point in base 10 notation is equivalent to multiplication by 10.

If you attempt to follow through the above multiplication, you will encounter one more difficulty—summing the partial products. This is because there are not only single, but multiple, carries in the addition and it is difficult to keep them straight. In machine implementation one usually accumulates the partial products as one goes along, although not for the same reason. The machine calculation would then look like this:

	0.11101	Accumulated	
X	0.11110	Partial Product	Multiplier digit
	00000		
	00000		0
	00000	x	
	11101		1
	111010	x	
	11101		1
	10101110	x	
	11101		1
	110010110	x	
	11101		1
Product	0.1101100110	x	

If the two numbers being multiplied are *signed* (having + and − signs) there are rules of some complexity involving 2's complements, but the above is sufficient to show the principles of multiplication.

Note, however, that this is only one of several methods available. There are others that the designer may choose to incorporate in the firmware.

In the preceding chapter it was seen that ratios are important in control systems design, and there are several ways of performing *division*. One method which is simple, involving only addition, subtraction, and multiplication, is *iteration*. If A/B is to be found, $1/B$ is found by the following formula, and the result multiplied by A to give A/B. The formula is

$$U_{n+1} = U_n(2 - U_nB)$$

That is, a trial value is selected for U_n when $n = 0$. U_{n+1} is calculated and then placed back in the formula. As this process is repeated and n becomes large, U approaches $1/B$.

While this method has been used in some digital calculators, it is too slow or inaccurate for most purposes. The method of *trial division* is one of the more popular. In this, the divisor is compared with the remainder (this can be done with the ALU functions in Table 3.8). If the divisor is the greater, no subtraction is actually performed and a 0 is placed in the lowest order of the quotient. If the divisor is not greater than the remainder, is it subtracted from the remainder and a 1 bit placed in the quotient. After each quotient bit is calculated, the dividend is shifted and the loop repeated.

Negative numbers introduce slight complications to these schemes. Furthermore, the divisor must be greater than the dividend (the quotient is less than 1) for most routines. An example of a microprocessor division routine is given in Chapter 7.

Square root is another important derived variable, used especially in flow control, and can be obtained by digital means similar to those for division. There is a square root iteration formula:[9]

$$X_{n+1} = \frac{1}{2}\left(X_n + \frac{a}{X_n}\right)$$

where X_n approaches $\sqrt{a}$ more closely as n, the number of iterations, increases. Also, there are quicker methods, similar to the square root algorithms learned in school, but we have already shown enough to prove our thesis. That is, any arithmetic calculations that can be performed by analog means can also be done digitally—quickly and more accurately.

We must recognize, however, that, while a 4 bit addition can be performed in 25 nsec by an ALU chip, operations like division and square root take considerably longer. As examples, 16 bit multiplication or division may typically require 400 to 500 μsec, while it may take as long as 1 msec to perform square root. Nevertheless, these are still negligible periods with respect to typical process time constants.

Dynamic Calculations, Integration and Differentiation

In all but the most elementary applications of automatic control, we are concerned with the dynamics or time-varying behavior of the process and control system. Thus a digital processor acting as a controller must be capable not only of multiplying (for the proportional factor) but also of integrating (reset) and differentiating (rate) actions. How is this accomplished by a microprocessor?

Early analog computers, and some digital types also, had special devices which performed integration. Classic examples are the mechanical ball and disk integrator used by Vannevar Bush in the pioneer digital differential analyzer (DDA) built at MIT in the 1930's, and the well-known operational amplifier analog integrator. A purely digital machine can approximate continuous integration very closely by assuming that the curve to be integrated, $Y = f(t)$, is made up of a large number of rectangular sections,

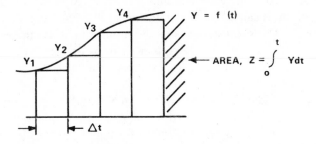

each of which is of width Δt. Each segment has the area $Y_i \, \Delta t$, and the integral is given by

$$Z = \sum_{i=0}^{n} Y_i \, \Delta t_i = \Delta t \sum_{i=0}^{n} Y_i$$

Therefore we need only add up the discrete values of Y at the start of each time interval Δt and multiply the sum by Δt. As Δt is made very small, the approximation becomes more accurate.

The diagram shows that there is always a small residual error in this approximation, represented by the approximately triangular area between the top of the rectangle and the true curve. The area of this triangle is

$$(Y_{n+1} - Y_n) \frac{\Delta t}{2} = \Delta Y \frac{\Delta t}{2}$$

Therefore a somewhat more accurate integration formula is

$$Z = \sum_{i=0}^{n} \left(Y + \Delta \frac{Y}{2} \right) \Delta t$$

With this rule, the sampling interval Δt need not be quite so small. In either case, it is not necessary to devise special circuitry for the integration function, since it can be accomplished by means of the addition, multiplication, and division routines already considered. Thus integration in a microprocessor is accomplished through a program designed into the firmware.

Differentiation is defined as the operation

$$\left(\frac{dY}{dX} \right)_{\text{at } X=X_0} = \lim_{\Delta X \to 0} \frac{f(X_0 + \Delta X) - f(X_0)}{\Delta X}$$

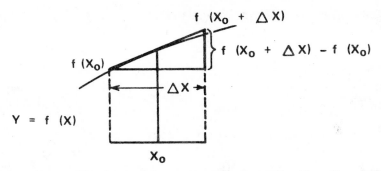

which represents the slope of the tangent drawn to the curve $Y = f(X)$ at X_0. A good approximation of this slope is therefore

$$\frac{dY}{dX} \doteq \frac{f(X_1) - f(X_0)}{X_1 - X_0}$$

The value so calculated by a digital computer, unfortunately, does not continue to become more accurate as $X_1 - X_0$ decreases, since $f(X_1) - f(X_0)$ also becomes very small, and the resulting calculation (with only a few significant bits left) may be far off. In some cases, more accurate values of the slope can be obtained by formal differentiation of Y in polynomial form, if the function is known, or by differentiating an approximation if only discrete points are specified, and subsequently evaluating the resulting algebraic equation.

In the general case $f(X)$ is not a known function and the first approximation given stands, using a judicious choice of ΔX (or Δt, since X is usually the time axis). This method is readily applied to the solution of control system dynamic equations, as seen below.

Take the case of a typical first order lag network. Assume it is desired to calculate by digital computer the output D as a function of the input X.

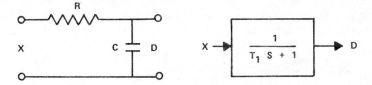

If the time constant $RC = T_1$, the transfer function in Laplace transform notation is as shown in the block. This can readily be converted to differential form by means of the inverse transform $SF(s) = df(t)/dt$, as shown. First,

$$\frac{D}{X} = \frac{1}{T_1 S + 1}$$

or $T_1 SD + D = X$

By the inverse transform for differentiation,

$$T_1 \frac{dD}{dt} + D = X$$

Putting the above differential equation in *difference* form, using the digital approximation,

$$T_1 \frac{(D_n - D_{n-1})}{T_s} + D_n = X$$

where T_s is the sampling time interval $T_n - T_{n-1}$.
Solving for D_n,

$$T_1(D_n - D_{n-1}) + D_n T_s = T_s X$$

$$D_n(T_s + T_1) = T_1 D_{n-1} + T_s X$$

$$D_n = \left(\frac{T_1}{T_s + T_1}\right) D_{n-1} + \left(\frac{T_s}{T_s + T_1}\right) X$$

$$= D_{n-1}\left(\frac{T_1}{T_s + T_1}\right) + D_{n-1}\left(\frac{T_s}{T_s + T_1}\right)$$

$$- D_{n-1}\left(\frac{T_s}{T_s + T_1}\right) + X\frac{T_s}{T_s + T_1}$$

$$D_n = D_{n-1} + \frac{T_s}{T_s + T_1}(X - D_{n-1})$$

Hence the most recent value of the network output D_n is obtained in terms of the previous value of D and the network input X modified by the sampling time and network time constant. This result is useful and economical of machine calculation time, as it builds on the previous value of D without requiring it to be calculated from scratch for each point. The output is continually calculated as in the following diagram.

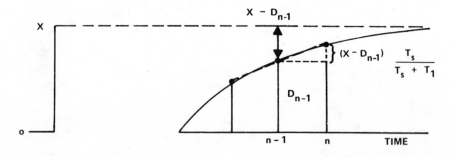

It can be seen that the rapidity of the successive approach of D to the asymptotic value of X is a function of the remaining error $X - D_{n-1}$ multiplied by the ratio $T_s/(T_s + T_1)$. Since the sampling time T_s is generally a constant, T_1, the time constant, correctly governs the lag of the output.

The Sampling Theorem and Sampled Data Systems

So far we have demonstrated that a controller containing a digital micro-processor can perform all the computations necessary for dynamic control. In order to use the digital computer, however, the input data must be in sampled form. A doubt may linger as to the effect of converting the analog process variables to digital samples and then back to analog form in order to actuate the final control element (most usually an analog-actuated valve or motor). Will we not lose some of the information in the signal? And even if we do not, what benefit is there in these seemingly extra steps?

The first question can be readily answered. If the sampling frequency (by which we mean the reciprocal of the interval between samples) is at least twice the highest significant frequency in the sample waveform, there is no loss of information. This is known as the *sampling theorem*.[10] As first expressed by Shannon: "Given a band-width limited signal $f(t)$ containing no frequency components beyond ω radians/sec, $f(t)$ can be recovered completely from the infinite sequence of impulse samples $f^*(t)$ separated by time intervals no greater than $\frac{1}{2}(2\pi/\omega)$ sec."

It is not possible to achieve the Shannon limit because we have neither an infinite string of pulses nor an ideal reconstruction filter. We can show in fact that, to recover at least the rms value from a *single* oscillation of frequency f, the sampling rate f^* must be at least $4f$. In practice, sampling frequencies 10 times the theoretical limit are common.[11]

Shannon's theorem does not say that frequencies in the sample above half the sampling rate cannot affect the sample, but rather that they must not be present if we are to achieve an undistorted sample. In fact, all frequencies present above $f^*/2$ are "*folded*" into the 0 to $f/2$ spectrum and are indistinguishable from it. That is, sample frequencies of $3f/2$, $5f/2$, and so on, appear to the sampler to be at $f/2$, and frequencies f, $2f$, $3f, \ldots$ appear to be 0, and similarly in between. This means, practically, that a low pass filter must precede the sampler in order to eliminate components above $2f^*$. Since, by definition, frequencies above this limit are not of interest, they constitute noise in the plant, which should be filtered out of the control system in any event.

To reconvert the sampled data to analog form, a *zero order hold*, some-times called a "boxcar" or sample-and-hold circuit, is usually sufficient.[12]

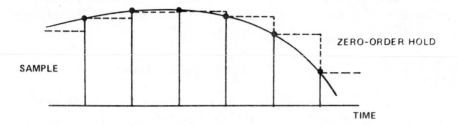

ZERO-ORDER HOLD

SAMPLE

TIME

The zero order hold merely holds the value of the sample constant until the next sample changes it. The resulting stair step can be further passed through a low pass filter (0 to $2f^*$) to reconstruct the smooth waveform. Higher order holds, such as first order (which extrapolates over the last two samples to produce the slope) can be constructed but are seldom needed.[13]

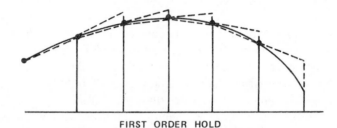

FIRST ORDER HOLD

Sampled data control systems can be analyzed, and their performance and stability can be predicted or analyzed by the same methods used for continuous systems. These techniques include the use of block diagrams and transfer functions and the stability criteria of Routh and Nyquist. (See references 5, 6, and 8 at the end of Chapter 2). Likewise, the Bode diagram can be used to design compensation. However, certain other analysis tools must be employed, primarily that of the Z transform, which is analo-gous to the Laplace transform for linear systems. In addition, as we have already shown, a difference equation can be derived for sampled data networks and used in systems analyses.

Since we are free to use a sampled data input to a microprocessor without loss of data or design capability, what are the advantages? The digital computer as a compensator is a completely arbitrary, reliable device and so offers the utmost flexibility in compensating difficult plant processes. In these cases, performance is possible that cannot be achieved with any linear, continuous control, for example, "deadbeat" control. Sampled data systems are especially appropriate when the controlled plant has considerable inherent dead time. If possible, the sampling interval should be chosen equal to the dead time. If the specifications on controlled response do not permit such a long sensing cycle, it must be reduced or the dead time shortened. However, with short dead time or sensing cycles, the performances of continuous and sampled data systems are essentially synonomous—in all cases the latter is perfectly acceptable. In these events, the appropriate choice is made on the basis of cost per loop, packaging, reliability, and other factors.

References

1. D. G. Larsen and P. R. Roney, "Computer Interfacing," *Am. Lab.* **6**(6) 67–68 (June 1974).
2. R. K. Richards, *Arithmetic Operations in Digital Computers*, Van Nostrand, New York, 1955, pp. 4–7.
3. *Ibid.*, Chap. 6.
4. 706 Computer User's Manual. Raytheon Computer, Santa Ana, Calif., 1977, Appendix F.
5. Richards, *op. cit.*, Chap. 4.
6. J. E. Whitesitt, *Boolean Algebra and Its Applications*, Addison-Wesley, Reading, Mass., 1961.
7. Circuit Type SN 74181, The Integrated Circuits Catalog, 1st ed., Texas Instruments, Dallas, Texas, undated, pp. 9-315 to 9-325.
8. Richards, *op. cit.*, 0. 292.
9. *Ibid.*, p. 292.
10. C. E. Shannon, "Communication in the Presence of Noise," *Proc. IRE.* **37** 10–21 (Jan. 1949).
11. V. E. Everleigh, *Introduction to Control Systems Design*, McGraw-Hill, New York, 1972, pp. 410–415.
12. J. T. Tou, *Digital and Sampled-Data Control Systems*, McGraw-Hill, New York, 1959. pp. 114, 130–131.
13. *Ibid.*, pp. 128, 137.
14. R. W. Peterson, *Error-Correcting Codes*, M.I.T. Press/John Wiley & Sons, New York, 1961, pp. 162–182.
15. P. H. Abelson and A. L. Hammond, *Science* **195**(4283) 1087–1091 (1977).

Four

Characteristics
of Microprocessors

A general purpose computer is a data processing machine. It comes complete with a convenient means of entering programs and data (by means of cards or a typewriter keyboard, for example) and for rapidly extracting the processed results, preferably in some neat form such as well laid-out, printed reports. When a computer becames smaller and cheaper, it is then called a *minicomputer,* or even a *microcomputer,* but is still concerned with processing data in accordance with programs devised by the user. When it ceases to be a general purpose processor and is dedicated instead to the control of some host device, such as an instrument, in accordance with a fixed program, it is no longer a computer but a controller. A microprocessor is an LSI chip or collection of chips which performs the arithmetic and logic and the control logic that instructs and sequences the ALU. The same microprocessor, then, can be part of a host machine or instrument and become its controller, or it can be a unit of a general purpose microcomputer.

Another important distinction that can be made is that a microprocessor-based controller is *dedicated,* that is, it is programmed to perform a single task, usually by the designer, not the user. The programming can be in permanent form (firmware). A microcomputer, however, is designed to be user programmed.

As we shall see, microprocessors are evolving into different forms to specialize in different tasks.

Some of the important features of microprocessors that differentiate them are:

Architecture
Word structure and length
Instruction set
Memory organization
Technology
Power, packaging, and other hardware considerations
Software and support available

We begin with a brief glimpse of the architecture of a microprocessor and then develop more background in the basic features before returning once again to the architectural configuration.

The overall organization of a microprocessor controller looks much the same as that of any other computer (Fig. 4.1). The microprocessor accepts from a random access memory (one that can be accessed in any sequence) the *program* of instructions to be followed. It performs what logical and arithmetic operations are called for on the data coming in from the real world, that in contact with the input-output (I/O) devices. The timing of the microprocessor may be taken from an internal clock or from an external real time signal. The temporary memory is of the read-write type, sometimes called RAM or R/WM (to avoid confusion with ROM). Except for special cases, these memories are semiconductor types, which means that the data stored in RAM or R/WM is "volatile," or is lost when power is removed. Thus programs are normally stored in ROM, which is nonvolatile, or backup power (batteries) is provided for RAM-

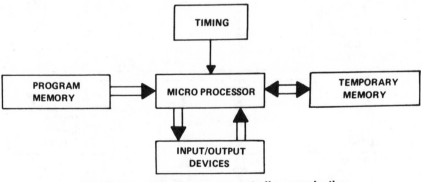

FIGURE 4.1. Microprocessor controller organization.

stored data. Alternatively, the program data may be held in a backup memory (tape or core) which can be quickly called on for restarting the program after power loss.

Figure 4.2 gives a more detailed picture of the microprocessor unit (MPU). The double line labeled "bus" represents the flow of data and the lighter lines are the control signals. The microprocessor consists of an ALU similar to the one discussed in Chapter 3, accumulators, and registers which hold data temporarily for quick operation by the other components of the MPU. Finally, the control decoder–sequencer interprets the program commands and issues detailed orders, called *microinstructions,* to each of the MPU components so that they perform the desired operation. In essence, the control decoder-sequencer is the microprocessor of the MPU.

In most cases, the MPU in Fig. 4.2 is laid out on a single silicon chip, the so-called one-chip microprocessor. We shall see, when we look at the architecture more closely, that there are MPU chips (slices) that can be stacked together to form processors of any given word size, however, these are more often used for micro- or minicomputers than for controllers.

Word Structure

Word length is the most obvious characteristic of microprocessors, because it strongly affects their one common characteristic—they must all be programmed before accomplishing anything useful. Word length determines

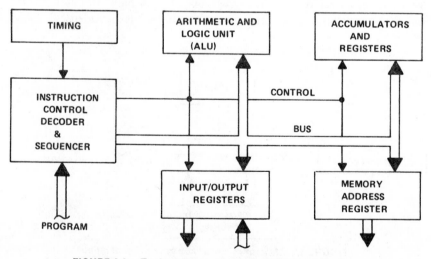

FIGURE 4.2.   Typical Microprocessor (MPU) architecture.

(usually) the accuracy of data, speed of calculation, and cost of memory, or the trade-off between these factors.

The basic memory element for digital systems is the bit, as we saw in Chapter 3. A word consists of N bits that can be stored, transferred, and manipulated by the MPU as a unit. N may be anything from 1 to 100, though for most MPUs with which we are concerned, 4 to 16 is the range.

Clearly, the more bits in a word, the more states it can have or, what is the same thing, the more information it can convey. Three bits can represent 2^3 or 8 states and four bits of the normal binary codes, given in Table 3.1 of the last chapter, can hold 2^4 or 16 numbers. A word of eight bits can then hold data numbers from 0 to 255 (decimal) or can point to as many as 256 different memory locations where other data or instructions can be found.

Some special nomenclature is used for processor words. If a word is divided into units of eight bits, these are usually termed *bytes,* although bytes of other sizes are known. By analogy, four bits have been termed a *nybble* (obviously, a small byte). The term "K," referring to memory size, formerly meant a multiplier of 1000, but it now means 2^{10} or 1024. Thus a 4K bit memory holds 4096 bits. This usually causes no confusion, but it pays to remember that a memory of 64K bytes, a not uncommon size, actually holds 65,536 locations, not 64,000.

The Intel 4004, one of the earliest microprocessors, first made commercially available in 1971, is a four-bit MPU, that is, its basic data word size is four bits. This is logical because the 4004 was originally designed as a custom LSI part for the calculators made by Busicom, a Japanese firm. With reference to Table 3.1 again, the four-bit word fits neatly into the BCD format, so that each four-bit word can represent a decimal number on a numerical display or keyboard. Other four-bit MPUs, such as the Intel 4040 (a later version), the Rockwell PPS-4, and the Fairchild PPS-25 have been used for scales, displays, and similar interface operations. Obviously, the four-bit format requires multiple operations for every function if numbers greater than one digit are to be handled. It is always possible for a 4-bit processor to achieve higher resolution than 1 in 16, but at the expense of repeating operations sequentially.

Eight-bit MPUs, with 256 states, are better suited to manipulate alphanumeric data, such as the American Standard Code for Information Interchange (ASCII). Thus they are widely employed for data communication. The Intel 8080, the RCA Cosmac, the MOS Technology 6500 series, and others (see Table 4.5 at the end of this chapter) are 8 bit processors. Since the word size implies data resolution of about $\frac{1}{2}\%$, there are many control applications for which they would be suitable. Several 12 bit

MPUs, including those made by Toshiba and Intersil (see Table 4.5), are available. They can handle data with a resolution of 1 in 4000, so are even better suited for control. For the highest control accuracy 16 bit microprocessors such as the National PAC and the General Instrument CP 1600 provide 65,536 states and alleviate the problem of data range, discussed later. Since two 8 bit bytes make up a 16 bit word, this format lends itself to byte manipulation which is efficient in terms of memory space, register size, and speed.

Various types of coding including binary, BCD, and octal, discussed in the previous chapter, are suitable for representation of numbers in four and eight bit machines. In addition, we must be aware of the hexadecimal (base 16) code, since it is often used for machine programming. To obtain the requisite number of symbols, the hexadecimal code uses the letters A through F in addition to the 10 decimal number symbols. Table 4.1 shows the relationship between hexadecimal, decimal, and 8, 4, 2, 1 binary positive integers.

To convert positive integers from binary to hexadecimal, the binary numbers need merely be grouped by fours and converted according to the table

Binary	1110	0100	1101	0011
Hexadecimal	E	4	D	3

and vice versa.

To convert hexadecimal to decimal, the former is expressed in terms of its base (Chapter 3):

$$4F2 = 4(16^2) + F(16^1) + 2(16^0)$$
$$= 4(256) + 15(16) + 2(1) = 1266$$

Negative integers must be treated according to the particular convention used for the MPU (see Chapter 3). In one system, the decimal numbers 0 to 4095 are represented by 000 to FFF; the negative numbers start with FFFF $= -1$ and continue downward through FFFE $= -2$, FFFD $= -3$, to F000 $= -4096$.

Decimal and hexadecimal fractions can be converted in the same way as integers, using negative base exponents. For example,

$$0.2CE = 2(16^{-1}) + 12(16^{-2}) + 14(16^{-3})$$
$$= 0.125 + 0.046875 + 0.003418 = 0.17529$$

Data words in machine format are in binary of course, since this is the

TABLE 4.1.   Hexidecimal Code

Decimal	Hexadecimal	Binary
0	0	0000
1	1	0001
2	2	0010
3	3	0011
4	4	0100
5	5	0101
6	6	0110
7	7	0111
8	8	1000
9	9	1001
10	A	1010
11	B	1011
12	C	1100
13	D	1101
14	E	1110
15	F	1111
16	10	10000
	and so on	

only way they can be stored in memories or registers. Integers can be stored with a sign bit:

Sign bit

where 1 is negative and 0 is positive, or in 1's complement or 2's complement form as explained in Chapter 3.

Table 4.2 contrasts these three methods.

TABLE 4.2.   Negative Number Storage

	Binary	Octal
Positive number	000 101	$+5$
Sign bit and magnitude	100 101	-5
1's complement	111 010	-5
2's complement	111 011	-5

To handle fractional numbers, the computer assumes a fictitious *binary point*; actually it is merely a rule for calculation and affects only the software, not the hardware. As pointed out in the previous chapter, the binary point is the separator between negative exponents of 2 used as multipliers and positive exponents; that is,

$$1001.011$$

represents

$$1(2^3) + 0(2^2) + 0(2^1) + 1(2^0) + 0(2^{-1}) + 1(2^{-2}) + 1(2^{-3})$$

The problem in computer storage is where to put the binary point. If it is fixed at the left side of the storage space, the machine cannot handle numbers greater than 1. If at the right, only integers (no fractions less than 1) can be treated. The solution used in many large computers with higher order programming languages, such as Fortran, is to use floating point arithmetic. The fractional number, say 141.9, is represented by an exponent and a mantissa:

$$0.1419 \quad \times \quad 10^3$$

Mantissa	Exponent
	+3

so that a 16 bit machine word representation could be

0	0011	00100100010
Sign	Exponent	Mantissa*
+	+3	0.1419_{10}

Although floating point representation is convenient and has been made available in some of the more recent and larger microprocessors (either as software or additional hardware), it is seldom used in control work because of the memory size, cost, and speed reduction penalties. Usually, we must live with fixed point arithmetic and scale our problems accordingly.

Other data formats are likely to be found in microprocessor applications. The double precision integer is most common. This is a means of considering two consecutive data words taken together as the most significant and least significant halves of a single word. These are sometimes called the *upper byte* and *lower byte,* respectively. For alphabetical and special characters, the ASCII (or teletypewriter code) is standard. For example, @ is represented by hexadecimal C0, the uppercase alphabet by C1 to DA, $ by A4, and numerals by B0 to B9.

---

* Decimal point assumed at left.

Instructions

All information used by the microprocessor is stored in the form of words, whether they represent a program of instructions or temporary data. The location of the program and data may be intermixed in the memory, as shown in Fig. 4.3, since the memory can be randomly accessed and location has no physical significance. In fact, the processor cannot distinguish between data and instruction words except by context. This does not mean they are identical; in fact, data and instruction words may have different (and even variable) lengths.

A typical instruction word may have a format like that in Fig. 4.4, where the word length is divided into *op code* and *operand* sections. The op code (operation code), tells the microprocessor what to do; it answers the question, "Do what?" The operand or operands are the *addresses* of the data on which the opcode operation is to be performed. In some MPUs, the operands may be the registers, or temporary memory storage locations, where the data addresses are to be found. In other words, they answer the question, "Where?"

At the lowest level of microinstruction, within the control decoder–sequencer, there are only four things that can be done with data:

Add
Move
Store
Compare

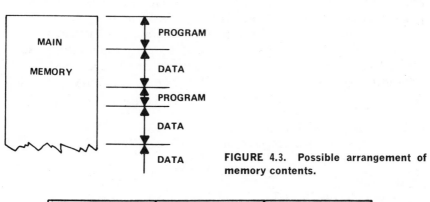

FIGURE 4.3. Possible arrangement of memory contents.

FIGURE 4.4. Indirect address instruction word.

In conjunction with the microprogram of the control decoder, these elementary operations can be sequenced into more useful and intelligible (to humans) *macroinstructions* which comprise the instruction set of the MPU. Generally, these are divided into eight classes:

Load/store
Arithmetic
Logical
Skip or branch
Shift/rotate
Transfer of control
Input/output

(In some architectures, shift and logical are microinstructions, instead.)

Occasionally these classes may be combined, for example, the General Instrument CP 1600 data bus structure does not distinguish between external devices and memory, hence load/store and input/output share the same instructions.

Load instructions transfer the contents of memory locations into selected registers, while *store* accomplishes the opposite—from register into memory.

Arithmetic operations are commonly performed on two operands: one may be in register and the other in memory, or both may be in registers (register-to-register add, for example). Other operations that can be microprogrammed are subtract, multiply, and divide.

It must be emphasized at this point that there is currently no standardization of instructions for microprocessors. Each manufacturer creates his own instruction set, so that a microprogrammed or firmware divide in one may be eliminated in favor of some other feature in another. What is not furnished in firmware may be supplied by the manufacturer in software, or may be programmed with perhaps greater efficiency by the user.

Logical operations include those of AND, OR, EXCLUSIVE OR (see Chapter 3) on two operands. For example, an OR may be:

Operand 1 (register)	10111001
Operand 2 (register or memory)	10001100
OR	10111101

Skip instructions are carried out in two steps. First an operation, logical or arithmetic, is performed on the operands. Second, the result is tested against some condition, such as "zero" or "negative." If the condition is met (true), the test is passed and the program skips the next instruction, otherwise, the skip is ignored.

A skip may also be unconditional, as SKIP 1 (the next instruction is passed over).

Shift operations involve the transfer of all the bits in a word one or more places to the right or left. If there is an implied binary point anywhere in the word, the shift is equivalent to multiplication or division by 2. There are a great many possible shift instructions. An ordinary or *"logical" shift* loses bits at the end toward which the word is shifted, and zeros are added to the empty end. *Rotate* implies that the bit lost at on end is added to the other. Shifts may or may not include the carry bit (recall the description of binary addition in Chapter 3). An arithmetic carry involves special rules for the sign bit.

Shifting is useful not only for arithmetic and scaling but permits the packing and unpacking of large amounts of binary data in one word, or bit-by-bit Boolean operations.

A transfer of control instruction or *Branch* is more powerful than Skip in that it may transfer control to a considerable distance ahead of or behind the current program step. Branch operates on the results of the previous instruction, for example, branch on carry, branch on not zero, branch on overflow, branch on greater or equal. A branch can also be unconditional. A *conditional branch* is probably the most powerful instruction of any stored program computer and provides it with the unique ability to alter its own program in accordance with results obtained from a computation.

Instructions that do not require going to memory to obtain data are known as *register instructions*. Since these eliminate the memory fetch cycle of an MPU, they take less time, typically two thirds or one half less. One operand instructions include such operations as increment (add 1), decrement (subtract 1), complement (1's complement), and negate (2's complement). Two-register operations include register add, exchange register, stack, and so on.

Because of the lack of agreement and uniform definitions for instruction sets, the vendor-supplied number of instructions is a poor index of an MPUs versatility. As we note later, it is possible to alter the basic instruction set on some machines.

Simple Programming Example. Assume an instruction word of the format in Fig. 4.4 which consists of 10 bits. Four bits are used for the op code, which can then define 16 types of instructions. The operand fields consist of three bits each and refer to registers in which the actual address or memory location is held; that is, the register contents are a "pointer" for the data location.

This technique is called *indirect* or *register addressing,* and is a powerful means for overcoming the limitations of a fixed word machine in addressing data in memory. Thus 3 bits can locate eight registers, which, if they are 16 bits long, can address 64K words of memory.

To resume the example, it is desired to solve the equation $Z = X + Y$. We then must be able to locate X and Y, add them together, and store the result in a location called Z. Assume that the addresses of X, Y, and Z have been stored by previous operations in three registers which we designate by the octal numbers 2, 4, and 6. As part of the instruction set, we have defined the following three machine opcode numbers and mnemonics, the latter being used by the programmer to define the operations because they are more easily remembered than the binary machine code.

Op Code	Mnemonic	Meaning
1010	MVI*	Load data from address held in operand 1 into register operand 2.
1001	MVO* (move out)	Move contents of operand 1 into address specified by operand 2.
0011	ADD	Add register specified by operand 1 to operand 2 register and hold result in 2.

Then the program, starting at instruction location 100, would read:

	Machine Code	Mnemonic	Meaning
100	1010 010 011	MVI* 2,3	Load data at address pointed to by register 2 (X) into 3.
101	1010 100 101	MVI* 4,5	Load data pointed to by register 4 (Y) into 5.
102	0011 011 101	ADD 3,5	Add registers 3 and 5 and store in 5.
103	1001 101 110	MVO* 5,6	Move contents of register 5 into address pointed to by 6 (Z).

Another MPU with a similar instruction set might use a full 10 bits for direct memory addressing (1K locations) and use the mnemonics LDR for "register load" and STR for "store contents of register in memory," rather than MVI and MVO. If we had previously stored in locations 201 and 202 the values of X and Y, respectively, and assigned location 203 to Z, the program would read:

	Mnemonic	Meaning
100	LDR R2,201	Load X into register 2.
101	ADD R2,202	Add X to Y.
102	STR R2,203	Store $X + Y$ in 203.

Thus we obtain some simplicity at the expense of some flexibility. Which constitutes the better architecture and instruction set depends on the nature of the problems and the timing of the micro operations.

Paging and Indirect Bits

Another useful technique of adding memory addressing capability in a fixed word length instruction is *paging*. In this method, a small number of bits is allowed for direct addressing, say 7 ($2^7 =$ octal 177 or decimal 127 address locations). This constitutes the number of words in a "page" of memory addresses (0 to 127). A sector bit or bits is then assigned to indicate the "page number." The full address is then acquired by taking into account the page and word numbers, as shown in Fig. 4.5.

The benefits of direct and indirect addressing can also be combined by using a specific bit for signaling an indirect address. If 0, the address is direct; if 1, the operand points to the address that contains the data; since the first address has no opcode in its instruction, all its bits can be used for addressing.

Indexing

This technique grants the programmer further flexibility by permitting him to modify the operand address with the contents of another register (or registers), called the *index register*. For example, the two might be added. If an instruction using an index register R3 containing the number 10 was programmed as

$$ADD\ R2, 175\ (R3)$$

then, to register R2 would be added to the contents of memory location $175 + 10 = 185$. Since R3 can also be modified by the program, say by adding 1 (incrementing) after each operation, it is very convenient in handling data organized (in the memory) by lists or *arrays*. For example,

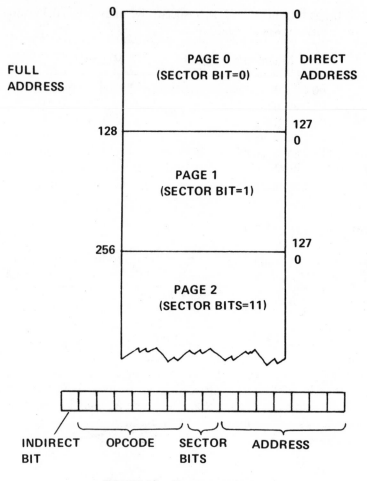

FIGURE 4.5.   Memory paging.

a program to copy and relocate all the data contained in a list stored at locations 2300 to 2200 to new locations 200 to 100, could use the index register in the following manner:

Location Name	Program Statement	Meaning
LOOP	LDR R2,'100'	Load number 100 in R2.
	LDR R1,2200 (R2)	Load contents of address 2200 + R2 into R1.
	DECR R2	Subtract 1 from R2.
	BPL LOOP	Return to location LOOP.

Architecture Revisited

At this point it will be instructive to take a more detailed look into the architecture of the microprocessor controller. If the designer is going to program the MPU in an assembly language like the mnemonics we have discussed, which bears a direct relationship to the machine language, he must have a very good idea of the organization of the processor, and especially its data flow paths. It is possible to program some MPUs in higher level languages, such as Fortran or dialects of PL/I, but we reserve this discussion for a later chapter. Suffice it to note that higher level languages permit the programmer to flowchart and code the problem in easy-to-understand symbols similar to those used in ordinary mathematics and logic, but that these must be translated into many more lines of machine code by means of *compiler* programs using larger computers. It is accepted that this automatic translation is not, in the present state of the art, as efficient as a human programmer working at the assembly language level, and that anywhere from 10 to 100% more program memory (instructions) will be required to do the same job. Hence a designer seeking to apply MPUs should be able to use either technique.

Control Unit Operation.   As pointed out at the start of this chapter, the control unit is the heart of the microprocessor. As shown in Fig. 4.6, it

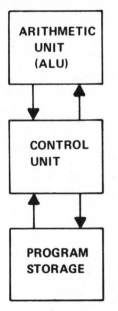

FIGURE 4.6.   Control unit function.

directs the ALU to perform the correct arithmetic or logic operations and commands the program storage to transmit the next instruction. The control unit senses the condition of the system—equality, sign of result, presence of stop signals—in order to generate its control commands.

Figure 4.6 does not show any provision to input data or to output results. These are shown in Fig. 4.7, along with a more complete data path (shown by double lines) including the temporary storage.

When this diagram is rearranged as in Fig. 4.8, it resembles the basic sketch of the microsystem (Fig. 4.1). The units that make up the MPU per se are enclosed in dashed lines; light lines represent control signals, and double lines show flow of data.

Figure 4.8 shows only one version of MPU architecture, which is more or less typical. Other MPUs are data bus oriented and do not distinguish between input-output and memory addressing, each coming through the data bus by means of the same registers. This architecture is employed

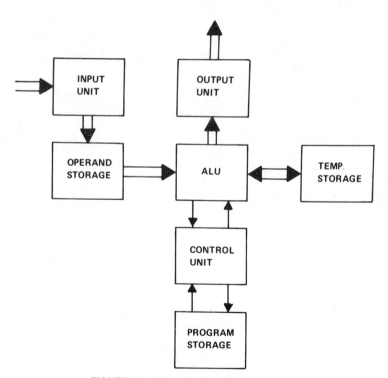

FIGURE 4.7. Input/output and data paths.

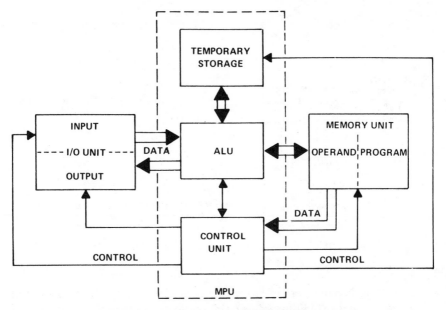

FIGURE 4.8.   Typical non-bus MPU architecture.

by the Motorola 6800, the 12-bit Toshiba TLCS-12, and the CP 1600 used as an example earlier.

The detailed operation of the control unit can be seen by reference to Fig. 4.9. An instruction enters the register after being transferred from the program storage memory. The instruction is then decoded by the control decoder into a sequence of instructions for other units. This sequence constitutes a *microprogram* which establishes the instruction set (e.g., 0011 is interpreted as ADD, and all the register operations that cause an ADD are sequenced). The program counter holds in memory the address of the next instruction. Ordinarily, the program counter automatically increments by 1 after each new instruction is read. However, if there is a jump, or transfer of control, the program counter contents are replaced by the new jump address called for in the program.

Timing.   The microprocessor and the operation of the control decoder (sequencer) are intimately tied in with the machine timing. The cycle is the basic unit of machine timing, and consists, at a minimum, of two operations:

Instruction fetch
Instruction execute

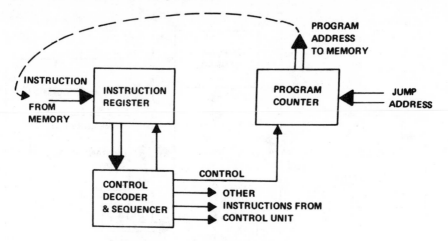

FIGURE 4.9.   Control unit operation details.

Fetch can be considered the reading of an instruction. To illustrate the concept, assume a childproof aspirin bottle has instructions on how to open the cap. Reading the instruction is equivalent to *Fetch*. Instruction execute is represented by the act of opening the bottle.

If an operand is involved, the cycle consists (at a minimum) of:

Instruction fetch	Read label on bottle.
Operand fetch	Recall your age. Should you take a child's or adult's dose?
Execute subcycle	Take required aspirin.

Each subcycle, fetch or execute, is composed of one or more *microcycles*. The microcycle is the basic timing unit of the computer. If, for example, an instruction fetch requires obtaining two bytes of memory, it will require two microcycles. Typically, an instruction fetch may require one microcycle; a decode, one microcycle; a register add, one microcycle; and a jump to subroutine, two microcycles. Then a two-register add, not requiring memory, would occupy the following time, assuming a 2 μsec microcycle:

Instruction fetch	$1 \times 2 = 2$ μsec
Decode	$1 \times 2 = 2$ μsec
Add	$1 \times 2 = 2$ μsec
Total add	$\overline{6}$ μsec

A memory add would take a longer time, because of the operand fetch. A jump would require $2 + 2 + 4 = 8$ μsec. Note that the operation time given by the manufacturer is often the microcycle time. A more meaningful figure is the time required to accomplish a full cycle, say a register add.

ALU

The basic form of the ALU is seen in Fig. 4.10. The accumulator is a register that can hold one operand while another is being fetched for addition. The nature of the adder was described in Chapter 3. Recall that there is no subtract operation at this level. Subtraction involves complementing and adding and is performed according to the particular conventions (software) used by the machine—in other words, it is defined in the microprogram.

Figures 4.11 and 4.12 show the remaining elements of Fig. 4.8. The memory structure consists of two single word registers. The memory address register (MAR) contains an address to read into or out of the memory, while the memory data register (MDR) contains the data to be exchanged. The I/O part (if used) consists of registers that interface with the ALU.

When all the elements in Figs. 4.9 to 4.12 are interconnected, the result is a complete microsystem, as shown in Fig. 4.13, for which the comments

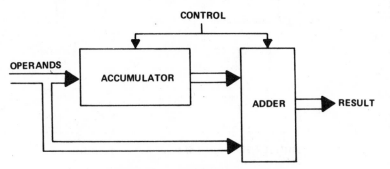

FIGURE 4.10. Basic ALU operation.

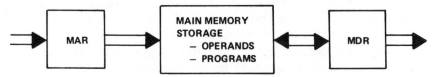

FIGURE 4.11. Memory registers.

FIGURE 4.12.   Input/output register.

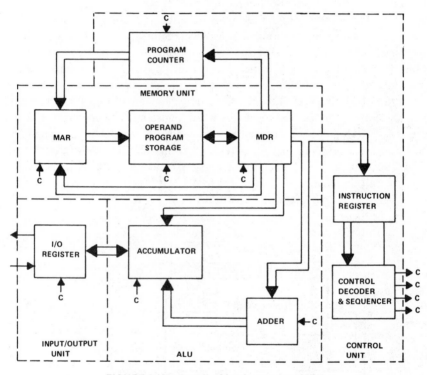

FIGURE 4.13.   Detail of basic non-bus MPU.

made concerning Fig. 4.8 also hold. This is not bus-oriented architecture but resembles many existing systems. It is often possible to see the various sections shown in Fig. 4.13 in the actual layout of the chip, as implied by the dashed lines. Supplementing the units described, other features such as an internal clock, special output flip-flops (sometimes called *flags*), and additional registers are often placed on MPU chips. Some of these added features are now discussed.

Additional Architectural Features

Multiple accumulators or registers to hold partial results (without requiring the memory fetch cycle time to move data in and out) save time, program steps, and ROM or program storage memory. Four registers are considered optimum, although some MPUs have more.

Multiple or special purpose I/O parts are considered valuable in some architectures because they permit communication with many peripherals. If data bus I/O is used, this consideration is invalid.

An extremely valuable feature in many applications is direct memory address (DMA). Normally, memory is accessed by external devices through a specific program. In the event that large amounts of data transfer are needed, such as hierarchal computer-computer connections or disk data transfer, DMA saves much time and programming, since it permits direct communication with the memory (via hardware) independent of the control unit and operating program.

Index registers were discussed earlier. Multiple index registers may be even more helpful by giving more flexibility to the programmer than furnished by one. Two are often recommended.

Interrupts. It is important in many control applications to give attention to external events, for example, alarms of abnormal conditions. Because these events may cause one to break into a program, they are called *interrupts.*

Basically, there are three ways to handle interrupts. The machine can be programmed to scan sensors and look for external events on some regular predetermined cycle. This may require excessive machine time in some cases and, depending on the cycle, the response to the event may be slow. However, this method is perfectly satisfactory for such applications as detecting the closure of a switch or the change in state of a relay.

Second, the event can be given priority or override of the basic program. In this case, it is important to save the address of the last regular instruction so that the machine can return to the program sequence after the event has been serviced.

Interrupts can also be handled by special hardware.

Combinations of these methods can be used. We must also face the problem of priority among interrupts.

If there is only a single priority level, all interrupts can be handled through one location. A "poll" can be taken of locations specified in a table, to determine the location of the event.

If multiple levels are provided, priority must still be established between two simultaneous interrupts. This can be resolved by addresses (in a data bus system) or by hardware.

Stacks. *Push-down, push-pop,* and *LIFO* stacks are designations for a group of registers so arranged that several sequential addresses can be entered into the stack and retrieved on command in reverse order of entrance, "last in first out." These are extremely useful devices for handling interrupts with priority. The address of the next program step is stored in the stack in the event of an interrupt and retrieved after the interrupt has been serviced. If a higher priority interrupt occurs during the service of the first, the address of that part of the interrupt program can also be saved, so that the machine returns to the first interrupt program and then to the main program.

Exactly the same stack logic can be used to handle *subroutines,* another important software concept. The subroutine is an independent program which can be used in several parts of a main program and is *called* (by a jump to its address) whenever required. The call must also arrange to place what would have been next normal program step (if there had been no call) in storage, as in the stack. When the subroutine program has been completed, it will "return"; that is, it will call the main program address that was saved from its temporary storage and continue the main program.

If a stack is used, subroutines can be *nested.* A subroutine can call another subroutine, placing the next address of the first subroutine in the stack on top of the main program return address. This can be repeated several times, so that as each nested subroutine is completed, control will return through the subroutines and to the main program in inverse order of calling. Figure 4.14 attempts to show this action diagrammatically.

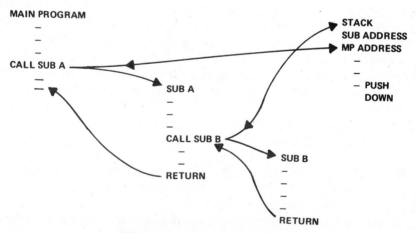

FIGURE 4.14. Operation of a stack.

Stacks are also useful for other purposes, such as in the storage of partial results of calculations, or of lists and arrays of data.

Microprogramming.   We have pointed out several times that the instruction set of an MPU is established by the control unit, and that the actions taken by the control decoder and sequencer are established by the microprogram of that unit. In many MPUs, this program is an integral feature of the chip and is not subject to change by the user. Several current machines, however, separate the microprogram and put it on a replaceable ROM chip. The instruction set can then be altered or enlarged. If a programmable read-only memory (PROM) is used for the control memory, the system can be programmed by the user. The ultimate in flexibility would be the use of an *electrically alterable ROM* (EAROM) for the control memory, which can be reprogrammed by paper tape I/O, for example, to change the computer's instructions whenever desired. With microprogramming, a machine can be made to "emulate" a much larger device, say a minicomputer, and use its software, although at a considerable speed penalty. For example, a microcomputer can be given higher level instructions such as divide, decimal arithmetic, floating point, binary-to-decimal conversions, a programmable real time clock, and so on. Most of these features are found in microcomputer systems, rather than controllers.

Bit Slice Architecture.   For completeness, we mention bit slice architecture (Fig. 4.15). Instead of a single chip containing a fixed word length MPU, computers based on bit slices are made up of several chips, each containing the ALU, memory addressing and data registers, and so on, for a limited number of bits, 2 or 4. A single control unit and microprogram service all the slices. The computer can then be expanded horizontally to have any size word from 2 bits on. This grants maximum freedom to the computer designer, since the word length can be tailored to the application. Slices are primarily used by minicomputer designers for 8 to 32 bit word computers and are furnished with very little of the application support desired by most control engineers.

Technologies

The term "technology" refers to the method of manufacturing the integrated circuit (IC) logic structures we have been discussing. Transistors and integrated circuitry can be formed on an insulating substrate (chip)

DATA AND ADDRESS BUSES

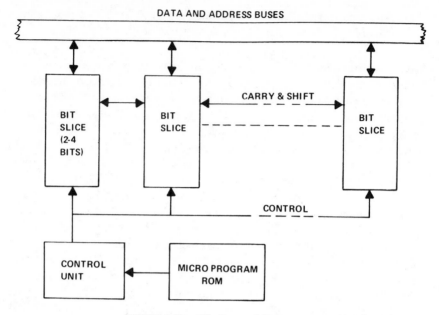

FIGURE 4.15.   Bit slice architecture.

by several techniques, of which the metal-on-silicon (MOS) method was the earliest used for MPUs. Essentially, the technology for LSI is the same as that for manufacturing semiconductor memories. Without knowing too much about the process, a design engineer can evaluate a particular manufacturer's MPU technology by his success in producing memories; these can be compared with others on the basis of speed, cost, size, reliability, and other easily measured attributes. MPUs, however, are more difficult to compare directly because of architectural differences.

Rough guidelines highlighting the differences between various technologies can be gathered from Table 4.3. This represents merely the state of availability at this writing. As can be seen from the dates given, the field is moving extremely rapidly—for example, Arthur D. Little predicts a doubling of logic density before the end of this decade.

MOS devices utilize field effect transistors, as contrasted with the earlier bipolar types which depended on the junction between N- and P-type semiconductors. A field effect transistor uses an electric field to control the flow of majority carrier currents in a channel. In a PMOS channel the conductors are holes (absence of electrons), and in an NMOS channel they are electrons. The gate, or conductor, which was originally aluminum metal (but is silicon in later devices), is deposited on a silicon dioxide

TABLE 4.3. Current and Potential Technology for MPUs

Technology	Date of MPU	Typical Add Time (μsec)	Typical Chip Power (W)	Density (gates/ mm)*	Power Delay (pJ)*
PMOS					
Metal gate	1971–1972	4–12.5	1	50	450
Silicon gate				90	145
NMOS					
Silicon gate	1973–1974	2	0.5	95	45
Depletion load				107	38
Double polysilicon†					175
CMOS-Silicon	1974	5–6	0.01	45	45
VMOS/DMOS†				225	20
TTL (bipolar)	1974	0.2‡	7	10	—
SOS/CMOS†	?	(0.7–1.5)	(0.01)	275	0.1
I²L-2 level	1975	0.5–0.65	0.5	150	0.10–1

* *Electronics* **49**(9) 76 (April 1, 1976).
† MPU not yet available.
‡ Cycle time.

insulator which in turn overlies the channel. The field effect resulting from the application of voltage to the gate suppresses or permits current flow in the channel. The construction resulting from a simple buildup of layers of various materials (semiconductors, metal, insulator) allows an entire structure consisting of thousands of interconnected transistors to be deposited through masks created by a photographic reduction process, allowing an extremely high density of components.

The very high impedance of a PMOS transistor logic gate allows it to retain a charge for at least several milliseconds. While the memory is thus volatile and must be refreshed periodically, the interval between periods is long enough so that the data processor is not slowed down too seriously. The long cycle time typical of PMOS MPUs is mainly a result of the slow migration of holes as current carriers.

NMOS devices represent an important improvement in three different respects: speed, power, and available density. This results almost entirely from the superior mobility and efficiency of electron flow in the N channel. Otherwise, the operation of NMOS devices is a mirror image of that of PMOS devices.

Complementary (CMOS) field effect devices are an arrangement of both PMOS and NMOS devices on the same substrate. The chief advantage lies in very low power dissipation, about $\frac{1}{100}$ that of PMOS devices. Furthermore, CMOS devices can be operated with one power supply instead of the two usually required for PMOS devices. The basic CMOS inverter consists of two MOS transistors in series, one N channel and the other P channel. The inputs to these two are in parallel, so that switching one on turns the other off (see Fig. 4.16). Hence the output can be switched from 0 to +V with no current drawn from the supply except during the actual switching instant.

Transistor-transistor logic (TTL) MPUs utilize bipolar logic supplemented by Schottky diodes, located so as to enhance the speed of operation. As indicated in Table 4.3, this speed increase is achieved at the expense of a significant rise in power. Bipolar MPU chips available at this writing are mostly bit slices, and their high power needs make them of primary interest to minicomputer designers.

Ion injection logic (I²L) is another form of bipolar integrated circuitry. The technology results in device densities nearly as great as MOS and power needs as low as NMOS. The I²L MPU currently available is a four-bit slice.

Silicon on sapphire (SOS) refers to the use of a sapphire substrate instead of silicon dioxide, resulting in very low power requirements and high density. Aside from the use of sapphire, the technology is the same

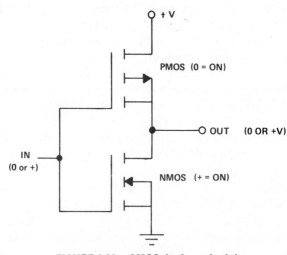

FIGURE 4.16.   CMOS device principle.

as that for MOS. P-, N-, and CSOS devices are possible. At this writing, there are no SOS MPUs generally available.

Other variations of MOS, the V-channel and double diffused technique (see reference to Table 4.3) are being developed.

Practical Design Considerations

Early microprocessors such as the Intel 4004 were packaged in 16 pin DIP sizes because other packages were not available. This requirement put a great strain on the design and inhibited performance. For example, only four pins are available to send 12 bit addresses to memory, receive 8 bit instructions, and transmit 4 bit data words. The requirements of multiplexed (time-shared) and bidirectional buses meant much internal circuitry for timing and sorting signals, and the resulting loss in speed was in part responsible for the long cycle time. Currently, MPUs are packaged in 18 to 42 pin DIP sizes, with 40 pins as the mode. Consequently, there is room for separate data and address buses with higher speed, and less external interface circuitry is needed.

Power supplies needed are a function of the technology. Typically, bipolar and some NMOS require +5 V; CMOS, +5 to +12; PMOS, −12 and ±5; NMOS, +12 and +5 or ±5.

Clocks are needed with some MPUs; others are included on the chip. Intel 4000 and 8000 devices require a two-phase clock, and National a four-phase clock.

Memory

Memory is the most important additional requirement for most MPU applications. RAM (or R/W) memory is used for working storage, insertion of problem constants and program options, and as a data base. Memory can be static or dynamic, the latter being cheaper but requiring more expensive logic for refresh functions.

Technologies are the same as for the MPU—TTL, NMOS, PMOS, and CMOS. Memories are organized by words and word size; the most prevalent is the 4096 × 1 (4K words times one bit/word) RAM, and other common sizes are 1024 × 1, 256 × 4, and 128 × 8. Magnetic core memories are used for special purposes, such as a backup for the volatile semiconductor RAM.

ROM for low cost, high volume is mask-programmed by the vendor. This is quite expensive and requires that no errors be present in the mask or the work must be done over. Several types of field programmable ROMs are available—those using a fusible link high current write (TTL or MOS) cannot be reused, while others can be erased by ultraviolet light or x rays (space charge MOS) and reprogrammed. Due to higher cost, they are primarily used in low volume or developmental applications. EAROMs have been mentioned. One type of read mostly memory (RMM) is an amorphous semiconductor which can be used for slowly changing data. An interesting possibility is the use of a CMOS R/WM with write lines disconnected and a battery backup. The low power requirements of CMOS make this feasible.

When To Use MPUs

For control purposes, the MPU must be considered one of many alternative means of implementing the required logic. Among the possibilities are

Analog logic, mechanical, electrical, or pneumatic
Random logic, hard-wired ICs or discrete components
Ordered logic, use of a programmed ROM (e.g., logic tables)
Custom LSI
Microprocessor
Minicomputer
Time-shared central computer.

The factors that must be taken into account include job requirements (speed, accuracy), packaging (environment, power dissipation), volume to be produced, development time and cost, amount of change or flexibility needed, complexity and theoretical knowledge of the problem, skill and knowledge of development personnel.

TABLE 4.4.   Comparison of Logic Alternatives*

	Development, Tooling Cost	Production Cost	Flexibility	Size
Random logic	1	4	3	4
Ordered logic	4	2	4	2
Custom LSI	5	1	5	1
MPU	2	3	2	3
Minicomputer	3	5	1	5

* The lowest score represents the most favorable condition.

If the choice is between a microprocessor and discrete ICs, a rule of thumb is to consider MPUs for any sequential logic design requiring more than 30 to 50 hard-wired ICs and some arithmetic or logic, and having more than a trivial number of steps in the flowsheet.

Table 4.4 is a subjective comparison of the various methods of implementing DDC, the lowest score representing the most favorable condition. It is clear that the MPU is not the best or only answer for all conditions, but it does have a favorable combination of qualities that make it nearly always a choice that must be considered as a solution.

MPU Selections

In the present state of rapid development of many new MPUs, it would be foolhardy to attempt a definitive listing of available machines. Table 4.5, however, is offered as an attempt to show the amount of choice. The data in this table were gathered from a variety of sources, including manufacturer's literature, and no pretention is made of completeness or absolute timeliness, nor is the accuracy of the specifications warranted by the writer. In all cases, the reader is cautioned to obtain the latest data from the manufacturer before proceeding further.

TABLE 4.5. MPU Data

Data Word Bits	Name	Manufacturer*	Type	Instruction Word Bits	Address Capacity, Words	Instruction Execution (μsec) #	Number of Instructions	Technology	Power Required (V)	CPU Pins	CPU Chips	Available Software‡
2	3001	I	2-bit slice	9		0.17	40§	Bipolar	5			PL
4	AM 2901	A	4-bit slice	9		0.1‖	54	Bipolar				
4	PPS 25	F				62.5	66	PMOS	5, −9			
4	4004	I	First MPU	8/16	4K	10.8	46	PMOS	15	16	1	CA(F), CS(F), S
4	4040	I	Improved 4004	8/16	4K	8.0	60	PMOS				CA(F), CS(F)
4	GPC/P	N	4-bit slice	16	64K	4.9	43	PMOS	+5, −12	24	5	CA, CS
4	CPS/I	M				2.7**		NMOS				
4	ME 7114	M				15	48	PMOS	+5, −12	24	1	CA, SA, PL, S
4	μCOM-4	NE	Calculator chip	8/16		3.5	55	NMOS	+5, −12			
4	RP-16	R	4-bit slice	48		1.0	§	Bipolar	5			CA(F), CS(F), PL +
4	PPS-4	RO		8		4	50	PMOS	17	42	1	CA, CS
4	TMS 1000	T	Mask ROM‖	8		50	43	PMOS		40	1	
4	SBP 0400	T	4-bit slice	9		0.35–0.53	45††	IIL				
4	TDY 52A1	TE			256K	50**	§	PMOS	5, −12	16	1	
8	Mini-D	B	See M 6800	12								
8	S 6800	AM		8/16/24	64K	2	72	NMOS	12, −5	40	1	SA, CA, CS
8	F8	E		8	64K	2–4	66	NMOS	12, 5	40	1	
8	CP-800	F		8/16/24	64K	2–4	100	NMOS	12, 5, −3	40	1	CA(F), CS(F), C(PL), TE, PL
8	8008-1	G		8/16/24	16K	12.5	71	PMOS	5–9	18	1	(PL), CA(F),
8		I	First 8-bit MPU	8/16/24	64K	2	48	NMOS		40	1	CS(F), TE, SA
8	8080	I					110	NMOS				
8	6500	MO	Similar to M6800	8/16/24	64K	2	57	NMOS		40	1	SA, CA

8	MK	MK 5065		8/16	32K	4.2	51–81	PMOS	–12, ±5	40	1	CA(F), SA
8	MT	M6800		8/16/24	64K	2	72	NMOS	5	40	1	
8	N	PACE	8/16 bit data word	16	64K	8.5	45	PMOS			1	Same as IMP-16
8	N	CMP-8		8	64K	1.6	74	NMOS		40	1	
8	NE	μCOM-8	Similar to 8080	8/16	64K	1.5	60	CMOS	5–12	40	2	CA, CS +
8	RC	COSMAC		8/16/24		6	109	PMOS		42		CA, CS, CA(F)
8	RO	PPS-8		8/16/24		4	75	NMOS	5	40	1	CA(F), CS(F)
8	S	2650				4.8		NMOS				
8	S	PIP				2		NMOS				
	W		8/16 bit data word	16		3.5	70					
12	A	CK-114		12	4K	5		PMOS		28/40	1	
12	IN	IM 6100			4K	5	50	CMOS	5	40	1	Uses PDP-8 software
12	TO	TLCS-12		12/24		7	18	NMOS	5, –5			SA, CA, S
10	G	CP 1600		10		2.4	68	NMOS	5, ±12	40	1	CA(F), PL, S +
16	NE	μCOM-16		32		1.6	§	NMOS				
16	TO		For custom minicomputer	1–32		0.3 ‖	117	NMOS				
16	SM					0.25**		Bipolar				
16	TE	TDY-52B1		16		10**		PMOS				

* I, Intel; A, Advanced Micro Devices; F, Fairchild; N, National Semiconductor Corp.; M, Microsystems International; NE, NEC Microcomputer; R, Raytheon; RO, Rockwell; T, Texas Instruments; TE, Teledyne; B, Burroughs; AM, American Microsystems; E, Electronic Arrays; G, General Instruments; MO, MOS Technology; MK, Mostek; MT, Motorola; RC, RCA; S, Signetics; W, Western Digital; IN, Intersil; TO, Toshiba; SM, Scientific Microsystems.

† SA, Self-assembler; CA, cross-assembler; CS, cross-simulator; (F), Fortran; C, compiler; TE, text editor; PL, program library; S, simulator; (PL), PL/M; +, others.

‖ Microprogrammed.

§ Per microcycle.

Register-register add except where noted.

** Per cycle.

†† Microprogrammable by user.

Five

Software for Microprocessors

Alexander B. Sidline, Principal Engineer, Process Control Division, Honeywell Inc.

Application Program

An automobile cannot move purposefully without a driver. All the elements that power and control the automobile are present in the vehicle itself. But to use it effectively, intelligent instructions have to be supplied. Only the driver knows where to go and how he plans to get there. Along the way, the driver must also react to road situations—a traffic light, a turn to avoid a rolling ball, and so on. If we compare the body of the driver connected to the various components of the automobile, such as the steering, accelerator, and brakes, to a microcomputer, the driver's intelligence is analogous to the software.

As a process control example, a controller was discussed in Chapter 2 and elsewhere. In its simplest terms, the controller set point is equivalent to where the automobile-driver system wants to go, and the process variable to what the driver sees on the road. In many computer-directed applications, the set point continually changes: Now we must drive along Maple Street, and when we reach Chestnut we must turn left; along the way, probably not consciously, we accelerate, correct for the automobile veering to one side, speed up by pressing on the accelerator (after checking the variable of whether or not a traffic officer is present), and so on, until we get there. This analogy describes the idea of an application program.

Software Level

Since software is a construct, and only humans are capable of handling constructs, the language of software can be considered a bridge between the human mind and the machine. How close the instructions are written to a point at which the machine can actually understand them defines the *level of the software*. We recall from Chapter 4 that the microprocessor fetches an instruction from memory, decodes the strings of 1's and 0's it receives, and performs the operation. Then it proceeds to fetch the next instruction from memory. The machine thus can understand instructions only at the most elementary machine language level. Writing software at any other level requires the additional step(s) of bringing instructions down to that level.

Language Processing

This brings us to another area of software: how to handle instructions written by a human being and convert them to the machine level. The software accomplishing this fall into the category of *language processing software*. Terms such as "compilers," "assemblers," and "link loaders" are often used. These are general purpose packages of instructions previously written to translate the instructions of application programs, written in some higher level, to the machine level. Software thus aids other software. To be somewhat more specific, let us discuss the various levels of software.

Level 1, Special Purpose.   The highest level implicit here, is a *special purpose level*. Suppose a microprocessor is running a process control program. An operator may decide to change its set point, examine the amount a valve is open, or change the process gain. These tasks can be done by pushing buttons, typing in commands on a console, or in some other way making changes or requesting information designed to interface with the operator. Data are modified in the operating program which is accessed by its logic at the machine level so that the correct things happen. This can be considered high level special purpose software.

However, most computer programmers would not regard this as a level of software. Instead, they talk of "high level languages," "assembly languages," and "machine languages." What do these words mean? Recall that the more closely a concept is expressed in human language (and the further away it is from machine language), the higher is the level of the language.

Level 2, High Level. A *high level language* is what most people not familiar with the techniques of programming understand to be computer programming. Popular high level languages are FORTRAN, PL/M, ALGOL, and BASIC. There are of course many more, but the common factor is that they are written in something resembling English or common mathematical symbols. For example:

INTEGER SETPT, PV, GAIN
READ(1,00)SETPT
IF(SETPT.LT.0)GO TO 200
C1 = (SETPT − PV)*GAIN

The above high level instructions are in FORTRAN, which is a contraction of "FORmula TRANslator." They instruct the computer to read a value from device no. 1 and place it in some location identified symbolically as SETPT. At the time of writing the program, the programmer does not know and really does not care where SETPT is physically located in memory. However, one may want to know later during the debugging or "fix-up" stage where it is. The next step in the program is to check if the value in SETPT is negative, that is, less than (.LT.) zero. If it is, then go to statment line 200 (not shown) to fetch further instructions. Otherwise, go to the next statement which is

C1 = (SETPT − PV)*GAIN.

This statement says in effect: Fetch the value SETPT; subtract from it the value of PV located somewhere in memory. Sometime previously, a value was inserted into the memory location assigned to the symbol PV wherever it may be. Next fetch from memory a value GAIN and multiply it by SETPT − PV. Take the result and place it in some other location C1.

The above example was simple to write, but it implied many steps. For example, we did not discuss how the subtraction and multiplication was to be done. It depends on the machine (see Chapter 3). The above program appeals to human understanding and is not concerned with machine details.

A higher level language currently gaining acceptance is Intel's PL/M,[1] a language first designed to generate a code for the Intel eight-bit microcomputers—the 8008 and the 8080. Using PL/M, the programmer has sufficient control of the processor to meet the system programming needs without being concerned about details such as registers, memory, and stack, which are automatically controlled by the PL/M program. The design facilitates the use of modern techniques in structured programming, a disciplined style of programming which helps reduce programming errors and facilitates testing.[2]

PL/M is derived from PL/1, and its popularity has resulted in the development of other similar types of high level languages such as:

SMPL	National Semiconductor's IMP-16
PL/M 6800 and PL/W	Motorola's M6800
PLUS	Signetics 2650
PL/Z	Zilog Z-80[3]

Compilers

The microcomputer does not understand these series of letters and numbers, just as the human does not readily comprehend the 1's and 0's type of instruction in machine language. Note that we did not say that the human mind cannot understand in the absolute sense, but that the human must figure it out, painstakingly. In the same manner, a program called a *compiler* is written to read the collection of letters, numbers, and symbols known as the *source code* and translate it into a machine language, after which it is then called the *object code*. How this is done is complex but need not concern us here.

Thus a computer with the compiler software in its memory is needed to input a source code and translate it into an object code. If the compiler is in the microcomputer itself and is written in the microcomputer's specific code, it is called a *resident* or *self-compiler*. If the compiler is on another type of computer (called a *host*), it is called a *cross-compiler*. The compiler program is written in the language of the host computer, but its final output is in a language close to that of the microcomputer, after the linking of object codes, at the machine level. The term "linking" means joining together object codes, assigning physical locations to the various symbols the programmer used, and inserting them somewhere in memory.

At this point, the reader may ask, If this is all that is involved, why do other levels of languages exist? There are many reasons. The most compelling is that many microprocessor manufacturing companies do not initially have high level software ready. The trend, because of the relative ease of programming in a high level language familiar to many, is to create and provide compilers to translate to the object code. Unfortunately, at this writing, this has not been universally accomplished. In the *EDN Microcomputer Systems Directory*,[4] out of 67 manufacturers of microcomputers, many of whom use the same microprocessors, only about 28 claim a high level language.

Another reason is that a high level language, because of its general purpose nature, requires more machine coding steps than are necessary with a lower level language. This has the disadvantage of using more memory and, because of the extra execution steps needed, the final application program requires more real time to perform the job. How well the compiler translates instructions into a machine level language is a function of how well the compiler has been written for the particular microcomputer.

Assembly Language

Another level, called *assembly language,* is closer to the machine in its logical step-by-step execution. The use of assembly language can reduce the amount of memory needed and also speed up the execution of the application program as compared with a high level language. A knowledge of the properties of the machine is needed to code efficiently in assembly language. For each assembly language source line there is at least one corresponding machine language word. Some have two or three machine language words equal to one assembly language instruction. For example, the assembly language used by General Instrument's CP 1600 can be coded as shown in Fig. 5.1.[5]

```
REL    SUB1      ;RELOCATABLE MODULE NAME

REGS             ;DEFINE REGISTER SYMBOLS

EXT    READ,MPY  ;READ & MPY ARE EXTERNAL ROUTINES

EXT    GAIN,SETPT,PV,C1,S200  ;EXTERNAL SYMBOLS

GLOB   SUB1      ;GLOBAL SYMBOL

SUB1 PSHR R5          ;SAVE RETURN ADDRESS
     MVII 1,RO       ;PLACE 1 IN RO TO IDENTIFY DEVICE 1
     JSR  R5,READ    ;GO TO READ SUBROUTINE & FETCH
                     ;VALUE READ INTO RO &
                     ;RETURN TO THE ADDRESS IN R5
                     ;R1,R2,R3,R4,R6 UNCHANGED
     MVO  RO,SETPT   ;MOVE FETCHED VALUE TO SETPT
     TSTR RO         ;CHECK FOR RO LESS THAN ZERO
     BMI  S200       ;GO TO S200 IF RO IS LESS THAN ZERO
     SUB  PV,RO      ;SUBTRACT CONTENTS OF PV FROM RO
     MVI  GAIN,R1    ;MOVE GAIN TO R1
     JSR  R5,MPY     ;GO TO SUBROUTINE TO PERFORM
                     ;MULTIPLY, RETURN RESULT IN RO,R1
     MVO  RO,C1      ;MOVE MS PART PRODUCT TO C1
     MVO  R1,C1+1    ;MOVE LS PART PRODUCT TO C1+1
     PULR R7         ;RETURN TO CALLING PROGRAM
     END
```

FIGURE 5.1.   Source image, assembly language.

This program is the equivalent to the FORTRAN level source code example given earlier. In FORTRAN the statements would be compiled to produce a series of CALLs, which are instructions to jump to certain locations containing instruction steps used frequently in many parts of a program, and to return for more instructions after performing these steps. Every reference to a location in memory would require storing and fetching, a duplication of steps costing memory space and execution time. However, FORTRAN is more easily written and understood by both programmers and others once written. But, the assembly language is much more suitable for the finer manipulation of bits and is generally more flexible. It should aways be well documented with comments and preferably include a flowchart as support.

Assembler

Assembly language is still a source language. Its instructions are mnemonics. Memory and registers are assigned to symbols, and a microcomputer does not understand these symbols. Thus assembler software converting them from an assembly code to an object code is required. Operationally, the steps are similar to those of the compiler, since they both convert a source code to an object code.

The assembly process usually generates a listing, a repeat of the source code, along side of which appear the one or more machine codes. Memory locations are usually assigned relative to zero. That is, instead of specifying exactly where the program will be placed in memory, the addresses are arbitrarily assigned with the first instruction at zero and are subject to later change. See Fig. 5.2.

If SETPT is located in relative location 31, PV in 32, GAIN in 33, and C1 in 34, after linking the object code generated from the above source code to the object codes for the subroutine READ and MPY, it may be found that the code in our example has been loaded into location 2000; thus SETPT will be found in memory location 2031, PV in 2023, GAIN in 2033, C1 in 2034, and C1 + 1 in 2035. The READ subroutine may be located in 11000, and MPY in 12400, for example. The link loader then not only allocates object codes to a specific memory location but determines how far the program must jump when it encounters the JSR R5,READ and JSR R5,MPY instructions. In Fig. 5.2 the first column is the source line number, the second column is the relative memory location, and the third column is the memory contents in machine code, with the exception that X denotes the later insertion of the proper code after link loading.

1	000000		REL	SUBI	;RELOCATABLE MODULE NAME
2					
3			REGS		;DEFINE REGISTER SYMBOLS
4					
5			EXT	READ,MPY	;READ & MPY ARE EXTERNAL ROUTINES
6					
7			EXT	GAIN,SETPT,PV,CI,S200	;EXTERNAL SYMBOLS
8					
9			GLOB	SUBI	;GLOBAL SYMBOL
10					
11	000000	001165	SUBI	PSHR R5	;SAVE RETURN ADDRESS
12	000001	001270		MVII I,RO	;PLACE I IN RO TO IDENTIFY DEVICE
	000002	000001			
13	000003	000004		JSR R5,READ	;GO TO READ SUBROUTINE & FETCH
	000004	000400X			
	000005	000000X			
14					;VALUE READ INTO RO &
15					;RETURN TO THE ADDRESS IN R5
16					;RI,R2,R3,R4,R6 UNCHANGED
17	000006	001100		MVO RO,SETPT	;MOVE FETCHED VALUE TO SETPT
	000007	000000X			
18	000010	000200		TSTR RO	;CHECK FOR RO LESS THAN ZERO
19	000011	001013		BMI S200	;GO TO S200 IF RO IS LESS THAN ZERO
	000012	000000X			
20	000013	001400		SUB PV,RO	;SUBTRACT CONTENTS OF PV FROM RO
	000014	000000X			
21	000015	001201		MVI GAIN,RI	;MOVE GAIN TO RI
	000016	000000X			
22	000017	000004		JSR R5,MPY	;GO TO SUBROUTINE TO PERFORM
	000020	000400X			
	000021	000000X			
23					;MULTIPLY. RETURN RESULT IN RO,RI
24	000022	001100		MVO RO,CI	;MOVE MS PART PRODUCT TO CI
	000023	000000X			
25	000024	001101		MVO RI,CI+I	;MOVE LS PART PRODUCT TO CI+I
	000025	000001X			
26	000026	001267		PULR R7	;RETURN TO CALLING PROGRAM
27	000026			END	

FIGURE 5.2.   Listing image, assembly language.

We have touched upon levels of software and its language conversion
software. There is much more to it, but it is neither mysterious nor in-
comprehensible if broken down into elementary components and understood at that level. For completeness, it is necessary to say that there are
three other types of language conversion: interpreters, translators, and
macrotranslators. An interpreter looks at the source code and converts it
to a machine code every time it is encountered. BASIC often is handled
this way. A translator converts a higher level source code to an assembly
source code. This is then assembled to an object code. Even though this
requires an extra procedure—recall that a compiler converts a high level
source code directly to an object code—the finer steps of an assembly
language define the step-by-step program more closely to that of machine
language. It is easier to troubleshoot or debug the program without losing
sight of the overall picture. Memory utilization inefficiency is nevertheless
still present.

A macrotranslator converts the symbolic instructions of the microprocessor to a bit pattern recognized by the host computer software. These

bits are processed as if the instructions were written in the host computer language. After assembling the source program it may require further processing to reduce it to the microprocessor level. Thus software interfaces are developed to be used by the host computer's software at both its input and output.[6]

Choice of Language Level

A suggested general rule on choice of languages is:

1. If you know only one, use it.
2. If different programs have to be written for different products, the programming costs are high. Use a high level language if available.
3. If a program is written for a substantial sales volume product, or if execution timing becomes critical, use assembly language.

Let us illustrate a small program, a process controller's gain calculation. Let us examine it from concept down to coding and testing.

Before starting any coding, the requirements of this coding must be well defined. These may be in a project specification derived as a study, or a customer requirement, or a definition of a cog in some larger machine. For example, let us assume the gain function is defined by specifying that the difference between present and past errors (or misalignments of actual value from desired value), multiplied by the numerical value called "gain," determines the change in output. This change is to be negative if the control action is specified as reverse.

In addition, we specify the following program details:

Error is defined as PV − SP.
Output change is stored in DELOUT.
Gain constant is stored in K.
Final output is stored in OUT.
Process variable is stored in PV. Process variable is the feedback, such as actual boiler temperature, stored in digital form.
Local set point is stored in LSP. It is the desired control value, such as desired boiler temperature, stored in digital form.
Direct or reverse control is stored in DIRREV and is .TRUE. if direct or .FALSE. if reverse.
The PV may be the output of an A/D converter.
A general routine to obtain the digital value of the latest analog PV is handled by subroutine PVAD.

We can flowchart this algorithm as in Fig. 5.3. There are many steps prior to this portion of the flowchart and many following. To code this in FORTRAN, Fig. 5.4 can be used.

Since this short routine was written in FORTRAN, it really is no different from another computer's FORTRAN. Microcomputers are really not different from larger computers. This same program can be written in assembly language. For example, see Fig. 5.5.

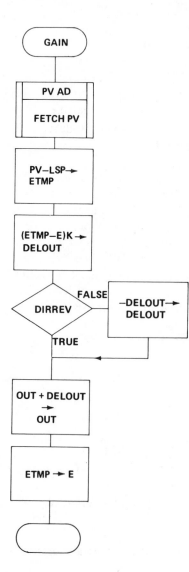

FIGURE 5.3.   Program flow chart.

```
10  C    THIS SUBROUTINE CALCULATES THE CHANGE IN OUTPUT
20  C    DUE TO GAIN ACTION AND STORES THE NEW WHOLE NUMBER IN OUT
30  C    THE NEW PV - SP IS STORED IN E, DESTROYING THE PAST SAMPLE VALUE
40  C    PREVIOUS OUT IS REPLACED BY THE NEW OUT VIA THE SUBROUTINE GAIN
50  C
60  C    TO CALL PROGRAM
70  C    CALL GAIN(OUT)
80  C
90  C    OTHER SUBROUTINES USED:  PVAD
100 C
110      SUBROUTINE GAIN(OUT)
120      LOGICAL DIRREV
130      COMMON PV,LSP,E,K,DIRREV
140      CALL PVAD(PV)
150      ETMP = PV - LSP
160      DELOUT = (ETMP - E)*K
170      IF(.NOT.DIRREV)DELOUT=-DELOUT
180 C    ADD IN NEW INCREMENT DELOUT TO THE PREVIOUS OUT
190      OUT = OUT + DELOUT
200 C    TRANSFER PRRESENT PV - LSP TO E
210      E = ETMP
220      RETURN
230      END
240
```

FIGURE 5.4. Source listing, high level language.


```
         SUBR  GAIN
         EXT   LSP
         EXT   E
         EXT   K
         EXT   DIRREV
GAIN  PUSH  R5            SAVE RETURN ADDRESS FROM CALLING PROGRAM
      CALL  PVAD,R5       SUBROUTINE PVAD WILL RETURN NEW VALUE
*                         OF PV INTO REGISTER R0
      SUBV  LSP,R0        PV - LSP -> ETMP. BINARY POINT IN 12TH PLACE
      MVR   R0,R3
      SUBV  E,R0          ETMP - E
      MVIV  K,R1
      CALL  MPY,R5        (ETMP-E)*K IN R0,R1.  BINARY POINT
*                         IN 19TH PLACE USING 2 WORDS OF MEMORY.  THE
*                         RESULT IN BINARY FORM IS
*                         SXXXXXXXXXXXXXXX XXXX.XXXXXXXXXXXX.  AFTER THE
*                         1ST BIT (SIGN), THE BINARY POINT IS LOCATED 19
*                         PLACES TO THE RIGHT.  THE PROGRAMMER MUST
*                         CARRY THIS INFORMATION IN MIND WHILE PROGRAMMING
      MVIV  DIRREV,R2     MOVE IN DIRECT-REVERSE FLAG INTO REG 2
      MVR   R2,R2         MOVE CONTENTS OF R2 BACK INTO ITSELF
*                         THIS SETS THE STATUS BITS (SIGN, ZERO, CARRY, OVFL
      BOP   GN2           IF POSITIVE, DIRECT CONTROL.  DO NOT CHANGE SIGN
      DNEG  R0,R1         ELSE IF REVERSE CONTROL, NEGATE CONTENTS
*                         OF R0,R1
GN2   MVIA  OUT,R4        MOVE IN ADDRESS OF "OUT" INTO R4
      DAD   R4,R0,R1      ADD "OUT" (A DOUBLE WORD IN
*                         B19 FORMAT) TO CONTENTS OF R0,R1
      SUBN  2,R4          RESTORE ADDRESS OF   OUT
      MVOI  R4,R1
      MVOI  R4,R0         RESTORE NEW VALUE OF   "OUT" INTO
*                         MEMORY LOCATION ASSIGNED TO   OUT
      MVOV  E,R3          RESTORE NEW VALUE OF   "E"  TO MEMORY
      POP   R7            RETURN TO MAIN PROGRAM WITH THE
*                         VALUE OF   "OUT"  IN R0, R1
      END                 END OF THIS SUBROUTINE


?
```

FIGURE 5.5. Source image, assembly language.

This program is more efficient in that less memory is used. For instance, ETMP in the FORTRAN program would have to be placed in a location dedicated to ETMP. Here ETMP is carried in register 3, until it is no longer needed as a unique piece of information. However, this program is not as readable or understandable as the one written in FORTRAN.

The above are source codes written in some form. Where do we go from here? At this time we must present it to some computer in some medium. Two popular media are punched paper tape and punched cards. The input medium depends on the computer system that will do the language processing.

Example of Compilation

Instead of enumerating the many types of facilities available, let us assume that a time sharing computer system is available to us. Let us further assume that someone else has already written a compiler or assembler suitable for the microcomputer in question.

In this case the above program will be punched on a paper tape which can be entered via a keyboard type terminal, such as a Teletype, into the time sharing system. Knowledge of the specific time sharing system is needed, such as signing on, file building, using special programs such as the compiler in question, editing for errors, dumping tape, and so on.

Let us look at an interaction. Having dialed a computer by phone from a terminal, we receive an acknowledgment. (For clarity, in the left hand column, all computer responses in the example are in lowercase, and operator interactions in uppercase. The question mark in the first field is a computer response requesting a command from the operator.)

please sign on
?ID 4257[XXXX]   Where [XXXX] could be some non-printing confidential characters authorizing access to the system

on at 1305, 04/06/19xx
?ENTER SGAIN   A tape, placed on the reader of the Teletype unit will to start feed through the sensor fingers, and a file will be built up at the remote time sharing computer. After the tape is read in, another command is given, such as

?FORTRAN SGAIN,OGAIN

What happens now? The source file SGAIN written into disk storage of the time sharing system will be acted upon by the compiler called into action by the FORTRAN command. Depending upon the compiler, it will most probably examine the source code for inconsistencies and statements the compiler cannot decode. Should such occur on the first try, which is very likely, lines of source code containing the errors will be printed out with some kind of explanation or diagnostic. How detailed the diagnostic is depends on how detailed the design of the error checking portion of the compiler was. Note that the errors picked up by the compiler are syntax errors, errors in "grammar" or the way the source phrases are put together. It cannot detect errors in logic perpetrated by the programmer.

Usually, finding such errors, the compiler terminates further processing after printing out the diagnostics. It is then up to the programmer to examine the error listing and decide upon the necessary corrections. The method of correcting a previously entered source file is a function of the time sharing system. A common correction method utilizes a text editor, another utility program of the system.

For example, suppose the following error occurred:

IF(NOT.DIRREV)DELOUT = −DELOUT
———————^

In this syntax error, the NOT operator should be preceded by a period. The correction interaction might be as follows:

?EDIT SGAIN
edit
CHANGE /(N/(.N/
IF(.NOT.DIRREV)DELOUT = −DELOUT (will be printed out)
QUIT
name output file
SGAIN
?FORTRAN SGAIN,OGAIN
?

At this time, let us assume that there were no syntax errors found in SGAIN. The compiler then generated and stored on a disk a new file in the object format, named OGAIN. Let us also assume that an object format of subroutine PVAD was previously compiled and assigned the file name OPVAD. The MPY subroutine is a library subroutine. For our discussion, let us further assume that one object file contains many library subroutines under the file name OLIB. The loader program will pick out the necessary portions from the file OLIB and ignore the rest of the library objects. The object codes must now be link-loaded.

?LOADER	
begin	
BO=BGAIN	Name of the binary (final) file.
MO=MAPFL	Name of file containing the memory map (see below).
ADDR='10000	Start address of program, octal 10000.
OBJ=OGAIN	
LINK	Link first module.
ADDR='11000	Start address of next module to be linked. If not specified, OPVAD will be assigned the first free address after OGAIN is linked.
OBJ=OPVAD	
LINK	
OBJ=OLIB	General library file.
LINK	
MAP	Generate memory map and write into file MAPFL.
QUIT	
?LIST MAPFL	

This command will list a memory map giving the absolute start of the subroutines GAIN, PVAD, MPY.

A memory map is a table of contents of the memory. It lists the addresses of key symbols, usually symbols denoting the beginning of modules. It indicates the area of memory occupied by a program, plus other memory-related information, such as free area.

A memory map may look as follows:

```
HIGH  = 11540
LOW   = 10000
START = 10000
GAIN  = 10000
PVAD  = 11000
MPY   = 11124
```

Machine Language Format: Paper Tape

?MPUNCH BGAIN will cause a paper tape containing the information in the microprocessor machine code in some special format to be punched out. Paper tape at present Teletype terminals is 1 in. wide and can contain eight holes plus a sprocket feed hole. Data containing up to 16 bits requires two rows of 8 bits each to form a 16 bit word. A possible format for the tape could be:

Leading blank tape containing only sprocket holes
Lower 8 bits of number of 16 bit words on the tape
Upper 8 bits of number of 16 bit words on the tape
Lower 8 bits of the start address
Upper 8 bits of the start address
Lower 8 bits of first instruction or data word
Upper 8 bits of first instruction or data word

. . .

Lower 8 bits of last instruction or data word
Upper 8 bits of last instruction or data word
Lower 8 bits of a check sum word
Upper 8 bits of a check sum word
Trailing blank tape containing only sprocket holes

See Fig. 5.6 for an illustration of a paper tape.

The check sum is a computation based on all the bits on the tape generated at punch time. Its purpose is to flag a punch error with a high degree of reliability when the tape is read by the microprocessor device or simulator.

When this tape is inserted into a microprocessor reader, another program, previously written and contained in the microprocessor memory, is the program for reading in the tape. What does this program do?

First it starts the tape reader on the microprocessor. As the reader drives the tape past its sensors, which detect whether holes in the tape are present or absent, initially the only information it sees is the sprocket

FIGURE 5.6. Paper tape of source.

hole punched. This portion is called the *leader*. The tape loader program reads this, decodes it as zero, and ignores it.

As the tape travels past the sensors, at what time should it read the tape? The microprocessor could read the same information hundreds of times before the tape advances far enough for a new pattern to appear under the sensors. A new appearance of a sprocket hole can trigger by hardware or software a new "read" signal. Thus each piece of data is read only once.

Having ignored all the null or zero information, the first nonzero information has the meaning of the lower byte or lower eight bits of the word count in the convention used. The next information is of necessity the upper byte of the word count. The tape loader program then combines the two bytes to form a 16 bit word containing the word count found in the tape. The maximum number of word counts then is 64K for a 16 bit microprocessor machine. Typically, the amount of memory utilized is considerably less than that.

The next two bytes of information form the starting address. Thus the first four bytes become two words. The count is used by the tape loader program to compute when the reader should stop accepting program data, for example, when the end of the information is reached. The start address is the first address where data or instruction on tape is inserted into memory. Subsequent pairs of bytes read in are stored in consecutive memory locations.

Finally, when the end of the information is reached, the check sum is also read in. While other information was being read, the tape loader program was computing its own check sum value. The two values are compared and, if identical, the information read in is reliable to a high degree of probability. If not identical, either the tape had a faulty bit, because of a misplaced or absent hole or the sensor or the microprocessor read in a bit that was not present because of a hardware defect or noise.

Note that it is possible for the check sums to agree and still have faulty information. The degree of verification is a function of the sophistication of check sum generation and checking and other factors (see Chapter 3).

Note also that nothing was said about the reliability of insertion of information into the microprocessor memory. A check on this would require a reading back from memory and a comparison with existing data just read in from the tape. Or else a second verification program, with the program read in from both tape and memory and compared for identity, would be required. If all information compares correctly, the transfer from tape to memory was reliable.

Microprocessor Development Systems

Recall Chapter 4 for a moment. Microprocessor memory usually consist of ROMs which are permanent in nature, and RAMs; the latter term really implies a read-write memory. Semiconductor RAMs are usually volatile, that is, they can lose all their information during a power outage unless backed up with secondary power. Alternatively, core memory could be used in lieu of semiconductor memory during the testing and debugging stage. Usually, only thoroughly tested programs have memory patterns (machine language 1's and 0's) transferred to ROM, PROM, or EAROM. These memories were discussed in Chapter 4.

Typically then, programs are first inserted into a read-write memory such as a RAM or the core for testing purposes. Manufacturers of microprocessors often sell kits which include such memory, means of reading in programs, and means of testing programs.

It is the means of testing the program that we now turn to. Programs can be tested by reading the user-generated program into a microprocessor development system built around the microprocessor, or reading the program into a simulator. The development systems are microcomputers which contain a sizable amount of read-write memory, as well as hardware and software debugging aids. A microprocessor-based development system has the advantage of using the actual microprocessor device. It can operate at the actual device speed and, where it is an important consideration, this is probably better than using a simulator. Special hardware design may be required for special user needs, such as the I/O specific to the intended product.

What does a development system do? Typically, the state of a microprocessor, such as contents of registers, program counter, and other status bits (e.g., as sign, overflow, carry, and zero) as a result of the immediately past operation, are examined after running part of the user program. Also, the memory contents may be examined. The user program can be run on a single instruct basis, e.g., "fetch from memory an instruction and perform it." The user can then examine the subsequent microprocessor state. The user program can also run through an indefinite number of instructions until the program counter containing the address from which the next instruction is to be fetched reaches a user-determined value, called a *break point*. The microprocessor state will then be examined as indicated above.

For instance, let us return to the GAIN subroutine (Fig. 5.5). Recall that this program subroutine starts at octal 10000, that is, the first instruction is located at address 10000. The subroutine GAIN is part of a much larger *calling* program which was previously entered into the debugging system. When GAIN is called by the main program a value of 10000 is entered into the program counter. Let us assume a single instruct mode of debugging. On pressing the "single instruct" (SI) button or giving a single instruct command, depending on the way the debugging methods are set up, a value located in R5 will be pushed into a stack. Here it will be stored as the return address of the main program that has called GAIN as a subroutine. Chapter 4 discussed methods of *nesting* subroutines. In this example the nested subroutine within subroutine GAIN is accessed by the instruction CALL PVAD,R5. This forces the program counter to the start of PVAD and places the return address to GAIN (10004) into R5, which is then temporarily placed in the stack above the value stored earlier. This frees R5 for other uses in the subroutine. (The same procedure applies when calling MPY, which is another subroutine nested within GAIN.)

The next single instruct request will change the program counter to the address of the first instruction in PVAD. In the example, this address is 11000 (see memory map); let us assume that PVAD had been previously checked out and is working. The purpose of PVAD is to convert a live analog signal into a digital value, that is, actuate an A/D converter, fetch its results, and place its contents into R0, and return to the calling program whose address is now located at the top of the stack.

If SI is continuously requested, the PVAD instructions will be performed a single step at a time. But since we postulated that PVAD is working satisfactorily, we would be better off inserting a break point at 10004. After instructing the debug system to RUN, two things should happen. One, the program should display the program counter address, 10004, after completing PVAD and returning to GAIN. R0 should display a digital value representing the converted analog signal. An SI at this time will subtract from R0 the contents found in LSP. This can be examined by requesting a look at R0.

A development system usually does much more. Not only can the registers and memory be examined, but they can actually be altered. If, for example, there is a programming error, the instruction can be corrected at the machine level by changing the instruction in memory. More typically, an error is due to insufficient processing of data. For example, if unexpected things happen because the contents of R0 are negative, and in actual practice this freak condition can exist, it may be necessary to take special action. Since the instructions are found in consecutive locations in memory, it is necessary to break into the user program. SUBV LSP,R0 and MVR R0,R3 using a total of three words, can be replaced by JMP PTCH (jump to a new location PTCH).

This location contains as its first two instruction the removed instructions SUBV LSP,R0 and MVR R0,R3. All this of course is in machine language, and the technique is called *patching*. All patching must be done at the final machine level, as mnemonic symbols no longer have meaning at this level. The patch illustration here is to test the behavior of the program in the special case of R0 being negative upon reaching 10004.

Usually the patch is temporary. It is a convenient means of modifying the program being tested temporarily to avoid holding up further testing. On completion of the test, all errors and omissions are corrected at the source code level, reassembled or recompiled, and link loaded, and a new tape in machine language produced. After the new tape is read in, the instructions will be located in different locations, usually displaced by the amount of the new insertion, without of course the JMP PTCH, which no longer serves a purpose.

At this point, it would probably hinder rather than help the reader to give further examples of this type of debugging. A debugging means is quite essential, and some very sophisticated aids have been produced either as software, hardware or, more usually, an effective combination of both. However, debugging is an experience that must be lived through and cannot be taught from books.

Debugging on a Simulator

Earlier, the term "simulator" was mentioned. A simulator is also a debugging tool, similar in function to development system debugging aids except that it is usually run on another computer system. It is a model of the actual microprocessor with real time replaced by simulated time; that is, corresponding elapsed time is stored internally. A simulator is often needed if the microprocessor is still in the developmental stage, the debugging system is not available, or it is desirable to check out the feasibility of a particular microprocessor for the function or program in mind. The simulator may be developed by the microprocessor house to run on another computer, often a time sharing system, or on some specific general purpose computer. The simulator is loaded with the program in the microprocessor machine language. It manipulates data to simulate the actual behavior of the microprocessor. A great deal of information can be processed by the simulator, because speed is not a constraint. It gives up real time processing by its very nature, so more information can be processed and checked to aid in debugging. For instance, it is relatively easy to detect illegal changes in certain parts of memory, such as a ROM area in the final product, and indicate via a diagnostic which instruction caused the fault. It can count the number of instructions processed between a start and a break point. It can sum the simulated time between the same interval. If a debugging system using the actual microprocessor were to do this, unless a parallel hardware means existed, real time would be compromised because of the additional time needed to handle the program being tested and do extra processing.

On the negative side, in addition to losing a real time capability, the simulator interfaces with inputs and outputs only with great difficulty. Sometimes it is not possible, and a substitute value to represent the I/O value must be inserted into the simulator memory or register in order to check out its effects on the program.

A compromise type of debugging package, using the better features of both hardware-based development systems and simulators, is becoming more and more popular. The debugging program is written in the same language as the user program to be debugged. Both programs are located simultaneously in memory. The debugging program controls the user's program.

The manipulation and display are similar to those for the previously described simulator running on another computer. Extra peripherals are needed such as a CRT (or even an ordinary oscilloscope with a Z-axis input), with appropriate character generation hardware, to display the microprocessor state at various user-requested stages. The software technique essentially is such that, during the command phase, all instructions and displays can be handled without running the user program. For instance, all registers and status bits can be displayed. Break points can be inserted into the user program. The start location can be inserted into the program counter, and the execute command given.

What then happens is that the user program is executed at real time until a break point is reached. Real time includes interacting with peripherals, such as A/D converters, D/A converters, transmission to other devices, alarm closures, sense line checks, and so on. A break point is usually handled in one of two ways. A software branch-out instruction to the simulator package may replace an actual instruction. This forces an exit from the user program to the debugging program upon executing the branch-out instruction. The debugging program then handles all the requested displays, replaces temporarily the removed instruction, and awaits further commands. As in the simulator on another system, it can examine and change memory and perform many similar functions.

The other method of inserting a break point involves replacing an instruction with a software *interrupt* or *trap*. Upon arriving at this address, an interrupt is generated and the user program switched to the debugging program. Both methods are equally good if the interrupt and the branch-out are single word instructions. If the branch-out contains more than one word, for example, if the first word is a branch and the second word a displacement, then the interrupt system is superior because the multiword branch-out method places certain restrictions as to where break points may be inserted.

A debugging package for the development system has the following drawbacks. Since real time operation does not permit it to monitor every instruction but only to describe the start and end points of a run, it is not feasible to do the following:

Monitor every instruction to obtain a count.
Monitor memory write violations.

Break point manipulation is possible only if the user program is in the read-write portion of memory. Programs in firmware (ROM) cannot have break point software inserted. Note, however, that programs being debugged usually are written into read-write memory until they are free from errors.

Some of the deficiences described can be overcome by extra hardware circuitry. Such circuitry can contain the break point information and monitor the program counter while the user program is being executed, without disturbing it in any way. Real time is preserved, and programs in ROM can be checked with the debugging program. Also, memory protection bands, such as groups of 512 words or 1024 words, can be monitored, with either a halt action or warning indication if a violation occurs.

In general, unless the resources of the application program developing company are large, and the intended microprocessor is not yet available, a debugging package for a development system is probably the preferred method of debugging.

Finally, at some time, the "good enough" point in the program development arrives. The point of perfection never does. It always appears possible to improve function and program efficiency or decrease memory utilization.

Unlike core-based computer systems, where the program can be easily modified by loading new software, the "good enough" point is more stringent, because it is usually desired to store the program in ROM, a very permanent action. PROM, which can still be changed (but less easily than software) requires more printed wiring board space and power to run so is generally a secondary choice.

Let us say that such a point in development is reached at which the programs have been thoroughly checked out by an independent checker, not the original programmer, all corrections have been implemented and rechecked again, and the time has come to prepare ROMs.

From the software point of view, the machine language of the program must be reformatted into the ROM manufacturer's format. Such a program may be present in the development package in the correct format of the microprocessor manufacturer. This supposes that an output medium such as a paper tape or a magnetic cassette exists. Some manufacturers require punched cards for ROM information to be conveyed.

A caution is in order. The user must double check that every bit of the information conveyed is perfect. This usually, involves having a read-back and verification program for the ROM format medium, since a bit may be incorrectly inserted or dropped because of noise or hardware malfunction. Once submitted, it takes several weeks to manufacture and deliver ROMs, and an error in the submitted ROM format, or in the actual program, could be very costly.

As a final note, microprocessor programming is quite similar to that of larger minicomputers. For a sufficiently large word structure, say 16 bits, there is little difference.

References

1. Trademark of Intel Corp., 3065 Bowers Ave., Santa Clara, Calif.

2. PL/M Programming Manual, Rev. A, Intel Corp., Santa Clara, Calif. See also J. E. Lewis and J. E. Davis, "Development of a Microprocessor-Based Clinical Analyzer," Preprint 76-510 of ISA International Conference, Houston, Texas, Oct. 10–14, 1976, Instrument Society of America, 400 Stanwix Ave., Pittsburgh, Pa. This paper is an excellent review of recent experience with the PL/M(R) version, pointing out difficulties such as high overhead in parameter passing and the necessity to use global variables, as well as its ease of use. A more general review is found in G. A. Kidall, "High-Level Language Simplifies Microcomputer Programming," *Electronics* **47** 103–109 (June 27, 1974).

3. R. M. Grossman, *Electronics*, **49** 108 (Apr. 15, 1976).

4. *EDN Microcomputer Systems Directory*, Cahners Publishing, Nov. 20, 1975.

5. Figures 5.1 and 5.2 reproduced with the permission of General Instrument Corp., Hicksville, N.Y.

6. A. Sidline, "Operating Systems Software Interfaces for a Microprocessor," *Digest of Papers, Fall COMPCON*, catalog 75CH0988-6C, IEEE, New York, 1975.

Six

Development of
Digital Control
Algorithms

In Chapter 2 we developed several control algorithms in a form suitable for analog controllers, utilizing differential equations derived from basic physical principles and the Laplace transforms. It is important for those using microprocessors to know how to transform these standard analog control forms into digital software (or firmware), as well as how to develop new control forms which can in some cases take better advantage of the digital processor's capabilities. These advantages are manifold and include such tangible benefits as a substantially infinite memory time constant which permits the use of exceptionally long reset times in a standard algorithm, the ability to compensate for long dead times in processes, and the capacity to implement deadbeat, optimum, and other control equations.

The transformation from continuous to sampled data (digital) control equations can be accomplished by the use of Z transforms or by means of difference equations. The latter approach is usually easier to understand and implement in simple cases, hence less subject to errors, so it is used here wherever feasible.

First Order Lag Filter

We used the difference method in Chapter 3 for a simple but useful example, the first order lag. An external, analog, first stage filter is necessary in nearly all digital control systems, because of the effect of aliasing or interference from high frequencies which is possible in all sampled data systems (see Chapter 3). Normally, a fixed low pass hardware filter is used in the data acquisition subsystem, followed by an adjustable digital filter. First order lags are commonly employed for both filters.

The steps in deriving any digital algorithm by the difference equation method are:

1.   Write the physically derived transfer function of the control equation in analog form, using the Laplace transform notation.
2.   Change Laplace notation to differential equations.
3.   Put in difference form, using the digital approximation:

$$\frac{dD}{dx} = \frac{D_n - D_{n-1}}{T_s}$$

where T_s is the sampling interval equal to $T_n - T_{n-1}$.

4.   Solve for the present value of the variable (with subscript n) using only past values of variables on the right hand side of the equation (subscript $n - i$, where i is equal to or greater than 1).

In the first order lag example the Laplace transfer function is

$$\frac{D}{x} = \frac{1}{T_1 S + 1} \qquad \text{(step 1)}$$

where D = output
$\qquad$ x = input
$\qquad$ T = filter time constant (RC)
$\qquad$ S = Laplace operator

Since the operator S is transformable to d/dt (Table 2.1),

$$T_1 \frac{dD}{dt} + D = x \qquad \text{(step 2)}$$

Changing to the difference form,

$$T_1 \frac{\Delta D}{\Delta T} + D_n = x$$

or

$$T_1 \frac{D_n - D_{n-1}}{T_s} + D_n = x \qquad \text{(step 3)}$$

since

$$\Delta T = T_n - T_{n-1} = T_s \qquad \text{(sampling interval)}$$

In most cases, some algebraic manipulation may be required to obtain a convenient solution. In this case, with a little ingenuity we obtain the solution

$$D_n = D_{n-1} + \left(\frac{T_s}{T_s + T_1}\right)(x - D_{n-1}) \qquad \text{(step 4)}$$

$$= D_{n-1} + K(x - D_{n-1})$$

This form of the algorithm is a most convenient one for microprocessor use. We need merely store the last value of the output D_{n-1}, subtract it from the current input x, multiply by a constant, and add the result to the stored D_{n-1} value. The new value D_n then replaces the old D_{n-1} value at the next sampling interval.

The filter constant K can be fixed or adjustable. If fixed, it will be stored with the firmware program. If adjustable, it can be computed separately and stored so as to be on call by the filter algorithm. Often the sampling interval (if variable) is determined by other than filter considerations and may be available as an input to another program. The time constant T_1 can be manually inserted by the operator. Or the value of K can be calculated externally (say by a nomograph) and inserted by means of a manual device.

Some time has been spent on this example, because it is uncomplicated and yet illustrates a complete procedure for digital algorithm development. We are now in a position to consider more complex functions.

PID Algorithm

Most process loops, where the plant transfer function has not been completely characterized (defined), are controlled by the ubiquitous PID algorithm or one of its variations.

As shown in Chapter 2, the ideal PID is the sum of proportional, integral, and differential elements or, in Laplace form,

$$\frac{\text{Output}}{\text{Input}} = \frac{V}{E} = K\left(1 + \frac{1}{T_IS} + T_DS\right) \qquad (2.13)$$

In the practical case, high frequency limits are set by a low pass filter (first order lag):

$$\frac{1}{1 + T_FS}$$

so that

$$\frac{V}{E} = \frac{K}{1 + T_FS}\left(1 + \frac{1}{T_IS} + T_DS\right)$$

Making the transformations shown in (2.15) and setting $T_F = \gamma T_2$, we arrive at the "real" or interactive form of the PID:

$$\frac{V}{E} = \frac{K_1(T_1S + 1)(T_2S + 1)}{T_1S(\gamma T_2S + 1)} \tag{2.14}$$

or

$$\frac{V}{E} = \frac{T_2S + 1}{\gamma T_2 + 1} K_1\left(1 + \frac{1}{T_1S}\right) \tag{6.1}$$

where V = output (to valve)

E = error $(PV - SP)$

T_1 = real integral time constant

T_2 = real derivative time constant

γ = rate amplitude constant

S = Laplace operator

K_1 = gain

Equation (2.14) is representative of most analog controllers. The second form, (6.1), permits the control equation to be implemented in software blocks and is more convenient for a microprocessor. Figure 6.1 shows the block approach.

Derivative Block.   With this approach, an algorithm can be derived separately for each block. Take the derivative block first:

$$\frac{D}{E} = \frac{T_2S + 1}{\gamma T_2S + 1} \tag{6.2}$$

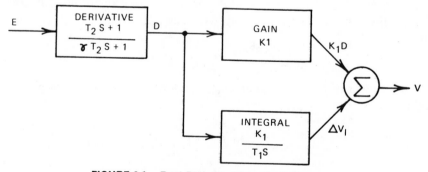

FIGURE 6.1.   Real PID algorithm block diagram.

where D is the derivative block output, Then,

$$(\gamma T_2 S + 1)D = (T_2 S + 1)E$$

$$\gamma T_2 \frac{dD}{dt} + D = T_2 \frac{dE}{dt} + E$$

Changing to the difference form, using

$$\Delta D = D_n - D_{n-1}$$

$$\Delta T = T_n - T_{n-1} = T_s \qquad \text{(sample period)}$$

$$\gamma T_2 \frac{D_n - D_{n-1}}{T_s} + D_n = T_2 \frac{E_n - E_{n-1}}{T_s} + E_n$$

$$D_n(\gamma T_2 + T_s) = \gamma T_2 D_{n-1} + T_2(E_n - E_{n-1}) + E_n T_s$$

$$D_n = D_{n-1} + \frac{1}{\gamma T_2} [T_2(E_n - E_{n-1}) + E_n T_s - D_n T_s]$$

To solve for D_n, the current value of the derivative in terms of the past values, further manipulation of the last equation is needed:

$$D_n \left(1 + \frac{T_s}{\gamma T_2}\right) = D_{n-1} + \frac{1}{\gamma}(E_n - E_{n-1}) + \frac{T_s}{\gamma T_2} E_n$$

$$D_n = \frac{\gamma T_2}{\gamma T_2 + T_s} D_{n-1} + \left(\frac{T_2}{\gamma T_2 + T_s}\right)(E_n - E_{n-1})$$

$$+ \left(\frac{T_s}{\gamma T_2 + T_s}\right) E_n$$

$$D_n = D_{n-1} - D_{n-1}\left(1 - \frac{\gamma T_2}{\gamma T_2 + T_s}\right)$$

$$+ \left(\frac{T_2}{\gamma T_2 + T_s}\right)(E_n - E_{n-1}) + \left(\frac{T_s}{\gamma T_2 + T_s}\right) E_n$$

$$= D_{n-1} + \left(\frac{T_2}{\gamma T_2 + T_s}\right)(E_n - E_{n-1})$$

$$+ \left(\frac{T_s}{\gamma T_2 + T_s}\right)(E_n - D_{n-1}) \qquad (6.3)$$

For small values of T_s ($\ll T_2$) we can make the approximation:

$$D_n \doteq D_{n-1} + \frac{1}{\gamma}(E_n - E_{n-1}) + \left(\frac{T_s}{\gamma T_2 + T_s}\right)(E_n - D_{n-1}) \qquad (6.4)$$

which is the desired form of the algorithm for the differential block.

Integral Block.   The integral block (Fig. 6.1) is much simpler to analyze. For integral action we wish the first difference ΔV_I of the output to be proportional to the input.

The Laplace form of the transfer function is

$$\frac{V}{D_n} = \frac{K_1}{T_1 S} \tag{6.5}$$

$$VS = \frac{K_1}{T_1} D_n$$

$$\frac{V_n - V_{n-1}}{T_s} = \frac{K_1}{T_1} D_n$$

or

$$\Delta V_I = K_1 \left(\frac{T_s}{T_1} \right) D_n \tag{6.6}$$

The ratio T_s/T_1 is often defined as K_I, the integral gain constant, so that K_1 is simply the system gain.

Summing the derivative output (multiplied by K_1) with the integral block output results in the complete three-term output.

Ideal PID.   The noninteractive or separated mode PID algorithm can be written directly from the differential equation resulting from (2.13) (see Fig. 6.2):

$$V_n = K e_n + K_I \sum_{i=0}^{n} e_i T_s + K_D \frac{e_n - e_{n-1}}{T_s} + V_m \tag{6.7}$$

where the summation is the difference equivalent of integration, and V_m is the average value position (offset). K_I, the integral gain constant, is equal to K/T_I in (2.13), and $K_D = K T_D$; thus the three gain constants are not independent.

Velocity Algorithm

Equations (6.1) and (6.7) are the position or whole value form of the real and ideal PID algorithms. In the event of temporary loss of signal to the process actuator, the correct position could be transmitted on restoration of the communication link, and the valve will "catch up" without any synchronization problem.

Another form of the PID algorithm is possible, which lacks this feature but has other valuable advantages. The incremental or velocity form is obtained by subtracting two successive values of V, that is, $V_n - V_{n-1}$.

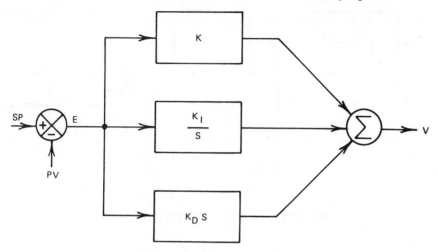

FIGURE 6.2.   Ideal PID algorithm.

Solving (6.7) for V_{n-1},

$$V_{n-1} = Ke_{n-1} + K_I \sum_{i=0}^{n-1} e_i T_s + K_D \frac{e_{n-1} - e_{n-2}}{T_s} \qquad (6.8)$$

Subtracting (6.8) from (6.7) gives

$$V_n - V_{n-1} = \Delta V_n = K(e_n - e_{n-1}) + K_I e_n T_s + \frac{K_D}{T_s}(e_n - 2e_{n-1} + e_{n-2}) \qquad (6.9)$$

One advantage is that the average valve setting V_m has disappeared, meaning that, when the controller is first started, the operator does not have to initialize the control loop by inserting this value manually. In the positional forms of the PID algorithm, if the controlled loop is switched from manual to automatic control, the process will "bump" unless the controller is aligned with the present valve position. The velocity algorithm is "bumpless." Another advantage is that the elimination of the summation eliminates the danger of windup, a condition in which the controller saturates its integral term when for some reason an error signal persists.

The bumpless feature of the velocity algorithm can be obtained in the real PID form by a small modification of (6.1) to

$$\frac{V}{E} = \frac{T_2 S + 1}{\gamma T_2 S + 1}\left(K_1 S + \frac{K_1}{T_1}\right)\frac{1}{S} \qquad (6.10)$$

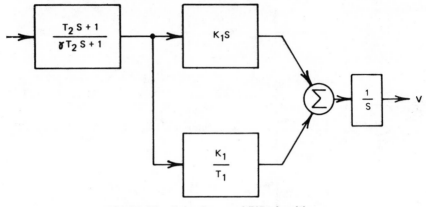

FIGURE 6.3.   Bumpless real PID algorithm.

The additional block $(1/S)$ is shown in Fig. 6.3. This form is basically a velocity algorithm integrated at the last stage. Windup prevention can be provided as an upper limit on the last block, by detecting saturation or in other ways.

Improved Derivative and Integral Computation

There are many further modifications and implementations of the basic algorithms. One particularly worth noting is a method of calculating digital differences for derivative terms. Noise may be a problem in first differences used with a position algorithm, and even more so in the case of second differences used with velocity algorithms.

The simple first difference (corresponding to d/dt in the analog case) is

$$\Delta E_n = E_n - E_{n-1} \tag{6.11}$$

and the second difference (corresponding to d^2/dt^2) is

$$\begin{aligned}
\Delta^2 E &= \Delta E_n - \Delta E_{n-1} \\
&= (E_n - E_{n-1}) - (E_{n-1} - E_{n-2}) \\
&= E_n - 2E_{n-1} + E_{n-2}
\end{aligned} \tag{6.12}$$

Since differentiation or its numerical equivalent, differencing, is a "roughening" process, it is sensitive to and accentuates data errors and noise. Hence some smoothing must be accomplished before the derivative is calculated.

We have already discussed the use of low pass analog and digital filters. A supplementary technique often employed is the use of interpolation formulas. By taking the values of several points equally spaced, an analytic differentiation can be performed, giving a much smoother derivative.

One formula that has been successfully employed with the velocity algorithm is the *four-point central difference* technique. Assume four points E_n to E_{n-3} equally spaced at the sampling interval

Define

$$E^* = \frac{E_n + E_{n-1} + E_{n-2} + E_{n-3}}{4} \tag{6.13}$$

Then,

$$\frac{\Delta E}{T_s} = \frac{\dfrac{E_n - E^*}{1.5T_s} + \dfrac{E_{n-1} - E^*}{0.5T_s} + \dfrac{E^* - E_{n-2}}{0.5T_s} + \dfrac{E^* - E_{n-3}}{1.5T_s}}{4}$$

$$= \frac{1}{6T_s} (E_n - E_{n-3} + 3E_{n-1} - 3E_{n-2}) \tag{6.14}$$

The amount of additional computation in this algorithm is minimal, but it requires storage for two additional past values of the variable E.

Although less vulnerable than the derivative term to noise and errors, the numerical integral or summation in (6.7) can also be improved from the standpoint of accuracy. For the rectangular integral

$$\sum_{i=0}^{n} e_i$$

can be substituted the trapezoidal rule

$$\sum_{i=0}^{n} \frac{e_i + e_{i-1}}{2}$$

Again, the price of the improvement is additional memory and more computation time.

Dynamic Compensation Algorithm

Before going on to more sophisticated algorithms, we derive a lead lag algorithm that is useful for dynamic compensation and a feedforward network.

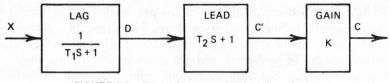

FIGURE 6.4. Dynamic compensation (lead lag).

The classic lead lag transfer function is

$$\frac{C}{X} = \frac{K(T_2S + 1)}{T_1S + 1} \tag{6.15}$$

This can be conveniently represented by three separate blocks, lag, lead, and gain, as shown in Fig. 6.4.

Taking the lag block first,

$$\frac{D}{X} = \frac{1}{T_1S + 1} \tag{6.15a}$$

$$(T_1S + 1)D = X \qquad T_1 \frac{dD}{dt} + D = X$$

$$\frac{T(D_n - D_{n-1})}{T_s} + D_n = X_n$$

$$D_n(T_1 + T_s) = T_sX_n + T_1D_{n-1}$$

$$D_n = \frac{T_1}{T_1 + T_s} D_{n-1} + \frac{T_s}{T_1 + T_s} X_n$$

$$= D_{n-1} - \frac{D_{n-1}(T_1 + T_s - T_1)}{T_1 + T_s} + \frac{T_s}{T_1 + T_s} X_n$$

$$= D_{n-1} + \frac{T_s}{T_1 + T_s} (X_n - D_{n-1}) \tag{6.16}$$

The lead block is

$$\frac{C'}{D} = T_2S + 1$$

$$C' = T_2 \frac{dD}{dt} + D$$

$$C'_n = \frac{T_2(D_n - D_{n-1})}{T_s} + D_n \tag{6.17}$$

And the gain block is

$$C_n = KC'_n \tag{6.18}$$

completing the algorithm.

Dead Time Compensation Algorithms

The algorithms discussed above are widely employed in process control, because they can be adjusted (tuned) to give nearly optimum response with many processes by manipulating the values of K, K_I, and K_D (or alternatively K_1, T_1, and T_2). The methods used for tuning are largely quasi-empirical and need not concern us at this point except to ensure, if we use these algorithms, that convenient means are provided for the operator to adjust the tuning controls. It is not necessary to know a priori the transfer function of the process.

An algorithm can also be designed from knowledge of the process response. Primarily, these are developed using Z-transform techniques. Some, however, may employ feedforward methods which require at least an approximation of the plant transfer function in order to construct a compensating model.

Many plants can be approximately represented by a first order lag plus dead time:

$$\frac{PV}{C} = \frac{Ae^{-LS}}{TS + 1} \tag{6.19}$$

A large value of dead time L can be exceedingly troublesome, causing long period oscillations which refuse to "line out" until after five or six dead time periods.

It was shown by O. J. M. Smith[1,2] that a feedback loop around a controller (which may use a PID algorithm) will compensate for many of these dead time effects, if the feedback transfer function is

$$\frac{A(1 - e^{-LS})}{TS + 1} \tag{6.20}$$

and the constants A, L, and T are the same as those of the process plant. The modified control loop with controller feedback is shown in Fig. 6.5. The primary problem involved in transforming this function into the difference form is the expression in parentheses, $1 - e^{-LS}$.

This can be represented first by use of the power series

$$e^{-LS} = \frac{1}{1 + LS + [(LS)^2/2!]} + \cdots$$

This expression to three terms can be further approximated by

$$\frac{1}{1 + LS + [(LS)^2/4]} = \frac{1}{[1 + (LS/2)]^2}$$

Then the transfer function [see (6.20)] can be adequately approximated by

$$\frac{A}{TS + 1} \left\{ 1 - \frac{1}{[1 + (LS/2)]^2} \right\} \tag{6.21}$$

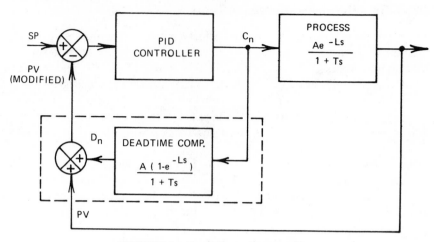

FIGURE 6.5.   Dead time compensation.

This expression can now be separated into blocks, as before, and a difference equation written for each one (see Fig. 6.6):

$$\frac{F_1}{C} = \frac{1}{TS + 1} \tag{6.22}$$

Since it is of the exact form of the lag block [see (6.15a)], we can immediately write a solution using (6.16):

$$F_{1,n} = F_{1,n-1} + \frac{T_s}{T + T_s} (C_n - F_{1,n-1})$$

But since the sampling time T_s is much smaller than the dead time T,

$$F_{1,n} \doteq F_{1,n-1} + \frac{T_s}{T} (C_n - F_{1,n-1}) \tag{6.23}$$

We can also write the difference equations for the next two blocks by inspection:

$$F_{2,n} = F_{2,n-1} + 2(T_s/L)F_{1,n-1} - F_{2,n-1} \tag{6.24}$$

$$F_{3,n} = F_{3,n-1} + 2(T_s/L)F_{2,n-1} - F_{3,n-1} \tag{6.25}$$

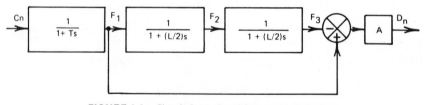

FIGURE 6.6.   Dead time algorithm approximation.

and

$$D_n = A(F_{1,n} - F_{3,n}) \qquad (6.26)$$

D_n is added to PV in order to modify the input to the controller.

The effect of dead time compensation on the performance of an ideal DDC controller is shown in Fig. 6.7a and b, the results of a computer simulation. The value of the controller T_s is $\frac{1}{3}$ sec, and the process dead time L and time constant T are 1 min each. The upper curve shows the effect of a 10% set point step disturbance at zero time with the PID controller tuned to the approximately best response. Figure 6.7b shows the effect

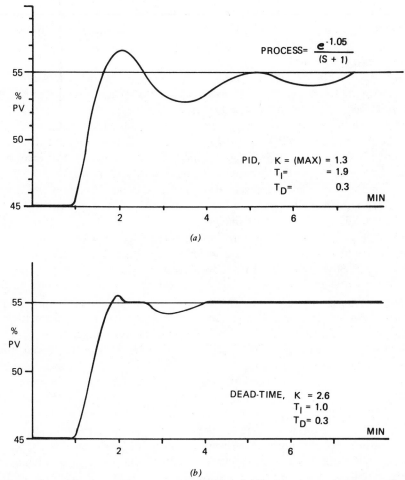

FIGURE 6.7. Effect of dead time compensation. *(a)* Best tuning, no compensation. *(b)* With compensation.

of adding the dead time compensator. The gain can be increased by a factor of 2, and the integral constant reduced, making the controller much more responsive. In terms of conventional error criteria, the absolute error integral (AEI) can be improved by 15 to 20%, and error integral multiplied by time can be reduced more than 40%. Closely similar improvements can be realized with load disturbances or by substituting a real controller.

Optimal Sampled Data Control Algorithms

We noted at the start of this chapter that there are two general approaches to the design of digital control algorithms, In the first, an intuitively satisfying physical control scheme, such as the PID, is developed in analog form and transmuted to digital form by means of difference equations. Tuning is required to fit a particular process or plant whose exact transfer function may not be known.

In the other approach, the transfer function of the plant is known or approximated closely, and its desired response to a particular input or disturbance is specified. The characteristics of a controller to produce this response are then back-calculated. In this way, much of the arbitrariness of the quasi-empirical PID method is eliminated. The response to the input may be specified as nearly ideal (optimal) for the purpose. For example, we can specify that the process variable respond to a step input of set point within one sample interval after elapse of the dead time without any overshoot—this is the best than can be achieved with any system.

Such a controller is often called *deadbeat,* "*bang-bang,*" or *minimal prototype*. The first designation, though often used, can be unfortunately confused with a deadbeat second order analog system, such as a damped pendulum. Since this kind of deadbeat system has a very slow response, it conveys the exact opposite of what a minimal prototype system actually does, which is respond with the greatest practical speed. "Bang-bang" response more graphically expresses the system's behavior, since ideally only two positionings of the valve or final control element are needed. However, "bang-bang servo" usually refers to a relay type, or one that has only two possible actuator positions. This is not the same as a minimal prototype system, hence the latter, somewhat academic term is preferred.

In general, what a minimal prototype controller does is precompute the position of the final control element to being the process variable to the desired position within one sample time after a disturbance is perceived. It then predicts and compensates by repositioning the valve for any overshoot that would ordinarily result from lags in the process. This behavior can be said to represent a type of feedforward behavior, a model of the process being resident in the controller. The predictive computations, which may be complex, make good use of the capabilities of a digital computer and its memory capacity and are well beyond the ability of conventional analog controllers. Thus a minimal prototype algorithm is well matched to the microprocessor.

Undesirable Features of Minimal Prototype Systems.   Minimal prototype designs are developed with the use of the *Z* transform, a sampled data technique similar to the Laplace transform for continuous differential equations. A feature of the *Z* transform is that it is defined only at the sample intervals. A possibility exists that oscillation may occur between these intervals, unless special analytic methods are used.[3] This is one possible difficulty of the minimal prototype controller.

Second, they are designed for specific plant transfer functions and for specific inputs as well. Therefore a controller designed for set point changes may not behave very well as a regulator, where the set point remains fixed and the disturbance is in the plant load. Furthermore, a controller designed for a step input may not behave well for a ramp. Thus minimal prototype controllers designed for continuous processes, where the duty is primarily regulation, may require a different algorithm if used for batch processes, where set points are ramped. To offset this, we have the capability of the microprocessor to operate with more than one algorithm.

Minimal prototype algorithms must also be physically realizable; that is, they must depend only on past and present values of inputs, not on future ones. Furthermore, enough energy must be available to drive the process from the computed output. This is often the limiting factor in real situations. We must inevitably refer to the *Z* transform to present these algorithms, but would be too much of a diversion to fully explain *Z* transform methods in this book. We therefore confine ourselves to using the results. Those seeking a more detailed explanation of sampled data techniques are referred to the works by Tou[3] and Koppel,[4] among others.

Minimal Prototype Regulator.   We stated above that a process transfer function must be assumed to derive a minimal prototype algorithm. We assume a first order process lag with dead time, represented by the transfer function

$$G_p(S) = \frac{K_p e^{-\tau_D S}}{\tau S + 1} \tag{6.27}$$

where K_p is the process gain, τ and τ_D are the process lag and dead time, respectively, and S is the Laplace operator. We assume further that the dead time is equal to the sample time T multiplied by an integer K.

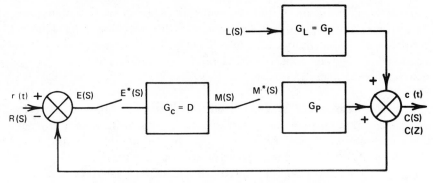

FIGURE 6.8.   Sampled data–controlled system.

A block diagram of the system is shown in Fig. 6.8. The load $L(S)$ enters the system through a transfer function $G_L(S)$ which we take as being the same as G_p. The starred values of error and controller output, $E^*(S)$ and $M^*(S)$, represent the effect of the sampling process, shown by the hypothetical switches in the schematic. For a regulator, $R(S)$ is fixed, and we represent $L(S)$, the load disturbance, as a step function, $1/S$.

The controller algorithm can be written as a finite difference equation:

$$m(nT) = q_0 e(nT) + q_1 e[(n-1)T] + q_2[(n-2)T] + \cdots$$
$$- r_1 m[(n-1)T] - r_2 m[(n-2)T] - \cdots \qquad (6.28)$$

where $m(nT)$ = present output of the controller at T, the sampling interval
$e(nT)$ = value of error at T
$(n-1)T, (n-2)T$, and so on = values of e and m at one, two, or more sampling intervals in the past

By applying the Z transform, this difference equation can be used to derive a sampled data transfer function for the controller:

$$D(Z) = \frac{M(Z)}{E(Z)} = \frac{q_0 + q_1 Z^{-1} + q_2 Z^{-2} + \cdots}{1 + r_1 Z^{-1} + r_2 Z^{-2} + r_3 Z^{-3} + \cdots} \qquad (6.29)$$

The variable Z is a function of the sampling time T and S, the Laplace variable, equal to e^{-TS}.

Note that once the controller transfer function is determined, the difference equation algorithm follows directly from the identity of the constants q and r and (6.28). We also have a check on the correctness of $D(Z)$, since, if expressed in negative exponents of Z, as in (6.29), it is physically realizable only if there is a 1 in the denominator.

To arrive at the correct expression for $D(Z)$, the output of the system C, the process variable, must be in accord with the physical situation. For a regulator, it is ideally desirable, but not possible, for C to remain zero at all times. Instead, the controller must return the process to zero PV in the shortest number of sampling intervals without causing oscillation and must have a physically realizable transfer function as just defined

The general expression for $D(Z)$ is obtained from manipulation of the block diagram (Fig. 6.8) and is

$$D(Z) = \frac{G_p L(Z) - C(Z)}{C(Z) G_p(Z)} \tag{6.30}$$

The expressions for G_p [see (6.27)] and $L(S)$ $(= 1/S)$ are known, so it only remains to determine the output $C(Z)$ and express $D(Z)$ in the form of (6.29)[5].

Physically, because of the dead time KT, the output must remain zero for K periods. At time KT, the controller input is still zero and, because it can change only at the sampling instants, it remains zero for $K + 1$ periods. At the end of this time, the output is

$$C[(K + 1)T] = K_p(1 - e^{aT})$$

where a is the reciprocal of τ. The controller will now perceive this error but, again because of the delay, its output will not begin to take effect until another $K + 1$ sampling periods have elapsed. At this time,

$$C[(2K + 2)T] = K_p[1 - e^{-(K+2)aT}]$$

The desired control action will now take place and restore the plant PV to zero for every interval greater than $2K + 2$.

Applying the Z transform to these expressions for $C(nT)$, and after considerable manipulation, one arrives at the equation for $D(Z)$:

$$D(Z) = \frac{Z^K}{K_p} \frac{Z(1 - e^{-aT}) - (Z - 1)(Z - e^{-aT}) \sum_{n=1}^{K+2} (1 - e^{-anT})Z^{-n}}{(1 - e^{-aT})(Z - 1) \sum_{n=1}^{K+2} (1 - e^{-anT})Z^{-n}} \tag{6.31}$$

Equation (6.31) is the general expression of a regulator transfer function for a first order lag process with dead time K times the sampling interval. In order to arrive at the difference equation algorithm of the controller a choice of K is made and the equation put in the form of (6.29) to evaluate the constants q and r.

Letting $K = 1$, for example, (6.31) reduces to

$$D(Z) = \frac{q_0 + q_1 Z^{-1} + q_2 Z^{-2}}{1 + r_1 Z^{-1} + r_2 Z^{-2} + r_3 Z^{-3}} \tag{6.32}$$

where $q_0 = 0$ $\qquad r_1 = e^{-aT}$

$$q_1 = \frac{(1 - e^{-4aT})}{K_p(1 - e^{-aT})^2} \qquad r_2 = e^{-2aT}$$

$$q_2 = \frac{e^{-4aT} - e^{-aT}}{K_p(1 - e^{-aT})^2} \qquad r_3 = \frac{-1 + e^{-aT} + e^{-3aT} - e^{-4aT}}{(1 - e^{-aT})^2}$$

and the correct algorithm form is

$$m(nT) = q_0 e(nT) + q_1 e[(n-1)T] + q_2[(n-2)T]$$
$$- r_1 m[(n-1)T] - r_2 m[(n-2)T] - r_3[(n-3)T] \quad (6.33)$$

This algorithm and a dead time process have been simulated on a digital computer, as shown in Fig. 6.9. The results of the simulation are plotted in Fig. 6.10. It can be observed that, for all sampling instants greater than $4T$ following the disturbance, the output C is zero. Also, it can be noted that there are no oscillations between the sampling instants. The requirements for a minimal prototype algorithm are thus met. The regulator algorithm for this process occupies 9 lines of FORTRAN code plus an additional 10 to define the controller constants.

Kalman Set Point Controller. A minimal prototype algorithm for set point control can be derived in the same way as (6.33), using Z-transform techniques. The result is known as a Kalman type controller, after R. E. Kalman, who first described such a method.[6] Gallier and Otto[7] reported the development of such a controller algorithm for a second order lag process with dead time, which is applicable to a large number of plants. The plant transfer function in Laplace form is

$$\frac{X(S)}{M(S)} = \frac{Ke^{-\tau_D S}}{(\tau_1 + S)(\tau_2 + S)} \qquad (6.34)$$

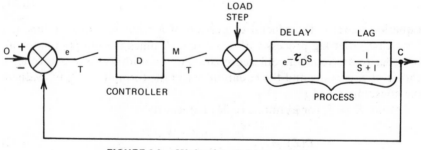

FIGURE 6.9. Minimal prototype control.

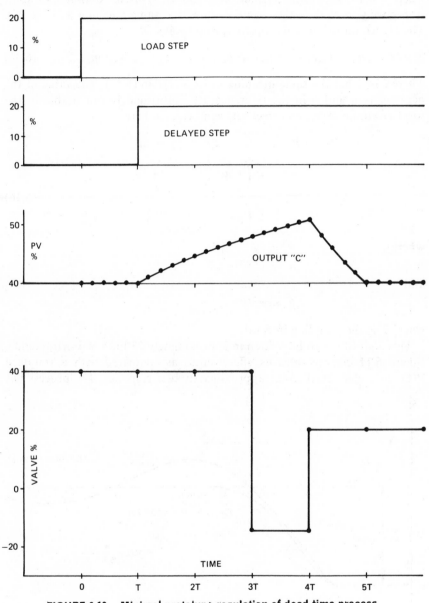

FIGURE 6.10. Minimal prototype regulation of dead time process.

where K is the gain of the system, $X(S)$ and $M(S)$ are the output and input, respectively, and the other symbols have the same meaning as in (6.27). The algorithm for minimal prototype controller is

$$m_i = b_0(e_i + b_1 e_{i-1} + b_2 e_{i-2} + a_1 m_{i-1-n} + a_2 m_{i-2-n}) \qquad (6.35)$$

where $i - 1$ has the same meaning as $(n - 1)T$ in (6.33). The value of the parameters a and b in the reference are unfortunately not usable in the form given, however, a correct set[8] can be given here:

$$b_1 = -(\alpha + \beta) \qquad b_2 = \alpha\beta$$

$$a_1 = K\left(1 + \frac{\alpha\tau_1 - \beta\tau_2}{\tau_2 - \tau_1}\right)$$

$$a_2 = K\left(\alpha\beta + \frac{\beta\tau_1 - \alpha\tau_2}{\tau_2 - \tau_1}\right)$$

$$(6.36)$$

where

$$\alpha = e^{-T/\tau_1}$$

and

$$\beta = e^{-T/\tau_2}$$

where T is the sampling interval.

This algorithm can be written in approximately 23 lines of Fortran code. Figure 6.11 demonstrates its effectiveness as compared with a standard PID controller tuned to the approximately best response. The process has

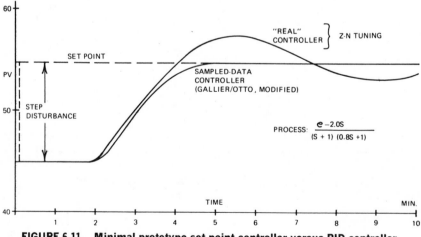

FIGURE 6.11.   Minimal prototype set point controller versus PID controller.

two time constants and a delay time equal to twice the longest time constant. The response of a minimal prototype controller to a 10% set point step is much improved over that of a PID controller.

References

1. O. J. M. Smith, *ISA J.* **6**(2) 28 (Feb. 1949).

2. O. J. M. Smith, *Chem. Eng. Prog.* **53** 217 (1957).

3. J. T. Tou, *Digital and Sampled-Data Control Systems*, McGraw-Hill, New York, 1959.

4. L. B. Koppel, *Introduction to Control Theory*, Prentice-Hall, Englewood Cliffs, N. J., 1968.

5. E. R. Rang, Honeywell Corporate Research Center, Bloomington, Minn., personal note to author, May 14, 1975. [The author is indebted to Mr. Rang for his derivations of (6.31) and (6.36), which were corrected from the published versions found in the literature, and for his generous permission to use them in this work.]

6. R. E. Kalman and R. W. Koepcke, "Optimal Synthesis of Linear Sampling Control Systems Using Generalized Performance Indexes," *Trans. ASME* **80** 1820–1826 (1958).

7. P. W. Gallier and R. E. Otto, "Self-Tuning Computer Adapts DDC Algorithms," *Instrum. Technol.* 65–70 (Feb. 1968).

8. E. R. Rang, unpublished memo, Sept. 19, 1975. See note in reference 5.

Seven

Digital Control of Instruments (Multichannel Spectrometer)

One of the earliest, most successful, and fastest growing applications for microprocessors is their use as integral components of analytic instruments; as dedicated processors of the large quantities of data generated in medical and industrial laboratories by these instruments and, in some cases, as controllers for the instrument functions themselves. Various sources have estimated a market of well over $1 billion for these instruments in the next decade, a growth of about 250% from 1976 levels. Well over half of these instruments will be highly automated, incorporating microprocessors.

The type of instruments that are candidates for this upgrading include optical spectrometers, chromatographs, and mass spectrometers, together with many specialized instruments, some of which, like the Fourier infrared spectrometer, depend almost entirely on computers to extract useful data from signals.

However, the majority of instrument microprocessor tasks are relatively simple in nature, involving elementary calculations, comparisons with standards, zeroing, and signal conditioning. The huge advantage of microprocessor-aided instruments is that these procedures can be absolutely standardized and are then not subject to error or variation from operator to operator. Another advantage is the uniformity of reporting format, usually taking the form of an alphanumeric printout under control of the microprocessor. An outstanding example is the application to the ubiquitous gas chromatograph (GC), one of the most versatile instruments in the modern analytic laboratory; a complete case history of a microprocessor-controlled GC is given in the next chapter.

Even simpler instruments, such as optical and atomic[1] absorption spectrometers have incorporated microprocessors with useful results. This chapter shows how a relatively uncomplicated device, an infrared absorption spectrometer, such as the nondispersive infrared (NDIR) spectrometer widely applied in the chemical process industries and in air pollution control,[2] can be successfully married to a microprocessor. At the same time it serves as an introduction to the types of problems and solutions encountered in more complex instruments such as the GC. A brief description of the instrument principle follows.

Absorption Spectrometers

Radiation passed through semitransparent substances is characteristically absorbed selectively, the amount of energy transmitted being a function of the wavelength as well as the depth of the optical path through the sample and the concentration of the absorbing material (Beer's law). Figure 7.1 is a portion of the absorption spectrum in the infrared region of an organic compound, ethylamine. Infrared spectra are generally unique and characteristic of particular organic and inorganic compounds as a result of the interaction of the infrared radiation with the molecular structure, exciting vibration and bending modes of motion and accounting for the energy absorption.

Absorption spectrometers fall into two categories, dispersive and nondispersive.[3] The former type spreads out radiation from a source in space, using a prism or grating, and selects a narrow wavelength by passing the dispersed radiation through a slit (this assembly being termed a *monochromator*). The resulting beam is passed through a cell containing the sample, and the transmitted radiation is measured by a photoelectric detector. As the monochromator setting is swept through a range of wavelengths, the spectrum (as in Fig. 7.1) can be plotted on a recorder. In the nondispersive type, *all* the radiation, not just a small passband, is passed through the sample cell. The transmitted energy is detected, and then the same amount of source radiation is passed through a reference cell (usually containing a nonabsorbing gas such as nitrogen); the two signals are then compared.

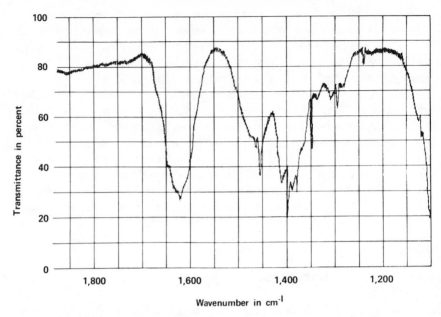

FIGURE 7.1.   Infrared absorption spectrum example—ethylamine.

Since the NDIR type utilizes all the energy from the source which covers a broad band of wavelengths, it consequently generates a larger signal and is more sensitive. It is therefore more suitable for gases and vapors, which generally absorb less energy than liquids in the infrared region.

Figure 7.2 pictures one of several conventional types of NDIR spectrometers. The source is a hot wire filament or Globar element; the radiation is alternately passed through the sample or reference cell by means of a motor-driven optical shutter (chopper). The detector is a pheumatic cell filled with a pure sample of the gas to be detected—the sample component of interest (COI)—and equipped with a diaphragm electrically connected as a condenser microphone. If the sample cell in fact contains some of the COI, the radiant energy falling on the detector will fluctuate in synchronism with the chopper rotation, since some of the energy is absorbed passing through the sample cell but not through the reference cell. This fluctuation is converted by the microphone to an electrical signal. Since the detector (filled with COI) responds only to the radiation absorbed by the COI, it is (relatively) sensitive only to that compound, ensuring *selec-*

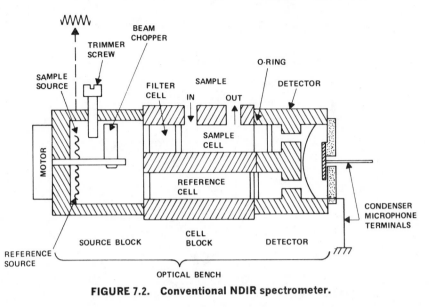

FIGURE 7.2. Conventional NDIR spectrometer.

tivity. The fluctuating signal varies in amplitude with the amount of COI present in the sample tube.

Although such a device is sensitive and selective, being capable of detecting many gases in the range of parts per million, it suffers from a number of shortcomings; the one that concerns us here is that only a single COI can be detected per instrument. In many industrial and technological situations, it is desired to monitor several components of the gas stream simultaneously and more or less continuously. To overcome these defects and expand the sensitivity of the NDIR instrument a variation of the concept is employed (Fig. 7.3). Instead of a pneumatic detector, a more sensitive and broad band solid state detector is used. The rotating chopper and gas-filled filter are combined; the *filter wheel* consists of pairs of these filters alternately interposed in the optical path of the infrared source, sample cell, and detector. One is filled with the COI and the other with nitrogen. When the COI filter is in the optical path, the amount of COI present in the sample cell affects the detector ouptut very little, because the radiant energy characteristic of that compound has already been largely absorbed by the concentrated COI in the filter cell, hence this filter is called the *reference cell.* When its place is taken by a nitrogen cell, called the *sensitive cell,* the amount of energy absorbed is proportional to the COI in the sample cell. Hence the detector output is in ac signal proportional to the COI

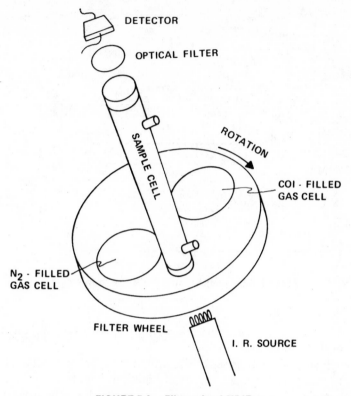

DETECTOR

OPTICAL FILTER

SAMPLE CELL

ROTATION

COl - FILLED
GAS CELL

N₂ - FILLED
GAS CELL

FILTER WHEEL

I. R. SOURCE

FIGURE 7.3.   Filter wheel NDIR.

in the sample cell and at the frequency of the filter wheel rotation or chopper. Since the selectivity of this instrument is obtained by means of the reference cell filter (plus optical filters to reduce interference) but without the highly specific detector in Fig. 7.2, the device can be multiplexed by employing several pairs of gas cells in the filter wheel.

The infrared gas analyzer[4] developed by Honeywell Inc. utilizes the above principle to achieve a multicomponent instrument design (Fig. 7.4). The illustrated version has three pairs of gas cells in the filter wheel (Fig. 7.4b), hence is capable of measuring individually three components in succession for each rotation of the wheel. The output of the detector preamp appears as in Fig. 7.4c, with one pulse appearing for each of the reference and sensitivity cells for components A, B, and C. For example, one commercial version measures and discriminates between CH_4 (methane), CO_2 and CO within 1%, even though the infrared spectra overlap and interfere to some extent (Fig. 7.5).

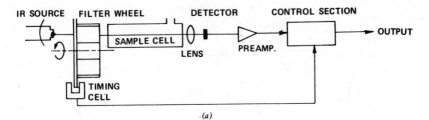

IR SOURCE   FILTER WHEEL   DETECTOR   CONTROL SECTION

SAMPLE CELL   LENS   PREAMP.   OUTPUT

TIMING
CELL

(a)

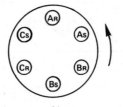

(b)

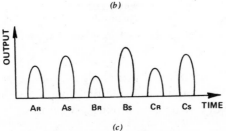

OUTPUT

A_R A_S B_R B_S C_R C_S TIME

(c)

FIGURE 7.4.   Multicomponent NDIR spectrometer. *(a)* Analyzer section and control section. *(b)* Filter wheel. *(c)* Detector output.

Instrument Equations and Signal Processing

The most precise spectrometers are those that incorporate a *double beam* feature; that is, one optical path from the source to the detector passes through the sample, and the other travels directly or via a neutral or nonabsorbing filter. The absorption of the sample is measured as a ratio of the direct and indirect paths. Thus any variations in strength of the source or of the detector sensitivity, together with the effects of film or dirt obscuring the main optical path, are canceled out by the ratioing process. In an NDIR spectrometer, a similar advantage is gained from the alternate presentation of the two filter cells used for each COI, hence it is desired to take the ratio of the signals obtained from each pair (Fig. 7.4c). The filter wheel NDIR spectrometer has been called a "double beam in time."

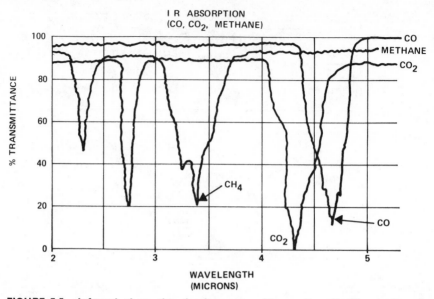

FIGURE 7.5.   Infrared absorption (carbon monoxide, carbon dioxide, methane).

If the detector delivers an electrical signal voltage proportional to the transmission or absorption of radiation along each optical path, it is desired to obtain an instrument output E_0 equal to

$$E_o = A \left(e_b - \frac{e_r}{e_s} \right) \tag{7.1}$$

where e_r and e_s are the reference and sensitive path voltages and e_b is a bias voltage added to the computed signal to give a zero reading when the concentration of COI is zero in the sample cell.[5] The division e_r/e_s in one version of the instrument is accomplished with analog circuitry using a voltage-controlled amplifier or automatic gain control (AGC), as in Fig. 7.6. The ganged switches represent gates synchronized by the chopper filter wheel, alternately energizing the sense and reference channels. When the sense (COI filter) channel is active, the AGC circuit acts through the feedback integrating amplifier to make the sense output E_s equal to the fixed bias voltage. Thus the gain of the AGC circuit is proportional to $1/e_s$. When the switches alternately gate through the reference signal, the AGC gain remains at $1/e_s$, owing to a long time constant, and

$$E_R = e_r \left(\frac{E_s}{e_s} + Z \right) \tag{7.2}$$

where Z is the zero adjustment for the reference channel.

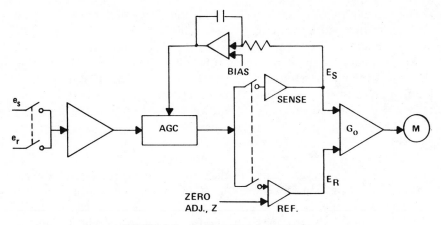

FIGURE 7.6.   Analog signal processing.

The complete expression for the output is obtained from the difference between E_R and E_S, since the differential amplifier G_o also has a long time constant compared with the pulse rates. Consequently,

$$E_0 = G_o \left[E_S - E_S \left(\frac{e_r}{e_s} \right) - Z \right]$$

$$= A \left(e_b - \frac{e_r}{e_s} \right) \tag{7.3}$$

which is of the same form as (7.1), A being equal to $G_0 E_s$ and

$$e_b = 1 - \frac{Z}{E_S} \tag{7.4}$$

Digital Data Processing

Although the analog circuitry developed for this device performs its task very well, there are several important advantages which may accrue from all-digital circuitry, specifically a microprocessor. First, the analog circuitry described, although time-shared between sense and reference channels, must be duplicated for every component; that is, a three-component analyzer requires three AGCs and associated amplifiers and gates. Second, a great deal of gating is required so that a certain portion of the circuitry is digital in any event. Third, time constants are long in order to "hold" voltages for subtraction and division—with time constants up to 12 sec a digital memory may save space and component dollars. Finally, an analyzer of this type is necessarily customized to the extent of being adjustable for different COIs, requiring changes in a few components.

With a microprocessor, programs substitute for custom hardware, and the large dynamic range possible often eliminates the need entirely. Also, the microprocessor allows signal processing techniques (such as filtering) to be added or altered with no new hardware, and digital processing generally adds to long term stability, particularly with respect to temperature changes.

For these reasons, let us consider what may be involved in applying a microprocessor to an instrument of this type. To make the problem more realistic, we assume a three-component instrument in which the filter wheel is driven by a pulse stepping motor, rather than continuously. Then the microprocessor has the additional task of synchronizing the filter positions and the signal processing task for the three COIs. As still another complication, let the analog signal from the detector preamp be integrated for a precise fixed period before digital conversion and further processing in order to increase the signal strength.

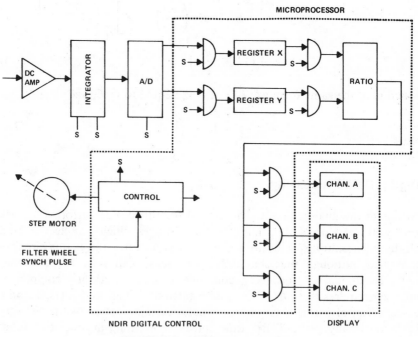

FIGURE 7.7.   NDIR digital control.

Initially, we neglect the problems of linearization, zero setting, span adjustment (system gain), and display, and consider that the end product of the signal processing task is the ratio of the reference and sense channel voltages, the variables in (7.3). A block diagram of the control-processing task (Fig. 7.7) shows the microprocessor tasks under consideration.

Generally, the time available for control and signal processing is more than adequate, considering typical microprocessor computing speeds. Table 7.1 indicates a typical time sequence for these operations, assuming each COI measurement is updated every 6 sec.

The next step is to generate a functional flow diagram for the operations, such as Fig. 7.8. In the hypothetical system it is necessary that the filter

TABLE 7.1.   Signal Processor Sequence Table

Milliseconds	Action Required
0	Reset sequencer (from filter wheel synch pulse)
0	Step filter wheel (motor)
200	Reset integrator and turn on
800	Integrator off. Store A/D output in register X
1000	Step filter wheel
1200	Reset integrator and turn on
1800	Integrator off. Store A/D output in register Y
1900	Compute register X/register Y ratio and gate result into channel A
2000	Step filter wheel
2200	Reset integrator and turn on
2800	Integrator off. Store A/D output in register X
3000	Step filter wheel
3200	Reset integrator and turn on
3800	Integrator off. Store A/D output in register Y
3900	Compute register X/register Y ratio and gate result into channel B
4000	Step filter wheel
4200	Reset integrator and turn on
4800	Integrator off. Store A/D output in register X
5000	Step filter wheel
5200	Reset integrator and turn on
5800	Integrator off. Store A/D output in register Y
5900	Compute register X/register Y ratio and gate result into channel C
6000–0	Reset sequence. Step filter wheel

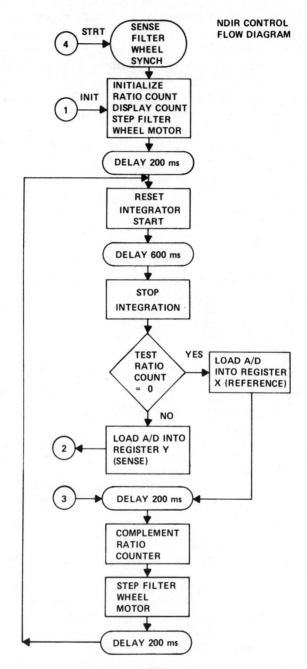

FIGURE 7.8. NDIR control flow chart.

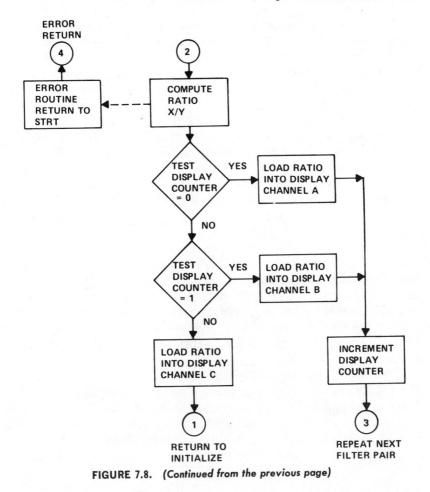

FIGURE 7.8. *(Continued from the previous page)*

wheel (containing three pairs of filters) generates by mechanical means a positive electrical signal (logic 1) when the no. 6 filter—the sense filter of the third COI pair—is in place. The presence of this 1 indicates that the previous measurement cycle of three components is complete and that the system is ready to begin a new sequence.

Having received this external signal, the program initiates the following actions. Two counters (registers), termed the *ratio counter* and the *display counter*, used for switching logic are set to zero, and a signal is sent to the stepping motor to rotate to the first filter, which is the reference filter of the first COI.

The program then delays for 200 msec while the first filter settles into place. At the end of this time, a signal is sent to the analog integrator to reset and begin integrating the preamplifier output. The integration continues until the program has measured a 600 msec delay, at which time the integrator stops. The A/D (Fig. 7.7) then holds the current output of the integrator in digital form.

The *ratio bit counter* is then tested. If it holds a 0, the A/D contents will be loaded into a register we shall call X. After a further 200 msec delay, the ratio counter bit is complemented—if it was 1 it becomes 0, and if 0 it becomes 1. The filter wheel is stepped (to the sense filter of the first COI), another 200 msec delay occurs, and the integrator is again zeroed and restarted. At the end of the integration, the ratio counter shows 1, so the A/D controls are loaded into register Y instead. The program then computes the ratio X/Y which is the e_r/e_s required for (7.3).

To anticipate, the division routine normally used by the microprocessor requires that the dividend be smaller than the divisor. In the physical configuration, the reference signal is always smaller than the sense signal, since the former results from the absorption of pure COI. Hence, if this inequality condition does not hold, there is an error, such as a failure of the filter wheel to step. If this condition is sensed, we enter an error routine which continues to step the wheel and test for the synchronizing position.

If there is no error, the value of the ratio is sent to the correct display channel, utilizing the display counter. If the display counter holds 0, the result of the ratio calculation is sent to channel A. The display counter is then incremented. If the counter holds a 1, the ratio is sent to channel B and the counter incremented again. If the counter holds more than 1, the ratio is loaded into channel C and the program is returned to the initializing step.

Microprocessor Selection

The choice of microprocessors was discussed in previous chapters. In this case, dynamic range and precision are important considerations, since signal changes of only a few thousandths of a percent can be measured. From this consideration, a 16 bit processor such as the CP 1600 is a good choice. A further advantage of this processor is the presence of eight program addressable registers (see Fig. 7.9) which permit the programmer a great deal of flexibility. Also shown in the figure are the four status flags for sign $(0 = +)$, zero, overflow and carry (S, Z, OV, C), which are controlled from the results of the ALU operations.

In the CP 1600 all operations to be performed are specified by 10 bit instruction words carried on the lower 10 bits of the 16 bit data bus. The structure of these codes is:

Op code	RS	RD
Four bits	Three bits	Three bits

where RS and RD represent three-bit codes specifying the *source* and *destination registers,* respectively. The four op code bits are decoded by the decoding and control (micro) ROM into 16 basic operations, 8 of which refer to external operations extending through the external data bus into the address space, to memory and peripherals (treated alike). The other eight are internal register-to-register instructions. The source and destination registers specified in the last two three-bit fields of the instruction refer to any of the eight addressable registers. Under certain conditions the last six bits are operation code modifiers instead of registers.

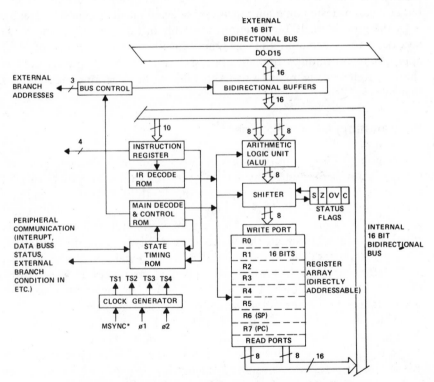

FIGURE 7.9.   CP 1600 basic microprocessor architecture.

All external addresses are reached by *register addressing*; that is, the register specified in the instruction contains a pointer to the location within the address space that actually holds or receives the data. Since the register holds 16 bits, up to 64K words can be reached directly, representing memory or I/O locations.

The 16 basic instructions and their op codes are shown in Table 7.2. The total number of useful instructions that can be generated from one or more of these basic instructions, is well over 100.

Software.   After selection of the processor (or as a parallel activity) the method of generating the software must be decided. The availability of software was discussed in Chapter 5 also, and some software information for specific processors was given in Table 45. The microprocessor selected has assembly type software available from the manufacturer, and CP 1600 cross-assembly software has also been developed by Honeywell for use with the H716 minicomputer.[6] Consequently, it is convenient to program this task in assembly language. As a further bonus, the assembler not only usually produces a listing with appropriate annotations and diagnostics,[7] but also can be tested on a microprocessor development system (Chapter 5).

Of the more than 100 instructions available in this language, only those necessary to understand this program, together with a listing of their appropriate mnemonics and meaning, is given in the Appendix to this chapter. Reference is made to the Appendix in the programming examples that follow.

Programming a Ratio Routine

Before going into the entire program, let us examine a segment that performs the key operation of division in order to obtain the required signal ratio e_r/e_s. Since the dividend is always smaller than the divisor, a simpler routine can be used which work only for this condition and will report an error if e_r is greater than e_s.[8] As a further simplification both signals must be positive, although this is not necessarily a software limitation.

In the example (Table 7.3) assume that $A = \frac{5}{16}$ and $B = \frac{1}{4}$ and we wish to find the quotient A/B which is equivalent to binary $0011 \div 0100$. Four bit accuracy is shown for this example, although any number of places can be taken. By means not shown, A is placed in register 2 (R2) and B in R5. R3 is reserved for the quotient Q, and R6 is used as a counter for the number of binary places to carry the division (four in this case).

The first step is to zero the register R3, which is accomplished by the instruction CLR R3 (see Appendix). The resulting condition of each register is shown in the first entry in Table 7.3.

TABLE 7.2.   Basic Instruction Set*

Mnemonic	Op Code	Meaning†
External reference		
MVOI	1001(RS,RD)	Move out. Send data from processor RD to location in RS in address space (memory or peripheral)
MVII	1010(RS,RD)	Move in. Bring data into processor RD from address in RS.
ADDI	1011(RS,RD)	Add contents of RS to RD; RS unchanged
SUBI	1100(RS,RD)	Subtract contents of RS (2's complement + 1) from RD; RS unchanged
CMPI	1101(RS,RD)	Compare. Examine value of RD minus contents of RS; RS and RD unchanged
ANDI	1110(RS,RD)	AND contents of RS to RD; RS unchanged
XORI	1111(RS,RD)	Exclusive OR contents of RS to RD; RS unchanged
B– – –	1000(– – – – –)	Branch on condition, using last six bits as modifiers
Internal reference (register-register)		
MVR	0010(RS,RD)	Move contents of RS to RD; RS unchanged
ADD	0011(RS,RD)	RS + RD → RD; RS unchanged
SUB	0100(RS,RD)	(−RS) + RD → RD; RS unchanged
CMP	0101(RS,RD)	(−RS) + RD; RS and RD unchanged
AND	0110(RS,RD)	RS and RD → RD; RS unchanged
XOR	0111(RS,RD)	RS ∀ RD → RD; RS unchanged‡
S– – –	0001(– –,RD)	Shift, using source register code bits as modifiers
Various	0000(– –,RD)	One operand instructions (including control instructions) using source register code bits as modifiers

* RS, source register; RD, destination register. (Note RS, for external reference instructions, is a pointer or address of location where data is to be fetched or moved.)
† Arrow means "insert into."
‡ ∀ means exclusive OR.

Next, we wish to ensure that A is less than B, or that $A − B$ is positive. This is accomplished by the second instruction CMP R5,R2, which temporarily subtracts R5 from R2 without changing either. In detail, this is a compound instruction. It requries 1's complementing B, adding 1 to make the negative or 2's complement, and adding the result $(−B)$ to A. If $A \geq B$, there is a carry bit, $C = 1$. If $A < B$, $C = 0$.

TABLE 7.3. Divide Routine Example

$$Q = \frac{A}{B} = \frac{\frac{3}{16}}{\frac{1}{4}} = \frac{0011_2}{0100_2} = 0.1100_2 = \frac{3}{4}$$

Quantity Register	A R2	B R5	Q R3	Carry C	Counter R6

Program	Comment	A R2	B R5	Q R3	Carry C	Counter R6
CLR R3	Clear quotient register	0011	0100 1011 +1 (1100)	0000		
CMP R5,R2	Test for $A < B$					
BOC ERR	Error if A not $< B$				0	
MVI # 4,R6	Initialize loop counter					4
CRC	Clear carry bit			0000	0	

192

			Remainder	Divisor	Quotient	
DV1	SRLC S1,R2	Shift dividend	0110			
	CMP R5,R2	Compare with divisor		(1100)		
	BNC DV2	Jump if C = 0				(1)
	SUB R5,R2	Subtract divisor if C = 1	$\dfrac{1100}{0010}$			1
DV2	SRLC S1,R3	Shift carry into R3			0001	
	DECR R6	Decrement loop counter				3
	BNZ DV1	Loop until counter is 0				
After three more iterations			0000	0100	1100	0
			(Remainder)	(Divisor)	(Quotient)	

193

The next instruction BOC ERR (or BOHE ERR) requires a jump to the symbolic location ERR (not shown in Table 7.3) if $C = 1$. This would put the system into an error routine.

If there is no branch, the program continues with MVI# 4,R6. This instruction moves the number 4, the number of places in the calculation, to the counter R6 where it will be used for control. (In actuality, these instructions do not all appear in the current version of the CP 1600 cross-assembler, as this coding was written for a prototype CPU. See Appendix note. Nevertheless, they serve to illustrate the method.)

The instruction CRC clears the carry, after which the dividend is rotated left with the carry bit (see Appendix), the equivalent of multiplication by 2. R2 − R5 is again examined with the CMP instruction and, if there is no carry (R5 is the larger), there is a jump to DV2 on the BNC command. Since there is a carry in this case, the next operation, subtracting R5 from R2, is possible and SUB R5,R2 takes place.

The next instruction shifts the carry bit into the LSB of R3 (the quotient) with SRLC S1,R3. R6 is then reduced by 1 (DECR R6), and if it is not yet zero, the program jumps back to DV1 on BNZ DV1. The reader can satisfy himself that three more iterations of this routine will put the correct value of the quotient 1100 into R3 and reduce the counter R6 to zero. Note that the binary point is assumed to be at the extreme left, so that 1100 translates to 0.1100 or $\frac{3}{4}$.

Main Program

Writing of the main program is facilitated by preparing a more detailed flowsheet from Fig. 7.8, specifying the microprocessor activities. In the CP 1600 or another microprocessor having multiple addressable registers it is advisable to include a listing of the registers in use at each step in the program. This could also be done on the coding form. External addresses can also be noted. Figure 7.10 shows the detailed flowsheet for this program. The main program is given in Table 7.4. Actually this program is written in an assembly language and so must conform to the rules of the computer that does the assembling (an H716 in this case). Also, instructions can be used that refer to the operation of the cross-assembling computer (the H716) rather than the microcomputer; these are in the form of *macros* (multiple instructions) and *pseudo-operations* (symbolic information).

The portion of the program starting with an asterisk in column 1 is descriptive comment and does not result in coding. The first three lines of coding merely define the assembly language and the memory location (relative). The symbols in the location field (columns 1 to 4) are labels

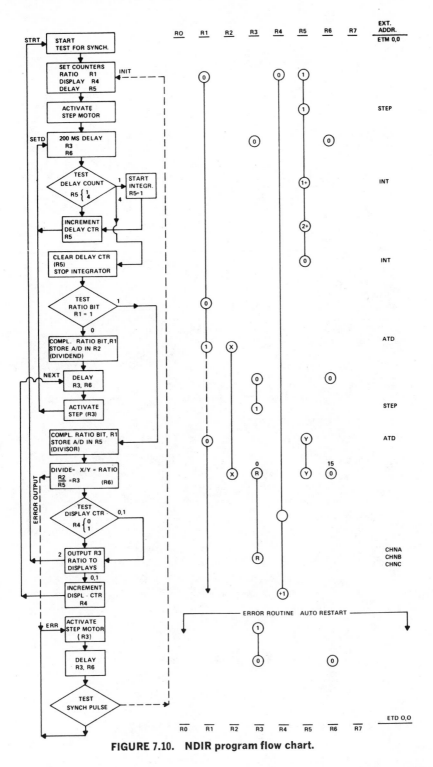

FIGURE 7.10. NDIR program flow chart.

TABLE 7.4. NDIR Control

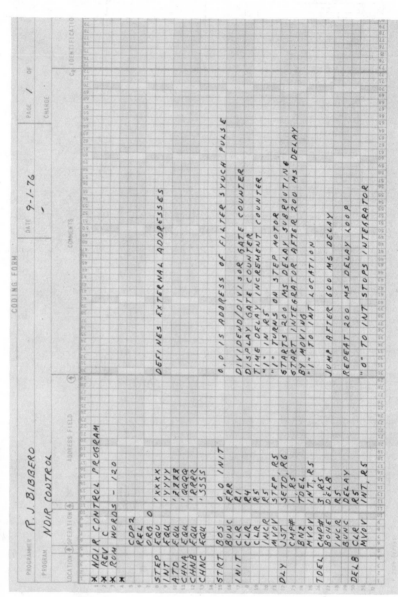

CODING FORM

PROGRAMMER R. J. BIBBERO PROGRAM NDIR CONTROL DATE 9-1-76 PAGE 1 OF CHARGE

LOCATION	OPERATION	ADDRESS FIELD	COMMENTS
*	*	NDIR CONTROL PROGRAM	
*	*	REV C	
*	*	ROM WORDS - 120	
*	*		
	CDPR		
	REL		
	ORG	0	
STEP	EQU	'XXXX	DEFINES EXTERNAL ADDRESSES
INT	EQU	'YYYY	
ATD	EQU	'ZZZZ	
CHNA	EQU	'QQQQ	
CHNB	EQU	'RRRR	
CHNC	EQU	'SSSS	
STRT	BOS	0,0 INIT	0,0 IS ADDRESS OF FILTER SYNCH PULSE
INIT	CLR	R1	DIVIDEND/DIVISOR GATE COUNTER
	CLR	R4	DISPLAY GATE COUNTER
	CLR	R5	TIME DELAY INCREMENT COUNTER
	INCR	R5	"1" IN R5
DLY	MVOV	STEP, R5	"1" TURNS ON STEP MOTOR
	JST	SETO, RG	STARTS 200 MS DELAY SUBROUTINE
	CMP#	1, R5	START INTEGRATOR AFTER 200 MS DELAY
	MVOV	TDEL	BY MOVING
	BNZ	INT, RS	"1" TO INT LOCATION
TDEL	CMP#	3, RS	
	BOHE	DELB	JUMP AFTER 600 MS DELAY
	INCR	R5	
	BUNC	DELAY	REPEAT 200 MS DELAY LOOP
DELB	CLR	R5	
	MVOV	INT, RS	"0" TO INT STOPS INTEGRATOR

TABLE 7.4. (Continued)

LOCATION	OPERATION	ADDRESS FIELD	COMMENTS
	SRLC	S1,R1	TEST LSB OF COUNTER
	BOC	LRG1	BRANCH IF "1" COUNTER
	SRLC	S1,R1	RESTORE GATE COUNTER
	COM	R1	COMPLEMENT COUNTER
NEXT	MVIV	ATD,R2	MOVE IN "REFERENCE" SIGNAL TO DIVIDEND
	JST	SETD,R6	JUMP TO 200 MS DELAY
	INCR	R3	
	MVOV	STEP,R3	ACTIVATE STEP MOTOR
	BUNC	DLY	REPEAT DELAY AND INTEGRATION CYCLE
LRG1	SRLC	S1,R1	RESTORE GATE COUNTER
	COM	R1	COMPLEMENT
	MVIV	ATD,R5	MOVE IN "SENSE" SIGNAL TO DIVISOR
	CLR	R3	START OF DIVIDE ROUTINE
	CMP	R5,R2	
	BOC	ERR	EXIT TO ERROR ROUTINE, DIVIDEND ≥ DIVISOR
DV1	MVI#	15,R6	SETS 15 BIT ACCURACY
	ADD	R3,R3	
	SRLC	S1,R2	
	CMP	DV2	
	BNC	DV2	
	SUB	R5,R2	
	SRLC	S1,R3	
DV2	DECR	R5	
	BNZ	DV1	END OF DIVISION ROUTINE
	CMP	R6,R4	TEST DISPLAY COUNTER FOR "0"
	BGT	ONE	
	MVOV	CHNA,R3	IF "0" MOVE QUOTIENT TO DISPLAY "A"
	BUNC	LAST	

TABLE 7.4. (Continued)

198

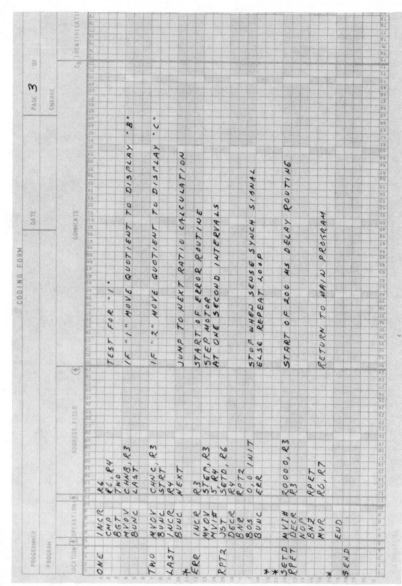

LOCATION	OPERATION	ADDRESS FIELD	COMMENTS
ONE	INCR	R6	
	CMP	R6,R4	TEST FOR "1"
	BGT	TWO	
	MVOV	CHNB,R3	IF "1" MOVE QUOTIENT TO DISPLAY "B"
	BUNC	LAST	
TWO	MVOV	CHNC,R3	IF "2" MOVE QUOTIENT TO DISPLAY "C"
	BUNC	STRT	
LAST	INCR	R4	
	BUNC	NEXT	JUMP TO NEXT RATIO CALCULATION
*			
ERR	INCR	R3	START OF ERROR ROUTINE
	MVOV	STEP,R3	STEP MOTOR
	MVI#	5,R4	AT ONE SECOND INTERVALS
RPTR	JST	SETD,R6	
	DECR	R4	
	BNZ	RPTR	
	BOS	0,0 INIT	STOP WHEN SENSE SYNCH SIGNAL
	BUNC	ERR	ELSE REPEAT LOOP
*			
SETD	MVI#	30000,R3	START OF 200 MS DELAY ROUTINE
RPET	DECR	R3	
	NOP		
	BNZ	RPET	
	MVR	R6,R7	RETURN TO MAIN PROGRAM
*			
$END	END		

which represent the symbolic address of the memory location. EQU is a H716 psuedo-operation which assigns a specific external location to the label, for example, STEP EQU '1437 assigns STEP to external word octal 1437. Thus, six lines define addresses in memory or external locations in the address space, for example, STEP is the address of the stepping motor drive flip-flops (external peripheral).

Similarly, the address for the start-stop driver of the analog integrator (INT), the analog-to-digital converter (ATD), and the digital display channel gates CHNA to CHNC, are defined.

With reference to the flowsheet, the STRT routine senses the presence of the signal signifying that the no. 6 filter is in place and the analyzer is ready to begin the first cycle. (The BOS (branch on sense) instruction refers to an addressable external multiplexer (MUX) in an experimental version of the microprocessor. This sense signal could be directly wired to the 0,0 address of the MUX. In the current CP 1600 the instruction BSNS could be used and the sense signal located with EQU as above.)

If the signal is not sensed, the program jumps to the ERR location with an unconditional branch (BUNC). This routine has the effect of rotating the filter wheels until the no. 6 position is found.

When the program branches to INIT, the register R1 is set to zero with the CLR instruction. R1 is selected as the counter to gate the ratio divisor and dividend signals into the correct registers when the divide routine is encountered. Similarly, R4 is chosen as the three-way display gate counter and is cleared. R5 is used to count increments of the time delay (200 msec) encountered in several places in the sequence in Table 7.1 and is also used for other tasks. In this case, it is incremented (INCR) to contain 1, and then the 1 is moved out to the location STEP to actuate the step motor. In this way, the no. 1 filter is put into position. (Recall that this is the reference filter of component A, containing 100% COI, therefore it will give the lowest signal and should be the dividend in the ratio calculation.)

The next coding is a JST (jump and store return) to the location SETD, which is the 200 msec delay subroutine. JST stores the address of the next instruction in sequence so that, when the subroutine has been completed, we can return to the normal sequence. The address is stored in R6, After subroutine SETD has been completed the contents of R6 will be transferred to R7, which is the program counter in this microprocessor (Fig. 7.8). The program will return to the address in the program counter.

The 200 msec delay (see subroutine at the end of the program) operates by moving a number (20,000) into R3, subtracting 1, and branching back to RPET until the number is reduced to zero (BNZ). The NOP (no operation) instruction adjusts the timing of the repeating cycle to approximately

10 μsec. At the end of the countdown, the program counter (R7) returns us to the main program, as explained.

At the end of this 200 msec delay the 1 that is still in R5 is moved out to the location INT, starting the external integrator.

The integrator is to be turned off after a delay of 600 msec or three increments of 200 msec. This is accomplished by comparing the contents of the time delay counter R5 with the number 3. If it is smaller, 1 is added to R5 and we branch back to DLY, which sends us to the subroutine for another 200 msec. When the 600 msec are up, we jump to location DEL 8, which clears R5 and stops the integrator by moving the 0 in R5 to INT.

The next step is to test the last bit of R1 we reserved as a ratio switch. By shifting the last bit (LSB) right, into the carry, we branch if it already contains a 1 to the place to store the sense signal. If the counter LSB is 0, however, R1 is complemented (COM) and the output of the ATD, recognized as the digitized integral of the reference signal, is placed in R2, the dividend location.

Next, we have a delay, an actuation of the step motor (MVOV STEP R3), and branch back to the delay and integration cycle (DLY). This time, the 1 in the LSB of R1 sends us to LRS 1 where we store the ATD output (identified as the sense signal) in R5.

We are then ready to enter the divide routine which was explained in Table 7.3. On completion of this segment, as we recall, R3 contains the quotient. The problem is to transfer the contents of R3 to the correct external address representing the display. R4 was chosen as the display counter and was cleared to zero at the start of the program. It is tested, and if it still contains 0; the quotient is moved out to the display for component A, CHNA. If it contains 1, then CHNB is chosen, and if more than 1, CHNC (see Fig. 7.9). This is easily accomplished by the coding following the division. At the end of the division, R6 contains a 0. If R4 also contains a 0, the CMP R6,R4 instruction bypasses the branch and moves R3 out to CHNA and returns the program to next filter wheel rotation and subsequent integration (after increasing the R4 counter by 1). Otherwise, it branches to ONE where R6 is increased to 1 and the comparison repeated, this time moving R3's contents to CHNB. If R4 contains more than 1 (the third time around), we place R3's contents in CHNC and return to STRT, to repeat the entire process with a move to filter no. 1.

Basically, this is the entire control and computation program, although a great many refinements are necessary to make it workable. One of these is the error routine mentioned earlier, which not only starts off the filter wheel in synchronism but returns it to the correct position if it somehow gets out of synch (detected by the division routine).

As an exercise, the reader can follow the nested loops of this subroutine, beginning with location ERR, and note how the filter wheel is stepped every second (five loops of 200 msec delay) until the no. 6 filter sense signal is found again.

Other Microprocessor Tasks

It is recognized that many other functions need to be implemented before a complete system is achieved, and that alternative means can be found to perform the above. For example, it is desirable to reduce drift by digitizing the signals at the earliest moment; consequently the integration or averaging step could be performed digitally and the ATD follow the preamplification. Filtering can be performed digitally by means of the first order lag described in earlier chapters. Another convenient device is the *spike filter*, which eliminates spurious short term noise peaks. This can be implemented by the algorithm

$$F_u = \frac{F_{u-1} + F_{u-1}}{2}$$

if $(F_u - F_{u-1}) > (F_{u-1} - F_{u-1})$.

Zero and gain adjustments are also required, in accordance with (7.1) and (7.3). This constitutes a problem in nearly every instrument application, as the adjustments should be easy to change and at the same time should not be volatile so that they are lost every time the power is switched off. This means that RAM cannot be used, and of course ROM is not possible since it cannot be altered once coded. Ths usual solution is to employ switches and diode matrixes to create the constants. If many 16 bit constants are needed, this solution may become expensive. Solutions to the problem can be found in RMM, CMOS, or newer memories such as the bubble type now coming into use.

Displays also generally require additional software. Usually an alphanumeric display operates in BCD rather than the microprocessor output. Routines for binary to BCD have been written for most microprocessors and may be available from the manufacturer. In the event that a printed output is desired, the microprocessor may also take control of this function, as described in the next chapter. When these duties are loaded on the microprocessor, it becomes necessary to find more elegant solutions to functions, such as timing, that occupy most of the processing time in this example.

References

1. L. P. Morgenthaler and T. J. Poulos, "A Microcomputer System for Control of an Atomic Absorption Spectrometer," *Am. Lab.*, **8** 37–45 (Aug. 1975). See also A. L. Robinson, *Science* **195** (4284) 1314–1318, 1367 (1977).

2. R. J. Bibbero and I. G. Young, *Systems Approach to Air Pollution Control*, Wiley-Interscience, New York, 1974, pp. 401–409.

3. S. Siggia, *Continuous Analysis of Chemical Process Systems*, John Wiley, New York, 1959 Chap. 6.

4. Specification Sheet No. SS-41-122, "Multicomponent Type Infrared Gas Analyzer M-300," Yamatake-Honeywell, Tokyo, Japan, 1976.

5. J. H. Garfunkel, A. M. J. Pearman, and E. R. Rang, "The Correlation Infrared Process Analyzer," Honeywell Research Center, Bloomington, Minn., Aug. 1975.

6. A. B. Sidline, "Operating System Software for a Microprocessor," *Digest of Papers*, *Fall COMPCON*, catalog no. 75CH0988-6C, IEEE, New York, 1975.

7. CDP3 Programmer's Reference Manual, System 700 Software, Honeywell Inc., 1975.

8. The writer is indebted to A. Kegg of the Process Control Division (Ft. Washington, Pa.), Honeywell Inc., who originated the program from which this adapted.

Appendix: Partial List of Instructions for CP 1600*

Some of the instructions given here have been taken from early versions of the CDP3-Honeywell software and are now obsolete. The manufacturer's latest literature should be checked for up-to-date instructions.

1. *Register—Register Instructions*

ADD	RS,RD	Add RS into R4. R3 unchanged.
SUB	RS,RD	Subtract RS from RD and put in RD. RS unchanged.
MVR	RS,RD	Move RS into RD. RS unchanged.
CMP	RS,RD	Examine RD minus RS to set status bits. RS and RD unchanged.

2. *Register—Address Space*

MVOV	SYM,RD	Move out RD to SYM (symbolic address). RD unchanged.
MVIV	SYM,RD	Move in value at SYM to RD.

*RS, Any source register (addressable); RD, any destination register (addressable); SYM, external location symbol; NMBR, a number (inserted by assembler); N1,N2, external test multiplexer address (nonstandard processor). Status bits (indicator flags): S, sign (+ is 0); Z, zero (1 if zero); OV, overflow; C, carry bit.

| MVI# | NMBR,RD | Move in NMBR (number) to RD. |
| CMP# | NMBR,RD | Compare RD with NMBR (RD minus NMBR) and set status bits. RD unchanged. |

3. *Shift—One Register*

| SRLC | SI,RD | Rotate left with carry. MSB shifted to carry and carry bit to LSB. |
| SRRC | SI,RD | Rotate right with carry. LSB shifted to carry, and carry to MSB. |

4. *Branch*

$\begin{Bmatrix} BNC \\ BOL \end{Bmatrix}$	SYM	Branch on no carry (branch on lower). Branch to SYM if no carry bit ($C = 0$) (unsigned).
BUNC	SYM	Branch unconditionally to SYM.
BNZ	SYM	Branch if not zero. Branch to SYM ($Z = 1$) if previous calculation did not result in zero.
BOC BOHE	SYM	Branch on carry (higher or equal). Branch to SYM if $C = 1$ (unsigned).
BGT	SYM	Branch on greater. Branch if previous comparison shows a greater number (signed).
BOS	N1,N2,SYM	Branch if logic 1 sensed (Nonstandard instruction).

5. *Jump*

| JST | SYM,RD | Jump and store return. Jump to SYM and store next instruction address in RD. |

6. *Special and One Register*

CLR	RD	Move zero into RD ($0 \rightarrow$ RD).
INCR	RD	$RD + 1 \rightarrow RZ$.
DECR	RD	$RD - 1 \rightarrow RD$.
NOP		No operation.
COM	RD	Complement (1's complement).
HLT		Halt processor after instruction is executed.
CRC		Set carry bit to zero.

Eight

Advanced Digital Instrumentation (GC Computing and Recording)*

S. T. Zawadowicz, President, Datalab, Inc.

Automated Processing of Chromatographic Data

To meet the expanding requirements of the materials and life sciences for effective chemical analysis, the use of various separation methods including GC has been growing rapidly. In the analytic laboratory field, chromatographic analysis has become the first choice of more than 20% of all analytic chemists (the largest single class of analytic methodology employed) and the subject of 2000 to 3000 technical papers published annually in recent years.[1,2]

Chromatography itself is an extremely sensitive and versatile method of analyzing complex chemical mixtures, which depends on the phenomenon of preferential absorption separating the constituent chemical species when the mixture is passed through an absorbing substance, for example, a column of silica grains. The separated molecules are detected as they emerge from the chromatography apparatus (nominally called an *analyzer*) by

---

* Material in this chapter describing developmental instrument concepts and software has been adapted from the American Society for Testing Materials (ASTM) Publication STP-578 (July 1975) with their permission and that of A. L. Kegg and Honeywell Inc.

an analog sensor (detector) which reacts to some differentiating property, such as heat transfer, giving rise to an electrical analog signal which can be graphically recorded and digitally processed. Each separate constituent gives rise to a peak on a graph—the relative position of the peak in time identifies the species by comparison to a calibration standard. The area under the peak is proportional to the relative or absolute amount of that constituent. Because of imperfect separation and detector limitations, peaks are often partly merged, forming shoulders or riders. In addition, baselines drift and tend to be noisy.

The chromatographer must detect the presence of peaks in the face of these disturbances and uncertainties, quantify them by integrating the area between the curve and a true baseline, and perform arithmetic calculations in conjunction with stored calibration data to identify the chemical species and determine their amount by calculation procedures called *methods*.

The data must then be reported in an acceptable format for the user. This cluster of functions, namely, data acquisition, integration, postrun calculations, and report generation, forms the quantizer portion of the analytic system (Fig. 8.1).[3]

Since gas-liquid chromatography's introduction in 1952, much has been accomplished toward the development of techniques and instrumentation for the basic chromatographic process itself, but it is in the second area, the quantitation of chromatographic peak data and the automatic production of analytical reports, that the most recent advances in precision and spectacular savings in human power have been demonstrated.

This chapter thus focuses on the description of systems designed to perform this quantitative task using a microprocessor as the key control mechanism for this advanced instrument.

A function that is not discussed, since it is too specialized to cover here, is that of digital control of the GC, shown as the dashed feedback line in Fig. 8.1. However, this function has been recognized and implemented by several manufacturers.

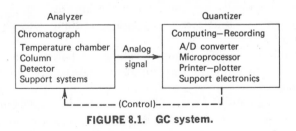

FIGURE 8.1. GC system.

A Brief History of Chromatography Data Reduction

Historical approaches are well documented in the literature. Early theoretical and experimental work established the relative accuracy obtained and effort required to manually quantitate strip chart recorder–generated chromatograms.[4,5] Manual integration techniques, including planimetry, triangulation, and "cutting and weighing" paper, require considerable skill, judgment and time consuming effort because of the number and complexity of peak shapes involved.

This early work also emphasized the fact that the limiting electromechanical characteristics of the recorder (principally bandwidth) and its inadequate graphical dynamic range were important obstacles to precision quantitative work. (Logarithmic graphical presentation, while bypassing the dynamic range problem, has not received widespread acceptance because its significant peak pattern distortion is disturbing to the chromatographer and introduces attendant difficulties in geometric area measurement.)

Ball and disk mechanical integrators (driven by the recorder servomechanism) reduce the manual effort by a factor of 2 to 3 and constitute a semimanual, low capital cost solution to the peak area measurement problem. This approach, while providing a permanent integration record alongside the chromatogram, suffers from the basic graphical limitations of the recorder medium.

Considerable developmental efforts were expended, during the 1960s, on transistor and IC hard logic–based digital integrators which could operate directly on the chromatograph's detector signal (independently of the recorder), and their capital cost was significantly reduced with the availability of ICs late in the decade.[6-8] This instrumental approach became widely accepted because of its inherent precision and wide dynamic range, unencumbered by the technical limitations of the recorder. The physical attachment of the digital integrator's strip printer output to its corresponding recorder-generated chromatogram also became an accepted part of the reporting format. However, since these separate documents required visual correlation and checking as part of an analysis, such a procedure was time-consuming and a constant potential source of operator error.

The digital integrator freed much valuable laboratory humanpower; but in most laboratory applications considerable area correction, postanalysis correlation, calculation, and final report preparation were still needed. Thus the raw area data had to be manually corrected to account for such factors as drifting baselines, fused peaks, detector response variations, and nonlinearity before such data could be used in postintegration calculations.

In summary, considerable time was consumed in these tasks after the sample had been completely chromatographed and processed by the digital integrator.

With dramatic reductions in price and improved capability, including the capacity for higher level languages, such as FORTRAN, it proved practical, in the late 1960s and early 1970s, to dedicate a general purpose minicomputer to the laboratory using multiple chromatographs.[9-12] This approach has achieved significant acceptance in large-sized laboratories, since the computational capability is under the direct control of laboratory personnel, a feature not available with the competitive approach of time-shared computer systems (programmed for a similar task and market).

The minicomputer, with a proper A/D interface, is of course capable of handling a wide range of integration and postrun calculation tasks on a multichannel basis, but it must generate a final analytic report on a teletypewriter, and this report is of necessity uncorrelated with the separate strip chart–generated chromatogram for the same analysis. Although such multichannel systems are more closely matched to the needs of larger laboratories, they still represent considerable capital investment and must be justified on a cost-per-channel basis, primarily.

More recently, special purpose computer systems have been developed which are optimized for GC analysis, in the sense of having a keyboard designed in chromatographic terms as an operator interface and dedicated GC programs stored in the ROM, so that the operator can set up parameters for a particular analysis by pushbutton entry. The Autolab systems of Spectra-Physics with these features have found rapid acceptance among users.[13,14] They provide processing of from one to four GC channels in parallel and use cost-effective, sophisticated digital integration techniques and extensivè postrun calculations (methods). These systems retain the strip printer technique of the digital integrator (and are called "computing integrators" by their maker), so that they are still open to the objection that they require physical attachment to the graphical recording. Also, the use of volatile memory in part requires the reloading of some methods files in the event of power failure.

A newer entry is the Hewlett-Packard "reporting gas chromatograph" (5380A) which combines a dedicated GC computing capability (provided by a microprocessor), a digital recorder on the same printout which replaces the separate analog trace, and a specially designed GC instrument controlled by the same microprocessor, closing the loop.[24] Another computer-controlled GC is the Perkin-Elmer Model 910. This manufacturer has also incorporated microprocessor control into nearly its entire line of line instruments, including infrared and atomic absorption spectrophotometers.[25]

In this chapter we do not discuss any of these instruments in detail, although some of the features considered may be common to several of them. Rather we focus on some of the more interesting concept and software features of the problem, using as an example an experimental device described by Zawadowicz and Kegg,[3] which can be termed a *computing recorder*. The object of this work was to prove the feasibility of providing a fully automatic, quantitated report, including the raw analog chromatogram, as a permanent, integrated record. This report should correlate all relevant numeric information with the corresponding analog trace, eliminate the opportunity for human error, and enhance the utility of the document for legal and scientific work by consolidating the data on one sheet.

System Requirements for the GC Computing Recorder

The evolutionary and comparative study of dedicated GC data processors implies a set of design or functional requirements which must be met by the instrument system if it is to be of maximum utility to the small single channel GC installation user. These requirements in turn imply certain design approaches which, in the present state of the art, are optimum or mandatory as stated in the list that follows.

1.   It is necessary to process the detector signal by the most accurate means; to accommodate low level signals and a large dynamic range $(1:10^6)$ while integrating the signal without loss; to perform sophisticated data acquisition operations, including digital filtering, in order to reduce detector noise without adding noise from the process; to accomplish complex decisions on-line (in real time), including the recognition of baselines, peak maxima, and rider and merged peaks; to separate and reallocate peak areas; and to maintain automatic control of parameters to compensate for peak width broadening during the chromatographic run (characteristic of many isothermal analyses).

Design implication: The detector signal must be directly digitized at the earliest moment, and a digital microprocessor of considerable power and capacity must be employed to "massage" the data into the desired form in real time.

2.   A chromatogram—an analog record—must be produced by the system in order to generate and preserve all the qualitative features familiar to the chromatographer, including noise, drift, skewness, and other background patterns, which assist him in adjusting the chromatographic conditions to the desired quality.

Design implication: To eliminate the possibility of losing subtle features such as very small peaks, shoulders, and noise variations, a good quality recorder mechanism should be operated independently of the analog detector signal rather than by reconstructing an analog trace from a digital signal that has already been filtered or otherwise processed and D/A'd.

3. The real time information extracted from the peak signals must be printed directly on the analog record adjacent to the peak to allow immediate peak identification and quantification, as well as a unified document.

Design implication: The recording paper and marking means must be adaptable to both alphanumeric printing and high quality analog recording; also, the digital processor must be capable of converting its signal to the appropriate code for alphanumeric printing.

4. The machine must rapidly produce on the same document a final analytic report for a limited number of peak components expressed in chemical units (amount or percent) generated by standardized computation methods commonly accepted by analytic chemists. Furthermore, the significant GC data processing parameters must be printed out as part of the permanent record.

Design implication: The digital processor must have an adequate repertoire of standardized calculation routines and sufficient memory to store both the methods and the temporary data needed for calibration and reporting of specific types of analysis runs.

5. The machine interface with the chromatographer must provide for straightforward control of the instrument and easy loading of necessary run and calibration data. The analysis method and routine for calculation and reporting must be simply selected by the operator and not require any program loading.

Design implication: Aside from the obvious need for human engineering at the interface, there is apparently a requirement for two kinds of memory in the data processor: a nonvolatile memory which will preserve the real time integration routines and the calculation methods after power shutdown, and a scratch pad type of memory for easily loaded individual run parameters, which may be volatile.

Implementation of the Computing Recorder.   The balance of this chapter reviews the overall design aspects of this microprocessor-based system and includes a description of the important chromatographic features and characteristics.

To recapitulate, the microprocessor approach was selected for three principal reasons. First, the cost-performance trade-off weighs heavily in favor of the microprocessor, compared with either hard-wired logic or a general purpose minicomputer. Second, the use of software type logic ensures relative ease of system modification and possible future expansion. Substantial changes in the instrument function can be effected by altering only the stored program in the computer memory. Third, the desirable fixed function, dedicated nature of a hard-wired system can be provided in a microprocessor system by storing the program in a fixed ROM (firmware). This permits the system to be operated like a typical laboratory instrument, having controls labeled in standard chromatographic terms, with no need for the user to learn to operate a computer or to learn programming in order to achieve successful results.

Furthermore, the ROM is nonvolatile, which satisfies the requirements for retention of the real time peak integration routines and calculation methods after power shutdown, without the need to reload the program.

It is evident that the microprocessor should perform as many operational functions in the system as possible. For example, timing for the alphanumeric printer, which would not be considered part of the computer function in a large scale system, is most efficiently controlled directly by the microprocessor. Also, the dedicated nature of the system permits the microprocessor to take on many supporting tasks to minimize operator-machine interface requirements.

The raw data flow diagram in Fig. 8.2 illustrates the nature of the extractive signal processing function on the incoming analog information (the processing support functions are not shown).

The system firmware is described in detail, in terms of its chromatographic processing implications, in subsequent sections of this chapter. Several detailed flow diagrams have also been included to indicate the relative ease of implementing highly sophisticated processing algorithms.

System Architecture and Peripherals.   The system becomes what might be viewed as a CPU at the hub of several dedicated peripherals such as an alphanumeric printer, a digitizer, status display lights, and a chart drive, all under its programmed control.

A conceptual block diagram is shown in Fig. 8.3. The processor reads the front panel switches to determine the values of operating parameters and acquires chromatographic signal data from the A/D converter. It must supply data to a status display, to a digital chart drive, and to a thermal printer. Through a separate isolated channel, the same chromatograph detector signal (analog) is used to drive a servo-system for graphic recording.

The function of the signal conditioning unit is to amplify the input signal by a gain of 10 in order to drive both the A/D converter and the recorder amplifier–servo. Source specifications derived from published studies[15]

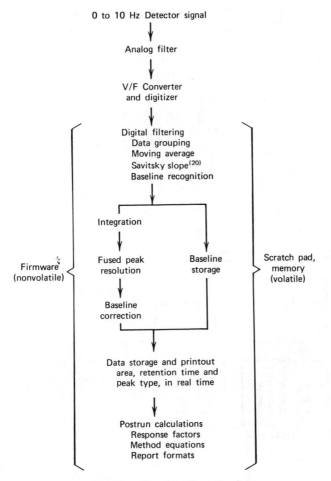

FIGURE 8.2. Raw data flow diagram.

of the characteristics of the chromatographic signal include such parameters as input noise of 2 to 100 μV peak-to-peak, signal bandwidth 0.005 to 5 Hz, and a linear dynamic range of 10^6. The signal conditioning output is required to be an amplified, precise reproduction of the input signal with appropriate rejection of common and normal mode noise. A notch filter tenuates power line noise by 60 dB. The accuracy of signal reproduction must be such that the specified A/D conversion accuracy is maintained. The input is differential with an operating range of -10 mV to 7 V. Signals more negative can be accommodated by biasing the input. The input

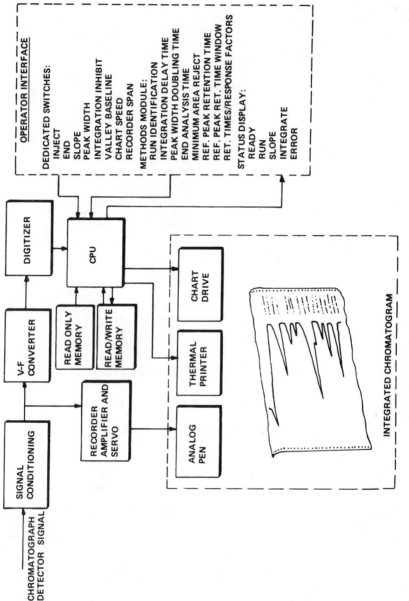

FIGURE 8.3. Computing recorder block diagram.

212

impedance is greater than 2 megohms. Noise introduced by the signal conditioning is specified at less than 3 μV peak-to-peak. The design bandwidth of the signal conditioning amplifier and input filter is 4 decades, and the upper frequency response is -3 dB at 5 Hz, accommodating the GC signal.

The requirements for the A/D conversion necessitate that the analog signal be digitized with an area resolution of 1 μV-sec and a linearity of $\pm 0.1\%$ of reading $\pm 0.005\%$ of converter full scale. This information must be stored and transmitted to the CPU on demand. Two common conversion types able to cover the wide dynamic range are the autoranging amplifier with a sampling converter and a wide range integrating converter. Since for noise considerations it is important to digitize the entire signal, a continuous sampling integrating type converter is preferred. One disadvantage of an autoranging scheme is loss of signal information during the time required for autoranging to occur. Also, a very high precision gain adjustment is needed to eliminate discontinuities in the output at the range crossover points, making that approach difficult to implement.

The A/D converter is conceived as two functional modules (Fig. 8.3), a voltage-to-frequency (V/F) converter and a digitizer to count the frequency pulses. The V/F converter takes the conditioned signal and produces a continuous pulse train having a frequency proportional to input voltage. The operating range is 1 Hz to 1 Mhz for an input of 10 μV to 10 V, yielding the desired dynamic range[16] of 10^6. The pulse train output of the V/F converter drives a synchronizer in which each V/F pulse is aligned with a 5 MHz clock pulse to ensure processor timing compatibility. The output of the synchronizer serves as the clock for a 17 bit binary counter. Parallel outputs from the binary counter connect to a storage latch. At the completion of a 100 msec interval (10 Hz sampling rate) the control circuitry strobes the counter data into the storage latch, where it is held until receipt of the appropriate function code from the microprocessor, whereupon these data are strobed onto the data bus. The control circuitry generates its signals in such a manner that they do not interfere with counting—no V/F pulses are lost.

Each sample represents the area under the signal in microvolt-seconds for that sample time. Because of the continuous data accumulation, all signal information is retained, representing a significant advantage in noise rejection over the processing performed by large computing systems in which, typically, the input signals are multiplexed and discretely sampled. The 10 Hz sampling rate was selected to optimize the system noise rejection. Since it is an integral submultiple of both 50 and 60 Hz power frequencies, excellent rejection of power line noise is achieved. Any aliasing effect due to sampling is eliminated by the 5 Hz filter in the signal conditioner;

however, the frequency response of most detectors makes the filter unnecessary.

Furthermore, the 10 Hz rate is adequate for the recovery of at least 99.99% of the area from a Gaussian peak 1 sec wide at half height points. For a theoretical Gaussian curve the literature indicates that a 2.4 Hz sampling rate is adequate. For real peaks, the rate required is between one and four or five times that, depending on the smoothing and filtering assumed, owing to noise and skewness. Thus, 10 Hz can account for all but the most extreme cases.

The operator interface should make the required manual data entry easy, while retaining flexibility for future system modification. Parameters that require more frequent manual entry can be entered through dedicated pushbutton switch banks, while less frequently adjusted parameters use thumbwheel swithches with function-select pushbuttons. All switch data come into the processor as data words whose interpretation is dependent on the program stored in the memory. Thus each switch function can be redefined by altering the stored program (firmware) rather than hardware. A simple status display, such as a row of five solid state lamps, conveys information about the instrument's operating state to the operator.

The analog recording amplifier and servopen mechanism should have an accuracy of 0.25% full scale and a full scale step response time of 0.5 sec. Recording means is an inkless trace on thermally activated chart paper with a heated stylus.

The printer produces 10 columns of alphanumeric data printed directly on the chart. It must be capable of printing while the chart is moving at its normal selected speed and in a line advance mode for rapid printout of of computed values following the analog run. For this reason, a digital stepping motor under control of the microprocessor is used to drive the chart. The print head consists of a linear dot array of 50 resistive elements bonded to a ceramic substrate. Selective energization causes the appropriate dots to heat, forming ten 5×5 dot characters on the thermally sensitive chart paper. The use of thermal techniques for both printing and analog recording provides an elegant and economical solution for both functions.

The digitally controlled forward motion of the paper combines with the selective activation of the 1×50 dot array to form alphanumeric characters (chosen from a set of 32 allowed by the five bit decoder). To prevent possible sticking, the chart is moved 1 step per character (10 steps per line), which imparts a slight skewness to the line. All this implies a degree of complexity in the printer and chart drive control. In an early design version, this control was implemented in discrete logic circuits requiring two printed circuit boards of logic. The processor sent a strip of character codes to the printer logic which then stored the information, decoded it, and caused the print head to operate with the proper timing. However, it was found that the microprocessor has a substantial amount of unused computing capability, a portion of which was allocated for printer and chart drive timing and for print character decoding. For example, when a character is to be printed, the microprocessor places on the data bus lines a bistate indication for up to 10 dots plus the column location data. These data are then stored in a latch, and a print pulse is initiated, causing the stored dot line to be printed. Dedicated circuitry is limited to providing one line of storage, print pulse timing, and power amplification.

In a similar manner, the digitally driven chart motor and associated interface circuitry is limited only to providing the capability to advance the motor one step upon receipt of the appropriate microprocessor command pulse. This circuitry is restricted to generation of the proper phase change and power amplification for single step motor advance. Complex speed control is left entirely to the microprocessor. In total, less than 300 words of memory are required for the print character decoding and for the printer and chart drive timing.

The microprocessor's basic parameters include 16 bit arithmetic, 5 μsec add time, an 8K address space minimum, multiregister architecture, and an *interrupt* or priority structure. General Instrument's CP 1600 meets these specifications, having seven general purpose 16 bit registers and 5 addressing modes. [17]

The address and data bus architecture permits the easy addition of peripherals, if desired, for system modification. Instruction words are 10 bits wide, while all data storage locations and working registers hold 16 bits. The result of minimizing the length of instruction words while retaining a 16 bit data manipulation capability is a reduction in memory requirements averaging 20% compared to a typical 16 bit minicomputer. This has been determined by comparing numerous programs written for both machines. The multiregister approach used improves coding efficiency and further reduces memory costs. With this approach, the programmer designing the firmware has a great deal of flexibility in data manipulation and avoids the bottleneck of single accumulator architecture.

As pointed out in earlier chapters, a most costly and time consuming task in the preparation of programs of any significant length for microprocessors is the hand coding of instructions in binary machine language. A higher level coding language (more oriented to the problem) improves the programmer's efficiency and speed. For this project, a *cross-assembler* program (see Chapter 5) was available. This program accepts high level instructions and automatically converts them to a tape containing the program in microprocessor machine code. The tape can then be used to store the machine code in the ROM.

The GC program is about 6000 words long. Variable data used in intermediate calculations, in data buffers, and for peak characterization are stored in 512 words of semiconductor RAM. This section of memory is sufficient for all temporary storage plus retention time, area, and peak type data for up to 98 peaks. (Retention time is the time, in seconds, for the chromatographic peak to appear at the detector, with respect to the sample injection time, t_0.)

At the option of the user, the memory can be used to store calibration data for specified peaks (expected retention time, window tolerance, and response factor) in methods files at the expense of real time peak storage. For example, the use of one or two files, each containing up to 20 calibrated peaks (previously identified peaks, with their associated retention times and response factors stored in memory), reduces the number of real time peaks to 66 or 34, respectively. Optionally, the addition of another 256 words of RAM permits various combinations of up to four files and 34 real time peaks or 162 real time peaks with no calibration files.

Program organization includes major routines and subroutines for reading and updating all the instrument's front panel controls. Examples include:

Status lights
End of run initiated
Peak width update
Chart drive
Peak width–slope switch
Integration inhibit

Other routines are dedicated to implementing various integration decision points. Examples include:

Baseline correction
Tangent
Peak valley
Baseline achieved
Auto slope
Moving average–slope
Horizontal baseline correction

Finally, subroutines for format instructions include such examples as:

Final printout
Printer

Real time print message
Area format
Basic parameter format
Error message print format
Peak number and area

Definitions of these representative subroutines are contained in a glossary at the end of this chapter.

A separate section of memory is dedicated for access to all routines and subroutines, via a thumbwheel data entry port, for all real time programming changes and all postrun calculation operations and printouts.

Real Time Data Processing

The important functions that must be performed in real time, that is, during the chromatographic run, are:

Smoothing of the analog detector and digitized signals
Detection of the baseline, time of peak onset, maximum peak height, retention time, and end of peak (baseline return)
Integration of area (microvolt-seconds) beneath the peak
Correction of area for baseline drift
Resolution of merged and rider peaks; separation and reallocation of areas
Printing of digital peak data (retention time, area, and so on) adjacent to the analog peak record, together with significant processing parameters and events as they occur

The peak data collected, stored, and printed as a result of these operations (peak area, retention time, identification number, and resolution type) can be combined with the data stored in the methods files, using the appropriate algorithms (analytic equations in this context) selected from the firmware by the methods files. These data are processed by the CPU and printed in the final analytic report desired by the chemist.

In this section we explain the operations performed in real time.

Signal Smoothing. A fundamental requirement for successful processing of a chromatographic signal by a computer-based system is the ability to filter noise from the input signal adequately, so that valid data are available to the computer. This function is handled by a combination of hardware and software techniques. Analog filtering over 5 Hz occurs prior to the A/D conversion to minimize noise at frequencies above the sampling rate[18] and to eliminate aliasing.[19] The choice of a 10 Hz sampling rate maximizes rejection of 50 to 60 Hz power line noise. The V/F signal is effectively integrated over the entire 100 msec sampling interval, which constitutes additional filtering of random noise. The remaining filtering is performed digitally by the microprocessor, using a cascaded combination of data grouping, moving averages, and least squares fit subroutines.

The integrated signal acquired from the digitizer is filtered further by a data grouping technique, but in this instance the degree of filtering is variable, adapted to the signal. Successive 10 Hz data samples are summed together to form a data group whose size is dependent on the peak width setting, which in turn is adjusted by the operator to the approximate width at half the height of the narrowest peak of interest in the chromatographic run. This causes the filter algorithm to produce 10 to 20 data groups across the half width of the peak (Fig. 8.4). The number of 10 Hz data samples in a data group is equal to the peak width number selected; that is, a setting of 8 sec creates data groups which are the summation of eight data samples. The filtering action is achieved by the averaging of this eight-sample group: The degree of filtering is then proportional to the number of data samples, that is, the peak width number. All further processing is performed using these averaged data groups.

The data grouping technique essentially optimizes noise filtering while minimizing the loss of smaller real peaks through overfiltering by adapting the degree of filtering to the width of the narrowest peaks of interest. The logic behind this scheme can be seen by comparing the requirements of narrow and broad noisy peaks (Fig. 8.5). The peaks are detected, and inte-

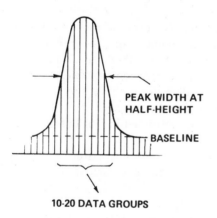

PEAK WIDTH AT
HALF-HEIGHT

BASELINE

10-20 DATA GROUPS

FIGURE 8.4.   Data grouping.

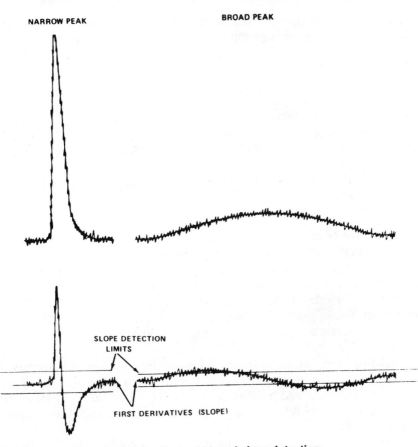

NARROW PEAK

BROAD PEAK

SLOPE DETECTION
LIMITS

FIRST DERIVATIVES (SLOPE)

FIGURE 8.5.   Peak width and slope detection.

gration is initiated on the basis that their slopes, or first derivatives, exceed a threshold value after filtering. Slope is computed after each data group is collected. In order to detect and integrate the smallest area peaks and recover the greatest amount of their area, it is clear from Fig. 8.5 that the narrow peak requires less sensitive slope detection than the broad peak. Furthermore, the broad peak requires the greatest amount of filtering. The narrow peak requires less filtering but a faster response—too much filtering could cause a narrow peak to be missed altogether. (In general, greater peak width settings mean more filtering—more 100 msec data samples per group.) It also corresponds to a slower response to slope measurement, because each data group takes longer to assemble. However, the slope sensitivity is greater, because there is more time between each data group for the slope voltage difference to build up; thus we achieve the following results:

	Narrow Peak	Broad Peak
Peak width setting (PW)	Small	Large
Degree of filtering (varies with PW)	Small	Large
Response item (varies with PW)	Fast	Slow
Slope sensitivity (varies with PW)	Least	Most
Ability to detect small peaks (varies with $1/PW$)	High	Low

These are the effects desired.

Although the PW must be initially set by the chromatographer (usually on the basis of observing the peaks of a preliminary chromatogram), the system can be made adaptive to the normal chromatographic characteristic of peak broadening during an isothermal run by inserting a time-based parameter (peak width doubling time) into the processor. This automatically updates the peak width setting, doubling it for each incremental period.

In this manner, consistent logical decisions during integration are based on a normalized peak width, since the peak width value directly affects both peak detection and baseline tests, and this value can be updated to maintain its relative relationship to broadening isothermal peaks during the run.

Since the derivative of a signal (its slope) is even noisier than the detector signal itself, the data are further filtered through a five-point moving average. This is computed for each data group by taking the average of the current and preceding four data groups. The slope is then calculated based on a quadratic least squares curve fit to the five most recent moving average data points, using the method developed by Savitsky and Golay.[20] Although this technique is quite generally useful and sophisticated (the reader seeking detail should refer to the original publication), its implementation in microprocessor firmware is straightforward. (Compare with the four point central difference technique of smoothing derivatives, Chapter 6.)

The flowchart in Fig. 8.6 shows the basic steps involved in taking the data grouping values and passing them through the moving average routine and on to the weighted slope calculation using the Savitsky-Golay algorithm.

Slope Setting. Other than peak width, the factor determining slope sensitivity (which we define as the slope value in microvolts per second establish-

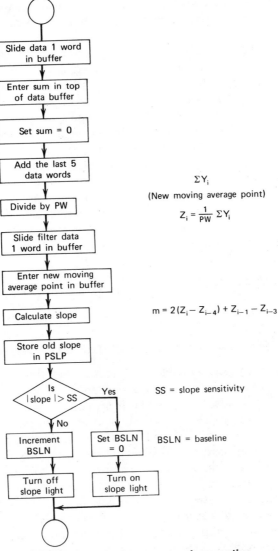

FIGURE 8.6. Moving average–slope routine.

ing the threshold between a peak and normal baseline) is the slope setting (in microvolts). The numerical value of this parameter is

$$\text{Slope sensitivity } (\mu\text{V/sec}) = \frac{\text{slope setting } (\mu\text{V})}{\text{peak width (sec)}}$$

Note that this number is actually the inverse of effective sensitivity—the smaller its value, the smaller the slope needed to initiate integration.

The peak width–slope setting flow diagram illustrates the sequence of updating these values and applying them to the moving average–slope routine (Fig. 8.7).

Slope setting can be manually entered before a run by using dedicated pushbuttons on the front panel. Values ranging from 2 to 254 μV can be selected. The normal procedure, following selection of the peak width parameter, is to enter successive trial values of slope setting until the "slope" light triggers on. This indicates a slope setting less than noise or zero signal drift of the detector. The setting, at this point, should be increased somewhat from this value, to avoid false triggering of integration. An automatic slope setting mode is also provided, actuated by the "auto" button on the panel. When this is depressed, the "ready" light on the top panel will remain off for 25.6 sec while the detector noise is being sampled at zero signal, and the slope (actually due to noise) is calculated after each data group. The slope setting will then be automatically calculated by the microprocessor, using the formula

$$\text{Slope setting} = K_1 \sqrt{\frac{\sum (\text{slope})^2}{n - 1}} \left(1 + \frac{K_2}{\sqrt{2N}}\right)$$

where K_1 = 3.0 to 4.5
   K_2 = 1.96
   K_3 = 256/PW setting = number of slope samples taken

This expression ensures with 95% confidence that the zero signal plus white noise will be between 3 and 4.5 standard deviations from the slope setting. In other words, there will be less than $\frac{1}{4}$% probability that the slope circuits will be triggered after any data group by white noise alone. Since, using the minimum peak width test (see next section), several consecutive data groups must exceed slope threshold for integration to begin. this is practically certain assurance against false peaks being recorded.

The basic flow diagram implementing this approach is shown in Fig. 8.8. The "ready" light is restored after the automatic slope subroutine has completed its cycle. If a run is not started, another 25.6 sec calculation will occur and be averaged with the first. The value selected (limit to from 2 to 256) is printed at the start of the run. At the end of the run, after the report is printed, the automatic slope setting is calculated anew.

Integration.   Peak detection, as explained earlier, is based on the magnitude of the signal slope. When the slope exceeds the front panel slope setting (in microvolts per second), integration begins. However, using a minimum peak width test, if a zero or negative slope is reached before five data

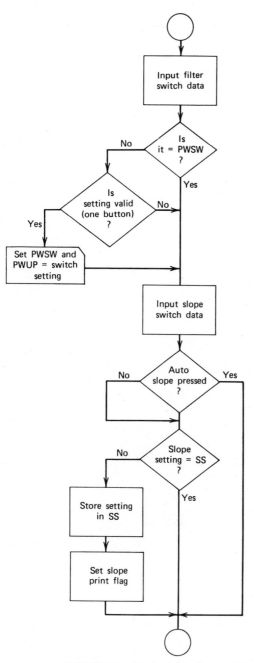

Input filter
switch data

Is
it = PWSW
?

No

Is
setting valid
(one button)
?

Yes

No

Set PWSW and
PWUP = switch
setting

Yes

Input slope
switch data

Auto
slope pressed
?

No

Yes

Slope
setting = SS
?

No

Yes

Store setting
in SS

Set slope
print flag

PW = current peak
width value

PWSW = last valid peak
width switch
setting

PWUP = Value to update
peak width when
possible

SS = slope sensitivity

FIGURE 8.7. Peak width–slope setting flow diagram.

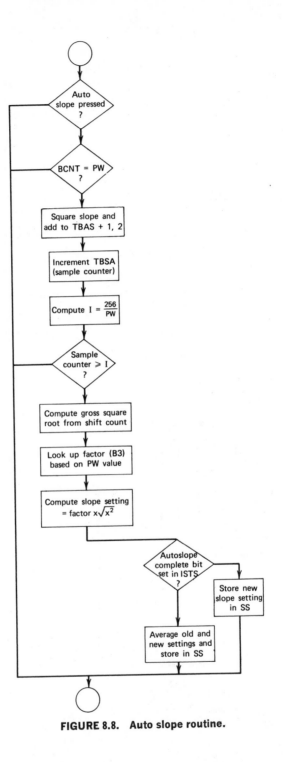

FIGURE 8.8. Auto slope routine.

groups or $PW/2$ sec have elapsed, the integration is assumed to have been triggered by noise, and integration is terminated. (It is possible to disable this test, as discussed in the section on real-time parameter control.) In this manner, noise spikes and baseline upsets are rejected. The value of $PW/2$ permits integration of all peaks whose width at half height is greater than one half of the peak width setting.

By using the memory capability of the digital processor, peak area data occurring prior to the time at which integration was initiated can be included in the area data. Four such prior data groups are added back when integration begins. This ability to recover area (commonly referred to as *area scooping*) provides a more complete integration than is possible with a conventional digital integrator. Figure 8.9 illustrates this process in somewhat exaggerated form.

Retention Time. At the crest of the peak, the slope calculation algorithm reaches zero value; the time of this event (the retention time) is stored, a sequential peak number is assigned, and both the peak number and retention time are printed on the chart next to the peak.

Baseline Tests and Area Correction. The baseline is reestablished under either of two conditions. First, if five consecutive slope calculations produce values less than the slope setting, a new baseline is established. Second, if negative baseline drift occurs, the signal level drops below the amplitude at which integration was initiated, and the tangent point is sought to terminate integration, as shown in Fig. 8.10. In either case, baseline correction occurs after a new baseline has been established. This correction is made linearly from the baseline prior to which integration was initiated to the current baseline. This nonhorizontal correction occurs for both positive and negative drifting baselines and is termed a *trapezoidal correction*.

If more than four peaks occur before the baseline is established, only the last four are treated with the trapezoidal baseline correction. All prior peaks in the group are corrected horizontally from the baseline amplitude at which integration for the entire group was initiated (see Fig. 8.11).

1–PEAK DETECTED
2–ESTABLISHED BASELINE   FIGURE 8.9. Area scooping.

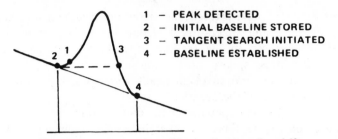

1 — PEAK DETECTED
2 — INITIAL BASELINE STORED
3 — TANGENT SEARCH INITIATED
4 — BASELINE ESTABLISHED

FIGURE 8.10.   Correction with negative baseline drift.

Resolution of Fused Peaks.   Fused peaks are resolved by one of two techniques: perpendicular drop and tangent resolution. In the perpendicular drop method, the areas of the overlapping peaks are divided by establishing a vertical line through the point of zero slope at the valley between the peaks, as shown in Fig. 8.12. The location of the point of zero slope is calculated by interpolating between the two slope values immediately preceding and following the transition through zero slope, as shown in the inset in Fig. 8.12. Thus the area resolution at the valley is not limited to the area of one data group but is calculated to within 1 μV-sec, just as if the peaks were fully resolved. This algorithm provides area repeatability for fused peaks superior to that obtained with the more conventional technique of partitioning to the nearest data group.

In the tangent method, the areas of the overlapping peaks are divided by a line computed from the valley point between the peaks to the point

1. CORRECTED PEAK AREA
2. TAPEZIODAL BASELINE CORRECTION AREA
3. HORIZONTAL BASELINE CORRECTION AREA

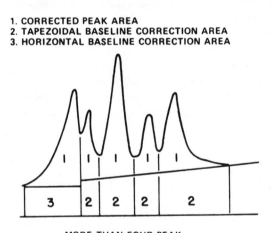

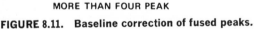

MORE THAN FOUR PEAK

FIGURE 8.11.   Baseline correction of fused peaks.

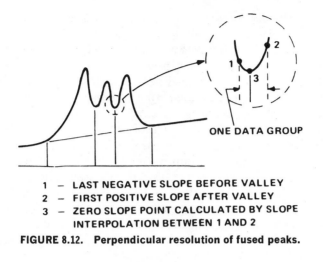

ONE DATA GROUP

1 — LAST NEGATIVE SLOPE BEFORE VALLEY
2 — FIRST POSITIVE SLOPE AFTER VALLEY
3 — ZERO SLOPE POINT CALCULATED BY SLOPE
      INTERPOLATION BETWEEN 1 AND 2

FIGURE 8.12. Perpendicular resolution of fused peaks.

of tangency, that is, the point where the signal slope (dy/dt) is equal to the slope of the line drawn from the valley point to the current signal point ($\Delta y/\Delta t$), as shown in Fig. 8.13. This is useful for skimming rider peaks from the tails of large skewed peaks, such as a solvent peak.

The criterion for determining whether perpendicular or tangent resolution should be used in a given situation was established on the basis of a study of overlapping Gaussian peaks.[21] It was found that perpendicular resolution yields a more accurate area allocation when the overlapping peaks have relatively equal widths, whereas tangent resolution is more accurate when the widths of the peaks differ greatly. The ideal criterion for choosing the type of resolution would place the decision point so as to minimize the area allocation error. While the width ratio of the two peaks

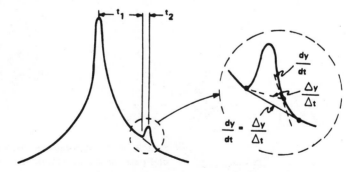

FIGURE 8.13. Tangent resolution of rider peaks.

at the error crossover point varies somewhat, dependent on the peak amplitude ratio and separation, a good width ratio value for minimum error was found to be about 8. This rule was implemented by comparing the time interval from the crest of the first peak to the valley point with the time interval from the valley point to the crest of the second peak (the ratio t_1/t_2 in Fig. 8.13), which is an approximate measure of the width ratio of the two peaks. Whenever the ratio exceeds 8, tangent resolution is used. Otherwise, perpendicular resolution is used to allocate the peak areas.

Combinations of tangent and perpendicular resolution are possible. In Fig. 8.14, for example, a group of fused peaks is riding on the tail of a solvent peak, The first of the fused peaks meets the tangent test just described (a width ratio greater than 8), hence the entire group of peaks is skimmed from the tail with tangent resolution. Skimming is performed from the valley point preceding the first rider peak to the tangent point on the tail following the last rider peak. Within the group of peaks, perpendicular resolution is applied.

One further mode of area correction is available, and useful when it is desired to skim multiple peaks from a large broad peak of no interest. This is termed *valley baseline correction* (Fig. 8.15) and forces the baseline to touch all valley points between each peak. This mode can be initiated by means of a latching switch or by a timed program.

Real Time Processing Parameter Control

Most of the parameters described above in the integration and real time processing of peaks are under complete control of the chromatographer and can be altered at any time. New parameter data are entered into the microprocessor RAM by any convenient means, in this design by the use of decimal thumbwheel switches, up to a maximum of eight, and four marked pushbuttons.

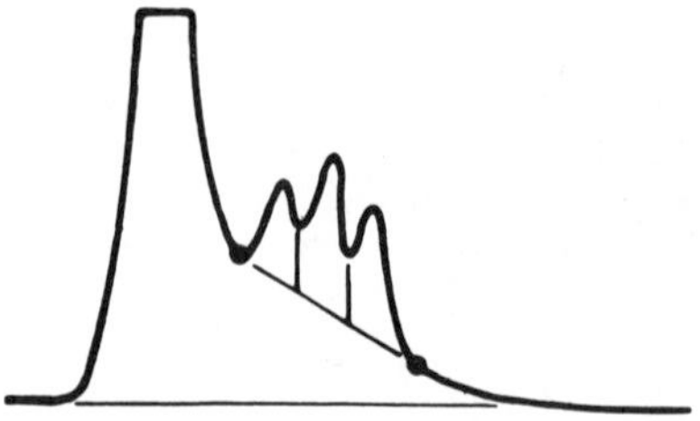

FIGURE 8.14. Combination of tangent and perpendicular resolution.

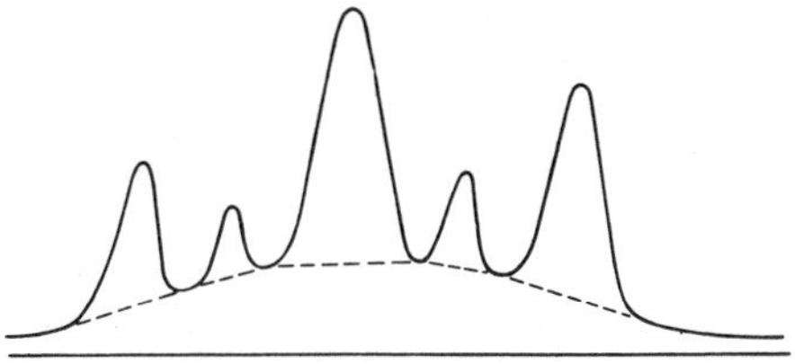

FIGURE 8.15.   Valley baseline correction.

The first five thumbwheels contain the numerical value of the data to be entered—the leftmost four represent the four significant digits, and the fifth is a negative exponent of 10 (i.e., it shifts the decimal point to the left). The sixth wheel in line is set to a *file number* (a file contains calculation parameters which are explained later), and the last two represent a two-digit *index number* which uniquely identifies the function or parameter to be changed.

The four pushbuttons are "enter," "list," "erase," and "calibrate." "List" merely requests the processor to print out the parameters or other data already stored in the memory. "Erase," in a similar manner, erases the stored data. "Calibrate" is used in postrun analysis calculations in which the methods module is also employed—its use is explained later. The first button on the right, "enter," is used for real time parameters.

The real time processing parameters that can be controlled by the operator and their index number are shown in Table 8.1.

Let us assume, for example, that it is desired to delay the start of integration until some time after injection of the sample, say 20 sec, in order to eliminate an air peak from the calculations. The integration delay parameter can accomplish this. To enter 20 sec, the first four thumbwheels are set to 20, the next (decimal shifter) is left at 0 (e.g., $\times 10^0 = \times 1$), the sixth wheel, the file number, is set at 1 or 2 (see discussion of postrun calculation methods), and the index number for integration delay, 12, is set into the remaining two switches. The result is:

$$0020 \quad -01 \qquad 12$$
20 sec   File 1   Integration delay

The "enter" button is then pushed. The 20 sec delay is entered into the microprocessor's scratch pad memory and a message is printed out:

$$I\ DL = 20$$

As shown in Table 8.1, a similar kind of message is printed for each parameter change.

TABLE 8.1.   Real Time and Postrun Parameter Control

Index	Function Accessed	Printout Format
10	Run identification	ID NO = XXXX
11	Method/format selection	MD-FMTXXXX
12	Integration delay	I DL = XXXX
13	End analysis time	END = XXXX
14	Minimum area reject	MN AR = XXXX
15	Peak width doubling	PW DB = XXXX
16	Peak width update time 1	PW TI = XXXX
17	Peak width value 1	PW 1 = XXXX
18	Peak width update 2	PW T2 = XXXX
19	Peak width value 2	PW 2 = XXXX
20	Valley baseline on	VB ON = XXXX
21	Valley baseline off	VBOFF = XXXX
22	Baseline test	BSLN = XXXX
23	Tangent test	TAN = XXXX
24	Minimum peak width test	MN PW = XXXX
30	Peak deletion	No printout
40	Reference peak retention time	R RT XXXX
41	Reference peak response factor	R RFXXXXE-X
42	Reference peak amount	RAMTXXXXE-X
43	Reference peak ret. time window	R WND XXXX
44	Component peak ret. time window	RT WNDXXXX
45	Sample amount	SAMTXXXXE-X
46	Scale factor	SF XXXXE-X
47	Component peak ret. time/calib. amount/response factor*	RT = XXXX CAMTXXXXE-X RE XXXXE-X

* The first value entered is the retention time; and the second value is the calibration amount ("calibrate" button) or response factor ("calibrate" button released).

Real Time Parameters.   The following is a brief description of the real time parameter functions directly modifiable by the chromatographer for a particular analysis.

> *End analysis time.* Automatically terminates the chromatogram at any time after injection of the sample up to 9999 sec. A final report printout is automatically initiated. This function is for unattended operation.
> *Minimum area reject.* Eliminates from calculations any peak having an area less than the number entered (in microvolt-seconds). In com-

bination with the minimum peak width test, this can be set to reject
spike noise or unwanted trace peaks.

Run identification number. This merely prints an identifying run number
on the report following the run. This parameter allows the number
to be reset to any value. It is automatically incremented by 1 each
time a run is made.

The following parameter-timed programs, together with the automatic
end analysis function, are particularly useful when the chromatograph
must be left unattended for long analyses.

Peak width doubling. This parameter has been discussed in the section
on signal smoothing. At the conclusion of each increment of the time
period entered by the chromatographer, the value of *PW* is doubled
and the filtering and slope sensitivity updated accordingly. For long
isothermal runs, this enables the integration parameters to keep pace
with the inherent broadening of peaks. The value of *PW* can be
changed only at the baseline, to prevent interference with the integration of a peak.

Peak width time program. PW, and its dependent filter and slope sensitivity parameters, can also be time-programmed to new values using
the indexes for the two update times (index no. 16 and no. 18) and
peak width values (index no. 17 and no. 19). An example of the use
of this capability is shown in Fig. 8.16. A broad peak nested within
a section of narrow peaks can be integrated with the updated value
of *PW* programmed to occur between t_1 and t_2. Both doubling and
update programs can be in effect simultaneously, subject to the
baseline limitation.

Valley baseline. When this timed program is effective, the valley points
between fused peaks are considered the baseline, just as if the "manual"
button for this function were depressed.

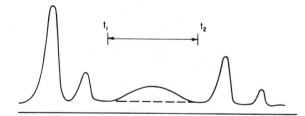

FIGURE 8.16.   Peak width parameter update.

The following functions enable the user to alter the basic decision parameters determining peak integration and resolution:

Baseline test. The normal value of 5 causes the baseline to be established when five consecutive data groups have slopes less than the slope sensitivity (SS/PW). Altering this parameter changes the number of test groups to a greater or lesser value, affecting the area recovery of trailing peaks, for example (Fig. 8.17).

Tangent test. Although the normal value of this parameter (causing tangent resolution to be selected when the skewed peak is more than eight times wider than a rider peak on its tail) has been selected as providing optimum area reallocations over an average range of peak types, special chromatographic conditions could make it desirable to change this criterion. A desired number of 0 can be entered in lieu of 8.

Minimum peak width test. As in the baseline test, the normal value of this parameter, 5, represents the minimum number of positive slope data groups that must be consecutively detected before a peak is accepted as valid. This number can be changed to 0, which will effectively disable the test (no rejection).

Whenever a parameter is changed, the new value is printed out in the format shown in Table 8.1. In addition, the values of all or selected parameters can be listed (printed out) by dialing the appropriate index and file numbers and using the "list" button. Data can be erased from the computer memory in the same manner, by using the "erase" button. For example, unwanted noise or impurity peaks can be deleted this way by entering

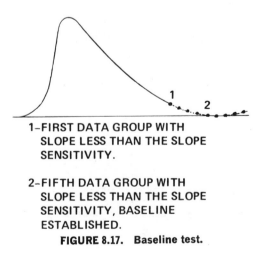

1–FIRST DATA GROUP WITH
SLOPE LESS THAN THE SLOPE
SENSITIVITY.

2–FIFTH DATA GROUP WITH
SLOPE LESS THAN THE SLOPE
SENSITIVITY, BASELINE
ESTABLISHED.

FIGURE 8.17. Baseline test.

the peak number and erasing—this eliminates that peak and area from any further calculations.

Real Time Reporting. During a run, the integrated chromatogram is printed out in real time, reporting the values of peak number, type symbol, area, and retention time for each peak detected adjacent to the analog record of that peak, together with other significant events associated with the integration as they occur.

The basic parameters defined as run identification number, slope setting, peak width setting, and chart speed are reported out with every analysis. The flow diagram for formatting this information is representative of subroutines designed for this task (Fig. 8.18).

Fig. 8.19 is an example of a real time report for a basic analysis. At the bottom of the chart, the first event, sample injection, is indicated by a "blip" or simulated event marker at zero time. Since the chart drive is now under control of the processor, it begins to move at this time and an internal real time clock is started. During the time it normally takes for the solvent (first) peak to pass through the chromatograph column, the preselected slope and peak width settings are printed. (If a file is used, the file number and mode will be printed here, as explained in a later section.)

When a peak crest is detected, a consecutive peak identification number and the retention time in seconds (up to four digits) are printed out next to it, in the margin. The first peak in Fig. 8.19 is number 1 and it crested at 37 sec, hence the printout is

$$1 \text{ RT} = 37$$

These data are printed as close to the peak maxima as possible, and so have priority over other real time reporting.

When the peak is terminated and the baseline corrected (which could occur at some distance along the chart because of intervening merged peaks, for example), the raw area is calculated and printed out, along with a symbol which indicates how the peak was resolved. (If integration was inhibited during this time, no area printout will occur.) In Fig. 8.19, the area of peak 1 is 12,6040 μV-sec. The symbol S signifies a skewed peak with a rider (peak 2) skimmed from it. Other symbols are:

(None)	Fully resolved peak, trapezoidal baseline
P	Fused, perpendicular resolution
T	Fused, tangential resolution
H	Fused, horizontal baseline correction
V	Valley baseline correction

Peaks 3 and 4, for example, are separated with a perpendicular drop (P).

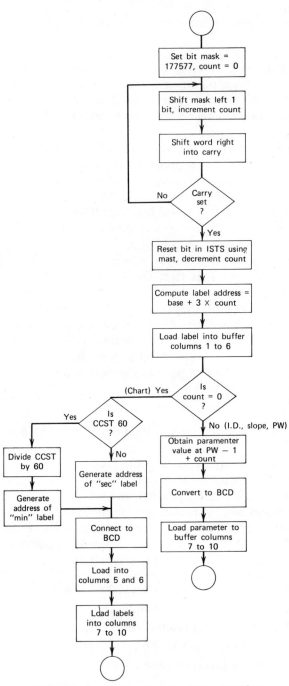

FIGURE 8.18. Basic parameter format routine.

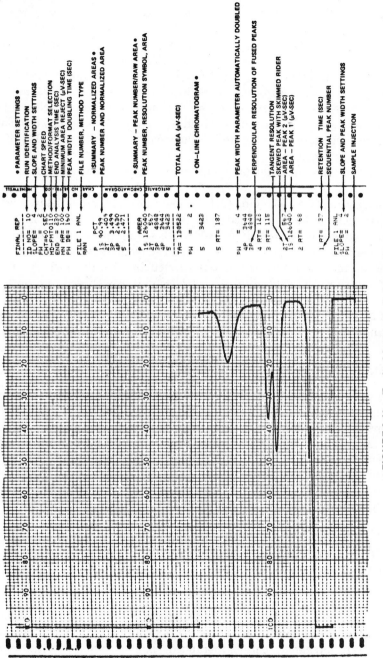

FIGURE 8.19. Typical integrated chromatogram.

235

The analysis was terminated by the preset value of the end analysis time parameter (230 sec). At this time the peak width is reset to its initial value, the total area (13,8522) μV-sec is printed, and the analog pen is driven full scale to provide a clean area for the final report. The succeeding information is printed in a rapid line advance mode, rather than at the analog chart speed. A raw area table is printed showing the peak number, peak type symbol, and area in top-to-bottom tabular format. Next a normalized area table is printed, in which the area of each peak is calculated as a percentage of the total area. Thus peak 3 comprises 3.499% of the total area for the run.

The two lines above the table indicate that the parameters in file 1 were used for the analysis, and the results were calculated using the raw area normalization (RAN) method (defined in the next section). Finally, a listing of parameter values is printed. The run identification number is 10, the slope setting was 4, The initial peak width setting (prior to doubling) was 2 sec, and the chart speed was 60 sec/in. The method-format value of 0110 indicates that the RAN method was selected and that the final report (one of several formats detailed in the next section) was chosen to report this level of detailed processing information. In particular, the analysis time was 230 sec, the minimum area reject was set at 100 μV-sec, and the peak width setting was doubled at 160 sec.

Postrun Processing and Reporting

One very important function for which the computing recorder is programmed is to produce four types of reports corresponding to four different forms of final quantitation as required by the analytical chemist. In addition, several different formats are selectable for presenting this information, depending upon the amount of detail desired. All these reports are printed in the rapid line advance mode (2 lines/sec) rather than at the selected chart speed for generating the chromatogram itself.

The four basic report methods that can be selected are:

RAN   Raw area normalization
ANRF   Area normalization with response factors
EST   External standard
IST   Internal standard (and variations)

For the purposes of method illustration, two similar mixtures, called a *calibration sample* and an *unknown sample*—but both of known composition—were prepared, chromatographed, and quantitated. The results shown here demonstrate the calculation algorithms and report formats for the four methods.

Raw Area Normalization (RAN). The simplest and fastest method is termed *raw area normalization* (RAN). It is the method of choice for preliminary analysis of an unknown sample. When no other method has been specified or the data needed for other methods has not been entered into the methods module, the computing recorder automatically computes RAN.

The method involves calculation of the percent area of each component (peak) of the sample, for example,

$$\text{Percent area}(i) = \frac{\text{area}(i)}{\sum\limits^{n} \text{area}(j)} \times 100$$

where i represents a specific peak and the summation is the total area of the n numbered peaks ($j = 1$ through n) recorded and not specifically rejected by one of the mechanisms already discussed.

Generally, the amount (weight, moles, or volume percent) of a component present is not the same as the area percent, because chromatograph detectors respond differently to different sample components; this is especially true for samples containing widely different classes of compounds, and of flame ionization detectors measuring lower molecular weight nonhydrocarbons.[22] However, with many samples that contain only homologous series of compounds, the correspondence of RAN percent area and percent weight is good, often better than 5% and sometimes better than 1%.

It is clearly necessary that all sample components of interest elute and be resolved into individual peaks in order for the RAN percent area to be quantitatively proportional to the percent weight. Hence the chromatographic conditions should be adjusted to give the best feasible separation.

If experience with standard samples proves that RAN is sufficiently accurate for the purpose, the method will be found extremely convenient, since the amount of sample (weight or volume) or the amount injected need not be known or reproducible. The analyst merely injects the sample and reads the percent area or percent weight from the final report portion of the integrated chromatogram.

Figure 8.20 is an example of such a report obtained using the RAN method. The calibration sample was known to contain (by weight):

	Grams	Percent
Benzene	4.395	6.582
Toluene	4.830	7.234
Ethylbenzene	4.335	6.492
Pentane (solvent)	53.210	79.691
	66.77	99.999

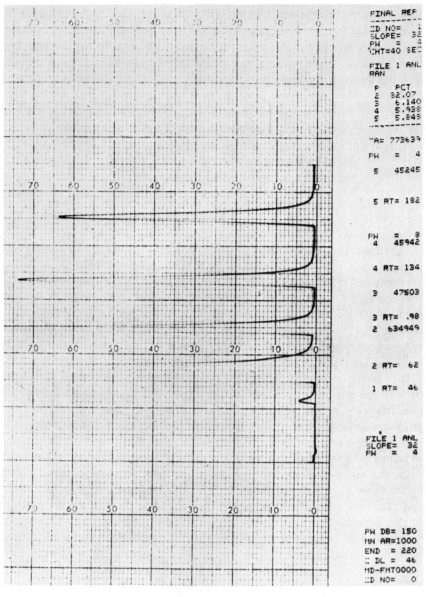

FIGURE 8.20.   RAN method (raw area normalization).

238

This 1 μl sample was chromatographed in a Bendix Model 2300 research GC, using a 10 ft $\times$ $\frac{1}{8}$ in. column of 10% SE-30 coated on 80/100 mesh Chromasorb P (nonacid wash). The initial column temperature was 125°C, programmed at 10°C/min to 160°C. The carrier gas was helium metered at 30 ml/min. A thermal conductivity detector was employed.

The computing recorder was set up with the following parameters: chart speed = 40 sec/in.; range (span) = 10 mV full scale; slope setting = 32 μV; peak width = 4 sec. In the lower part of Fig. 8.20 are the parameters for this RAN report format. MD-FMT0000 represents RAN (the first 0), and the next three zeros indicate a negative choice of a summary raw area printout, a detailed report, and a list of integration parameters. (These data, which are not desired for this run, are illustrated later.) The method and format are entered into the methods module by using the first four thumbwheels for the above selection and an index number of 11 to specify a method-format choice.

The integration delay (I DL) is shown as 46 sec; the end analysis (END) is 220 sec; the minimum area (MN AR) reject is 1000 μV-sec; and the *PW* doubling time (PW DB) is 150 sec.

In the report, the first peak (an air peak) is numbered, and its retention time of 46 sec is printed, but no area has been calculated because the integration delay extends up to 46 sec. Peak 2 is the solvent peak at 62 sec, which has an area of 63,4949 μV-sec; peak 3 at 98 sec is benzene; toluene is at 134 sec; and ethylbenzene peaks at 182 sec. The area of each is printed on the integrated chromatogram.

Immediately following the preset end of run at 220 sec, the total area (TA = 773639) is printed, and the RAN final report is identified and printed. The results can now be compared with the known percent weight.

"Unknown" Sample Analysis (RAN)

Peak	Component	Measured Area (%)	Known Weight (%)
2	Pentane	82.070	79.691
3	Benzene	6.140	6.582
4	Toluene	5.938	7.234
5	Ethylbenzene	5.848	6.492

In this case, the maximum difference between percent weight and percent area is less than 3%.

Above the analytic results, the final report lists the run parameters used: chart speed, *PW*, slope, and identification number.

Area Normalization with Response Factors (ANRF). To account for the varying response of some detectors to different chemical species, it is possible to apply a response factor to each component of the sample and obtain a corrected area percentage, which is a more accurate measure of the percent amount. A calibration chromatogram is first run on a carefully prepared standard, and the computing recorder automatically computes the response factor $R(i)$ for each component of interest:

$$R(i) = \frac{\text{amount}(i)}{\text{area}(i)} \times \frac{\text{area(REF)}}{\text{amount(REF)}}$$

Amount(i) is the amount of component i in the calibration sample. The reference (REF) is a component having a well-resolved peak, usually in the middle of the run, chosen as a reference by the chromatographer for the purpose of identifying each peak in subsequent analysis runs. Note that, if there is no reference, or one is not identified, the response factor becomes

$$R(i) = \frac{\text{amount}(i)}{\text{area}(i)}$$

The relative retention time RRT, defined as

$$RRT(i) = \frac{\text{absolute } RT(i)}{\text{absolute } RT(\text{REF})}$$

is used for peak identification. It is less subject to errors, such as operator lag in pressing the "inject" button and run-to-run variations in chromatographic conditions, than the absolute values.

The reference peak is identified as the largest peak within the retention time window (R WND), which is the percent tolerance around the reference retention time (R RT) allowed by the chromatographer. Similarly, the component peak is identified as the one closest to the center of the component peak time window (RT WND), which must also be selected. Having selected and entered all the required parameters for ANRF and computed the response factors through a calibration run, the ANRF method calculates the corrected area for each analysis run as:

$$\text{Percent corrected area}(i) = \frac{\text{area}(i) \times R(i)}{\sum\limits^{n} \text{area}(j) \times R(j)} \times 100 \times SF$$

SF is a scale factor which may be entered by the chromatographer to account for dilution, change in units, and so on. If none is entered, it is equal to 1.

The percent corrected area is equal to the percent weight if:

1. The calibration standard is accurate.
2. The detector response is linear with weight over the sample and calibration range.
3. All sample components elute and generate separate peaks.

If properly accomplished, ANRF gives greater accuracy than RAN and compensates for minor variations in chromatographic conditions. As with RAN, the amount of sample prepared or injected need not be known.

Figure 8.21 and the following illustrations show the use of ANRF. The format mode chosen (MD FMT 1111) represents the setting of the first four thumbwheel switches in the methods module: in sequence, ANRF method (first 1), area printed at end of analysis (second 1), integration parameter list in final report (third 1), and a detail report with expected retention times listed (last 1). As before, this format selection is entered in file 1 (in this instance), using index number 11.

Reading from bottom to top, in Fig. 8.21, the entries into method file 1 were:

Reference retention time (toluene)	R RT 134 (sec)
Reference amount (toluene)	RAMT 4830E-3 (4.830 g)
Reference window	R WND 10 (%)
Component retention time window	RT WND 3 (%)

Also, the three pairs of retention times and calibration amounts (RT and. CAMT) follow in sequence, each pair entered by index number 47 and the five data thumbwheels (the retention times were selected from Fig. 8.20). The peak calibration data can also be entered after an analysis by a slight modification of this procedure.

Note that it is possible to enter response factors directly from the literature (all referenced to the same compound) and thus eliminate the calibra-

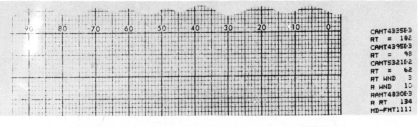

FIGURE 8.21. Entry of calibration amounts (ANRF).

tion step. In doing so, the same procedure is followed for data entry into the methods module, but the "calibrate" button is released and the response factor terms are substituted for CAMT values.

Following the entry of the calibration data in Fig. 8.21 and the calibration run, the response factors are calculated by pressing the "end" button again, with the "calibrate" button also depressed. The printout (final report) is seen in Fig. 8.22 with the requested format.

Reading from the bottom up, we have:

1.   A resume of the raw peak areas obtained in the calibration run

2.   Calculation of the response factors for each component, including the toluene reference (peak 4)

3.   An identification of the report (file 1, ANRF calibration)

4.   A listing of the integration parameters.

Above the final report is the optional detailed report. This lists the peak number, raw area, actual retention time (ART), and expected retention time (ERT). (If desired, RRT could have been displayed instead of the expected value.) The format of the detailed report table is as shown in its heading. This detailed report confirms that each calibration amount has been properly matched to its respective peak (retention time).

As a check on the system, an analysis type of report can be obtained from the calibration sample by releasing the "calibrate" button and again pressing the "end" button. The resulting report is identical to Fig. 8.22, except that percent corrected area is shown instead of response factor for each peak. The results will correspond to the percent weight calculated on the basis of the actual weights entered in the step in Fig. 8.21.

Figure 8.23 shows the results of an analysis run made with a different sample (the unknown sample), using the above calibration factors.

The integrated chromatogram is followed (reading upward) by the raw area report, the corrected percent area and file identification (ANRF analysis), the integration parameters, and the detailed report.

Note that the correct percent area and the actual sample percent weight (see accompanying table) are within about 0.1 % of each other. The accuracy

Unknown Sample Analysis (ANRF)

Component	Actual Weight (g)	Actual Weight (%)	Corrected Measured Area (%)
Benzene	3.1644	4.774	4.835
Toluene (REF)	4.8300	7.286	7.309
Ethylbenzene	3.9015	5.885	5.916
Pentane	54.3994	82.056	81.94

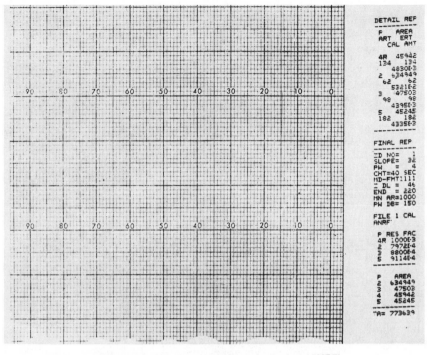

FIGURE 8.22. Response factor calculation (ANRF).

of this method, particularly if the pentane solvent is excluded, is far superior to that of the RAN method.

External Standard Method (EST). When a complex sample containing only a few components of interest to be quantitated, the EST method is convenient. Like ANRF, it is a two-step method: calibration followed by analysis. However, the results are reported in amount (grams or other units entered in the calibration step) rather than percent, as in RAN and ANRF. Only the COIs need be calibrated, and all components need not elute or produce peaks.

In calibration, a standard sample is chromatographed as before. One peak can be chosen as the reference peak if it is desired to use relative retention times to match analysis and calibrated peaks. After entering the retention time and calibration amount of the remaining COIs, the computing recorder calculates the response factors:

$$R(i) = \frac{\text{amount}(i)}{\text{area}(i)}$$

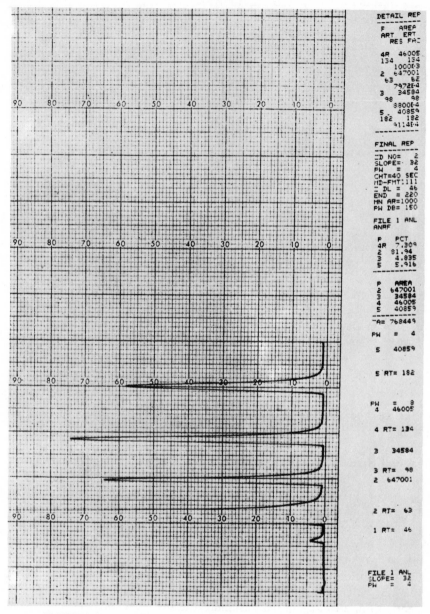

FIGURE 8.23.   ANRF method (using response factors of Figure 8.21).

When the analysis sample is chromatographed, the amount of each COI is computed:

$$\text{Amount}(i) = \text{area}(i) \times R(i) \times SF$$

The amount injected must be constant for calibration and analysis runs, although the absolute amount need not be known. The EST method is particularly suitable for high volume applications utilizing automatic injectors that provide precise volumetric control.

Internal Standard Method (IST).   IST results in the highest order of quantitation accuracy, because it compensates for the minor run-to-run and day-to-day variations in chromatographic conditions. It requires the addition of known amounts of a standardizing component to both the calibration and analysis samples; this component is not part of the regular sample and must form a separate peak. The variation of the system response (area per unit amount) to this internal standard is actually observed and computed during each analysis run and serves to compensate for changes in the response of the COIs due to these chromatographic system variations.

The IST compensation is effective for the COIs, because both tend to be affected in the same way by minor analyzer variations if the internal standard has been properly chosen. Hence the ratio, area(i)/area(REF), does not significantly change from run to run on the same sample.[22]

Several variations of the method can be applied, each of which requires the addition of a known amount of internal standard to the sample. The choice of IST variation (three in number) depends on whether a large or small number of samples is to be run, and whether or not samples are more easily handled volumetrically.

As stated, the internal standard chosen must not be a COI in the sample, but it should have a structure similar to the COIs and appear in about the same concentration. It should be well resolved, free of secondary peaks at or near its baselines but close (in retention time) to the bulk of the COI peaks under study.

The calibration is performed by preparing the known mixture, usually by weight, containing the internal standard and the COIs. The mixture is chromatographed, in the calibration mode, and the computing recorder calculates

$$R(i) = \frac{\text{amount}(i)}{\text{area}(i)} \times \frac{\text{area(REF)}}{\text{amount(REF)}} \quad \text{(for each COI)}$$

Amount(i) and amount(REF) are the known amounts of COI and reference added to the calibration mixture.

For analysis, an accurately known amount of the sample is blended with a known amount of internal standard and chromatographed. The computing recorder calculates for each COI:

$$\text{Amount}(i) = \frac{\text{area}(i) \times R(i)}{\text{area(REF)}} \times \text{amount(REF)} \times SF$$

where amount(REF) = amount of reference added to the analytic sample (at the macro level)

$$SF = \text{scale factor for dilution or unit conversion}$$

The insertion of a sample amount (*SAMT*), not explicitly stated in the above form, converts amount(*i*) to percent concentration by automatically multiplying the result by 100/*SAMT*. For IST, the volume need not be known or held constant.

Summary of Methods and Equations. Four general methods have been outlined in the preceding sections. These methods, RAN, ANRF, EST, and IST, give the chromatographer the capability to convert raw peak area information into concentration levels in accepted chemical units. These equations are stored in the methods section of the computing recorder's firmware.

In generalized form, they include:

RAN
   Analysis mode:

$$\text{Percent area}(i) = \frac{\text{area}(i)}{\sum \text{area}(i)} \times 100$$

ANRF
   Analysis mode:

$$\text{Percent area}(i) = \frac{\text{area}(i) \times \text{response factor}(i)}{\sum [\text{area}(i) \times \text{response factor}(i)]} \times 100 \times \text{scale factor}$$

   Calibration mode:

$$\text{Response factor}(i) = \frac{\text{amount}(i)}{\text{area}(i)} \times \frac{\text{area(REF)}}{\text{amount(REF)}}$$

EST (general form)
   Analysis mode:

$$\text{Amount}(i) = \frac{\text{area}(i) \times \text{response factor}(i) \times \text{scale factor}}{\text{amount(injected)}}$$

Calibration mode:

$$\text{Response factor}(i) = \frac{\text{amount}(i)}{\text{area}(i)}$$

IST (general form)
Analysis mode:

Amount(i)

$$= \frac{\text{area}(i) \times \text{response factor}(i) \times \text{amount}(\text{REF}) \times \text{scale factor} \times 100}{\text{area}(\text{REF}) \text{ amount}(\text{sample})}$$

Calibration mode:

$$\text{Response factor}(i) = \frac{\text{amount}(i) \times \text{area}(\text{REF})}{\text{area}(i) \times \text{amount}(\text{REF})}$$

The utilization of any particular method requires a separate procedure for sample preparation and varying amounts of analytic effort to obtain the desired level of accuracy. But this effort can now be devoted almost entirely to careful control of the analyzer, including the necessary efforts aimed at optimizing separations, and the routine tasks of postrun calculations relegated to the computing recorder.

Future of Microprocessor-Based Analytic Instrumentation

The microprocessor revolution is bringing significant benefits and new processing capabilities to the state of the art in the analytic instrument field. By virtue of their low cost, these processors allow functions previously relegated to implementation only on expensive computer systems to become part of a single laboratory instrument, in and of itself.

In chromatography, the synergistic effects derived from considerations of the hybrid analog and digital informational needs have resulted in advances in report generation and data presentation clarity. Many additional classes of instrumental analysis, ranging from infrared spectroscopy to atomic absorption[23,25] and mass spectroscopy, require considerable signal processing and real time alphanumeric reporting. These needs can also be served by such approaches as that examplified by the computing recorder.

In the future, total instrumental automation, sophisticated signal analysis and information extraction, real time analyzer control, and expanded analyzer applications will be the principal areas to benefit by further design attention and innovation.

At the most fundamental systems level, namely, at the analyzer and quantizer block level, it is profitable to reexamine the basic elements within the context of the processor environment. From such a frame of reference, "intelligent" instrumentation which carries out the process from sample to final answer with minimal operator intervention holds much promise. Several systems have already been designed and marketed with a measure of this capability. Such "smart" analyzers will find increasing acceptance for whole classes of analysis, especially where the marketing requirements demand a fairly balanced instrumental capability in both qualitative and quantitative areas. However, systems configurations centered around the "smart" recorder concept will also continue to evolve for applications with highly quantitative tasks and customized report generation needs.

One is struck by the enormous design flexibility inherent in the basic microprocessor approach, regardless of the systems thinking involved, and the instrument designer is continually impressed with the relative ease of altering algorithms, modifying formats, and redefining the instrument's controls (the operator-machine interface) as new ideas and concepts in operator needs and human engineering influenced design thinking.

In the long run, rapid acceptance of the microprocessor within the analytic instrument industry has been motivated by two basic factors: (1) significant economies at the manufacturing level, and (2) enhanced value added as a result of increased functional capability. Several electronics industry studies have documented the significant savings to be developed by partial or nearly total replacement of dedicated logic circuitry with the microprocessor approach. Also, a certain degree of marketing advantage will accrue to manufacturers that can claim microprocessor incorporation within their existing product lines. It is, however, in the area of tangible improvements, which will come only through concerted efforts at the development of application knowledge, that the exciting advances in instrumentation capability will occur.

The keys to successful new design efforts are a close and intimate knowledge of the application under consideration and considerable dialogue between user and designer to allow for a maximum understanding of the user's intentions and modes of thinking. With such knowledge, it is often possible to define new concepts in operator-machine interaction that virtually leapfrog the user over the more conventional and accepted ways of using and interacting with equipment.

Glossary of Representative Subroutines for Chromatography

Status Lights. Indicative of real time data acquisition and integration conditions. Subroutine tests flag conditions continuously and report system status to operator.

End of Run Initiated. Terminates integration process, updates status light indications, and initiates postrun calculations and report format subroutines.

Peak Width (Filter) Update. Adjusts peak width value to current manually set value, as allowed by other program subroutine flags.

Chart Drive. Digital motor drive pulse generation from the 5 MHz clock pulse, as flagged by chart speed settings and run or postrun operation modes (i.e., rapid line advance, hold).

Peak Width–Slope Switch. Inputs peak width and slope switch data from the front panel buttons), updates values, and sets flags for integration subroutine.

Integration Inhibit. Sets area inhibit bit based on front panel switch setting manually set for this function.

Baseline Correction. Corrects accumulated area information for drifting baselines through trapezoidal (nonhorizontal) subtractions from recognized baseline loci.

Tangent. Locates point of tangency of small peak riding on the trailing edge of a large skewed peak by testing for slope values greater than or equal to a tangent line drawn from the starting point of the rider peak. This routine allows the rider peak area to be skimmed off the large skewed peak.

Peak Valley. Recognizes valley points (in time and amplitude) for fused peak clusters, which allows for subsequent area allocation following baseline reestablishment.

Baseline Achieved. Clearance of all integration flags, including tests for fused peaks and back slope conditions plus cumulative slope values less than the slope setting.

Autoslope. Calculation of optimum slope value for a minimum acceptable probability of less than 0.014 of false triggering. Calculation based on assumption that chromatograph detection noise is modeled as white noise.

Moving Average–Slope. Subroutine that calculates the moving average value of incoming data groups and computes the weighted slope value of this digitally filtered data by the Savitsky-Golay algorithm.

Horizontal Baseline Correction. Fused peak area allocation construct which allows the trapezoidal (nonhorizontal) baseline correction for up to four fused peaks with any additional peaks (within a peak cluster treated horizontally (to conserve memory demands).

Final Printout.   Data conversion to BCD, formatting instructions, percent area calculation (each peak area over the total area) and printout of peak number, type, percent area and total area.

Printer.   Transfer of data to print buffer and formatting of two thermal dot data bytes per imprint cycle for character generation.

Real Time Print Message.   Formatting and printing of initialization values (run identification number, slope setting, peak width, and chart speed), plus peak retention time, peak type, and area information, during the analysis.

Area Format.   Conversion of peak area data (in mircovolt-seconds) to BCD form for storage in print buffer. Area information greater than 10^7 counts is restated in exponential form prior to code conversion and storage.

Basic Parameter Format.   Transfer of data and loading of lables (names) into printer buffers for printout routine, covering run identification number, slope setting, peak width setting, and chart speed setting.

Error Message Print Format.   Decoding of error flag condition and transfer of error message and label from memory for storage in print buffer. Error conditions covered include signal level in excess of input limitations, peak area exceeding area overflow limit, and negatively computed area.

Peak Number and Area Format.   Transfer of peak area and peak number into print buffer for printout after baseline reestablishment. Buffer holds data in event of priority interrupt from simultaneous command for real time peak retention data printout.

References

1.   D. A. H. Roethal and C. R. Counts, *Chem. Eng. News* **49**(47) 90 (Nov. 15, 1971).

2.   S. P. Cram and R. S. Juvet, *Anal. Chem.* **44**(5) 213–241 (1972).

3.   S. T. Zawadowicz and A. L. Kegg, "Definition, Functional Design, and Implementation of a Dedicated Computerized Laboratory System—The GC Computing Recorder," ASTM E-31 Meeting, 25th Pittsburgh Conference on Analytic Chemistry and Applied Spectroscopy, March 1974, ASTM Special Technical Publication, STP-578, July 1975.

4.   J. M. Gill and F. Tao, paper presented at the ASTM E-19 Meeting, St. Louis, Missouri, October 1965.

5.   D. L. Ball, W. E. Harris, and H. W. Habgood, *J. Gas Chromatogr.* **5** 613–620 (Dec. 1967).

6.   D. T. Sawyer and J. K. Barr, *Anal. Chem.* **34**(10) 1213–1216 (Sept. 1962).

7. R. D. Johnson, D. D. Lawson, and A. J. Havlik, *J. Gas Chromatogr.* **3**(9) 303–309 (Sept. 1965).

8. F. Bauman and F. Tao, *J. Gas Chromatogr.* **5** 621–626 (Dec. 1967).

9. F. Bauman, A. C. Brown, and M. B. Mitchell, *J. Chromatogr. Sci.* **8** 20–31 (Jan. 1970).

10. B. Dewey, III, paper presented at the Pittsburgh Conference on Analytical Chemistry and Applied Spectroscopy, Cleveland, Ohio, March 1969.

11. H. Hancock and I. Lichenstein, *J. Chromatogr. Sci.* **7** 290–292 (May 1969).

12. J. G. Karohl, 7th International Symposium of Gas Chromatography and Its Exploitation, Copenhagen, Denmark, Institute of Petroleum, London, England, 1968.

13. J. D. Hettinger, J. R. Hubbard, J. M. Gill, and L. A. Miller, *J. Chromatogr. Sci.* **9** 710–717 (Dec. 1971).

14. J. D. Hettinger, L. A. Miller, and R. S. Jacobs, paper presented at the Eastern Analytical Symposium, New York, N. Y., Nov. 1973.

15. F. Bauman, D. L. Wallace, and L. G. Brendan, "Interfacing Chromatographs to the Computer," paper presented at the Pittsburgh Conference on Analytical Chemistry and Applied Spectroscopy, March 1969.

16. T. P. Kelley, "Voltage to Frequency Converter," Internal Report, Honeywell, Inc., Fort Washington, Pa., Sept. 1973.

17. D. M. Stern, "The F/W Microprocessor Project," Honeywell Microprocessor Symposium, Minneapolis, Minn., August, 1974.

18. D. L. Wallace, *Am. Lab.* **4**(9) 67–71 (Sept. 1972).

19. R. S. Blackman and J. W. Tukey, *The Measurement of Power Spectra*, Dover, New York, 1959, pp. 31–37.

20. A. Savitsky and M. J. E. Golay, *Anal. Chem.* **36**(8) 1627–1639 (July 1964).

21. A. L. Kegg, "Study of Error Analysis of Perpendicular and Tangent Resolution of Overlapping Gaussian Peaks," Honeywell, Inc., Fort Washington, Pa., Dec. 1972 (unpublished manuscript).

22. I. G. Young, "A Review of Post-Run Calculation Techniques in Gas Chromatography," *Am. Lab.* **7**(2, 6, 8) 27–36, 37–44, 11–21 (February, June, August 1975).

23. L. P. Morgenthaler and T. J. Poulos, *Am. Lab.* **8**(8) 37–45 (Aug. 1976).

24. Series 5830A Reporting Gas Chromatographs, Hewlett-Packard, Avondale, Pa.

25. A. L. Robinson, *Science* **195**(4284) 1315 (1977).

Nine

Distributed Microprocessor Control Systems

Up to this point the emphasis has been placed on the use of single microprocessors to perform a repertoire of relatively simple fixed program tasks. There is a high probability that this kind of application will utilize the major share of microprocessor chip production in the future, because of its economic advantages over competing electromechanical and discrete electronic methods. Spark advance (plus many other tasks) in automobile applications, and home video games in the noncontrol field, are typical of the jobs that will employ a large share of microprocessor chips.

But there is another mode of microprocesser use that may well prove to be of much greater significance in the long term, even though the number of chips so employed may be considerably less. This application involves systems in which many microprocessors are linked together to form a *distributed control system,* or what is called in the data processing field a *multiprocessor.*

There are two possible kinds of control-computing device architectures utilizing multiple digital processors in parallel.[1] One is the parallel data structure, such as that of the ILLIAC IV (the current single quadrant version), which can perform full 64 bit arithmetic on 64 independent arguments simultaneously, utilizing 64 independent arithmetic units, but with only a single control, so that all the arithmetic operations are the same.

This machine is really no different from many other binary computers in which independent data word bits are simultaneously ANDed or otherwise operated upon. A true multiprocessor has a parallel control structure, each data element being driven by a separate control unit.

The philosophy of a control parallel multiprocessor or distributed control system has been described as being similar to that of the team approach taken by cooperating humans to solve a problem too large for one individual. There are three possible modes of interaction: hierarchal, "republican," and "democratic." A hierarchal system requires a leader, giving a continuous stream of commands. A republican system requires that all decisions be made by vote. Although the first system may be more efficient, it lacks reliability because of the possible failure of the leader, for example, by death or irrationality. The republican system is much more reliable, in that it can survive the failure of any individual, but the voting procedure is slow and inefficient. In a democratic system, goals and a leader are chosen for each task and, during the operation of that task, the leader's will is obeyed. By analogy, a distributed control system in which responsibility for each task is assigned to different processors in a control parallel structure is more reliable than a single or hierarchal processor, and nearly as efficient.[1]

Distributed control multiprocessors are more economical, in general, because slow computers are cheaper, even allowing for speed differences; that is, cost increases faster than power. This general rule has been demonstrated even more dramatically with the advent of the microprocessor. Therefore putting together many slower processors to achieve large computing power is more cost-effective than using one large machine. A multiprocessor requires no more peripherals than a single large unit for the same task; for example, much of the cost of a process control computer is in the data acquisition system (A/D, D/A), manual backup controls, and so on, which basically do not depend on the processor.

The cost of these advantages of multiprocessor distributed control is the cost of communication. Therefore the choice of a communication system must be carefully made to minimize the burden on system logic and operating time. Considering the cost of reliability, the multiprocessor again comes out ahead. This is because the cost of duplicating low powered components for redundancy is lower. The addition of a single extra small processor for redundant reliability in a multiprocessor system can provide the backup for many units and accomplish the same reliability objective as duplication of a single powerful unit (plus mechanisms to implement the spare switchover), which can be very expensive indeed.

Digital Multiprocessors in Distributed Control

Multiple processors are by no means novel in process control; in fact, the traditional method of implementing process control systems is with multiple analog controllers—one for each loop. Only in recent years have large digital computers taken over many multiple loop control functions, where they have brought attendant efficiency in solving complex problems of system optimization and interactive loops. At the same time they have brought with them problems of reliability to the point of necessitating analog controller backup in critical loops. What is new, then, is the distribution of this digital process control function among many physical units, which permits both logical tasks and physical location to be distributed in the plant in the most effective manner.[2]

Since cost has always been an important element in industrial process control, it has been necessary to await the microprocessor to put this concept on a feasible economic footing.

From a systems point of view, it can be seen that the single loop process control task is relatively undemanding and can be readily satisfied by either an analog controller or a preprogrammed digital processor. However, the control of an entire process or plant may be enormously complex, involving numerous dynamic interactions and reactions, some of which cannot be precisely defined. Optimum control of such a situation requires either a powerful computer able to perform the many necessary computations and support an impressive array of peripherals for process and operator interfacing or, alternatively, a control parallel multiprocessor or digital distributed control system able to accomplish the same task. While the control of a single loop is preprogrammable, that of the entire system is not. In the large computer, the programming must be accomplished by software, requiring a substantial knowledge of both computer and process. In the multiprocessor approach, the major amount of programming involves the interconnection of specialized task processors and the selection of individual control loop (preprogrammed) algorithms. If some of this interconnection can be made by software (as will be the case if a single microprocessor is time-shared with several loops), a proportionate amount of wiring cost will be saved, wiring being one of the most significant items of control system cost. If, after this configuration (the interconnection programming) is complete, there remain higher level control tasks, such as system optimization, these can be solved using larger computers connected in hierarchal fashion but assigned solely to these high level tasks—leaving the microprocessor's task assignments intact. In this way, the larger computer becomes merely part of the distributed control system with its own task assignment.

The benefits accruing from distributed process control utilizing multiple microprocessors can be summarized:

Improved control	More powerful control strategies can be implemented because of the more efficient allocation of tasks to separate processors
More reliable	Greater reliability at a given cost than with a single large computer, greater reliability than with individual loop controllers because of fewer parts, and greater reliability of the LSI microprocessors
More flexible	Interconnection flexibility plus a selection of preprogrammed functions stored in firmware permit configuration process situations more readily than with software programming.
Improved data integrity and display	Digital data format permits duplicate storage of data base as well as logical data checks. Data can be displayed in various visual formats best matching the operator task [Cathode ray tube (CRT) displays can provide the necessary flexibility, for example].

Communication between Distributed Control Processors.   The price of the advantages listed above, as stated, is the cost of communication. This is by no means a negligible item. In power and chemical process plants, the cost of the structure alone (wireways and trays) for a conventional two-wire, shielded signal cable can exceed \$8/ft and the installation labor \$40/ft. Consequently, the communication system must be carefully planned.

Several possible methods of intercommunication between units of a multiprocessor system are shown in Fig. 9.1. That shown in Fig. 9.1a, the star connection, is economical of cabling but is vulnerable to shutdown if the central communicator fails. The system in Fig. 9.1b is more reliable, since every unit is connected to every other and a processor failure does not affect communication between the others. The system in Fig. 9.1c, called a *data highway,* sends all messages over the same path but addresses them in code so that they are intercepted only by the interface (*I/F*) of the unit to which they are directed. The failure of any unit has no more effect than in the completely interconnected system in Fig. 9.1b. The data highway and interfaces may be redundant for additional reliability. The data highway is particularly adapted to coaxial cable,[9] which carries high

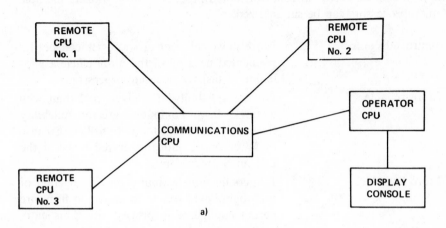

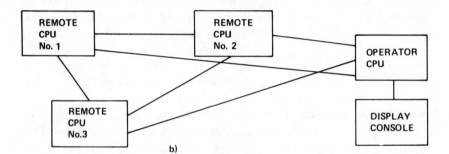

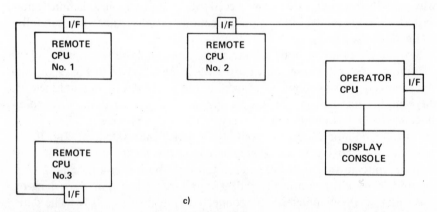

FIGURE 9.1. Distributed control processor interconnection schemes. (*a*) Star. (*b*) Totally interconnected. (*c*) Data highway.

speed signals with better quality and less noise pickup than conventional twisted pairs. High speed transmission permits the cable to be completely multiplexed, with substantial savings in view of the high costs cited above. Figure 9.2, for example, shows the hypothetical savings resulting from the use of a dual coaxial cable data highway compared to the use of individual cable pairs in a star arrangement.

Architecture of a Total Distributed Control System

A total system architecture for process control employing the multiprocessor concept must consequently encompass much more than a microprocessor controller and includes the communication system, data display, and interface with the operator (who is a necessary part of the system for reasons of safety and judgment), as well as the interface with the process for data acquisition and control.

J. M. Watson[3] has reported on the considerations leading to the architecture of the total distributed control system (TDC 2000) developed by Honeywell Inc. It is instructive to look into this system in some detail, as it is the first complete multimicroprocessor system to incorporate all the necessary aspects in a unified design and for this reason may be considered a paradigm of future development in this field.

A primary architectural requirement is a distributed data base. Information passed from one task to another requires additional characterization to be used in the new task. For example, temperature is converted by a thermocouple to electrical current and thence to meter deflection, however, this deflection is not useful to the operator unless he can interpret it with a calibration or scale. It follows that each separate task (microprocessor) must have associated with it its own local data base. Further advantages accrue when these data are redundantly stored and can be replaced in the original unit if lost by power failure, for example.

The basic functions are process regulation (regulatory control), primary alarms (limits), and determination of process trends. Data directly obtained or derived from these tasks may be used to interact all other tasks (such as operator display) with the process.

The operator has special requirements which must be met if the system is to match his capabilities and limitations.[4] Displays must be created to give a broad, overall view of the process state, permitting the use of human pattern recognition and prediction skills, and yet they must be capable of localizing down to specific loops and detail with minimum delay when

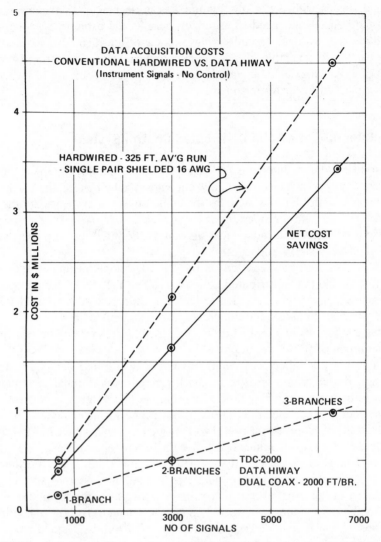

FIGURE 9.2. Data acquisition costs, conventional hard-wired versus data highway.

needed for manual control or intervention. Since very large panel boards are considered poorly matched to human capabilities and are inflexible, support of CRT operator facilities is indicated.[10] However, data must be presented by a secure and consistent method, regardless of the mode of control.

A higher level computer should not be required for safe operation of the process. But the microprocessor system should be capable of direct interfacing with such a computer where large quantities of data must be stored or manipulated in a single machine.

Security of Communications. The economic role of communications in distributed control systems and the advantages of the data highway approach are thus emphasized. It is not feasible at present to terminate a coaxial data highway at every sensor and control element, however, the economics favors bringing it out into the field to multiplexed process interface units located at each unit process, the interface units in turn being hardwired with short cable runs to the sensors and elements. This requires spreading the communication system over large areas of a process site and exposing it to severe electrical and meteorological environmental hazards. Considering also the large quantities of material and energy directed by industrial control systems, it is essential that no errors be tolerated. In consequence, prime requirements placed on the system include message security, environmental integrity, and adequate message handling capacity.

Security may be ensured to any desired extent by adequate coding, as brought out in earlier chapters. In this particular system, a 26 bit command and data word is supplemented by 5 security bits, the latter forming a coding scheme known as the 31, 26 Bose-Chaudhuri-Hocquenghem (BCH).[5]

This code has properties such that:

1. All burst errors of five bits or less are detected.
2. All combinations of one or two random errors are detected.
3. All single message inversions are detected.
4. 98% of six bit burst errors and 95% of all other burst errors are detected.

The efficacy of this code is supplemented by checks on individual bits, bit counting, and monitoring of total communication time by any one device. The net result is to reduce the error rate to better than one undetected error per 12 years by both theoretical and physical tests under the worst environmental conditions. The latter include exposure to broad band radiation at 30 V/m from 20 KHz to 500 MHz and tests per IEEE specification 472 for surge resistance on transmission lines.[6]

Channel Capacity. A consequence of the division of labor among processors units is that those devoted to regulatory control will have the highest rate of information transfer, because of the process dynamics. These messages are also localized within one plant or process. Watson[3] estimates a capacity of 2000 to 3000 data transactions per second as being required in the foreseeable future, about two to three times current large system requirements. For larger distances (interarea) only about 100 to 500 transactions per second are needed.

It is not simple to estimate the *net* capacity of a communication system serving multiple processors, because of the quasi-random nature of the message load.[7] For example, delay encountered by a message on a serial data highway, assuming purely random message inputs, is, in the steady state,

$$W = \frac{1}{\mu - \lambda} \qquad (9.1)$$

where μ = capacity of the transmission line for messages of average length (taking into account message protocol and recovery) in messages per second

λ = average rate of requests to use the highway in the same units

Since the message protocol can specify priorities or nonrandom elements, the delay may be less than this amount. In actuality, the TDC 2000 system grants priority to devices generally requiring more than 100 accesses to the highway per second; these include the CRT displays (operators' stations) and higher level computers. Lower priority devices (such as multiplexed sensors and status contacts) are polled by a traffic director unit every 10 msec.

Microprocessor Systems Architecture.   In conventional analog process control a great many different types of controllers are required to suit the individual requirements of each loop or group of loops. These differences encompass the control algorithm, the interconnection or control strategy (primary or cascade), the variations of indicators, and other I/O options. With microprocessors, a single physical unit can be programmed to perform all these tasks—the particular mode of operation being capable of selection and variation on-line (for convenience in starting up a process, for instance). A general type of microprocessor subsystem is shown in Fig. 9.3. It is possible to design such a structure with a series of standard printed circuit boards giving an extra dimension of flexibility; memory, I/O, and so on, can be added to or subtracted from any specific system. For example, extra RAM or ROM modules can be added as needed for a specific subsystem. The other dimension is of course the program which can be altered without physical change in the system.

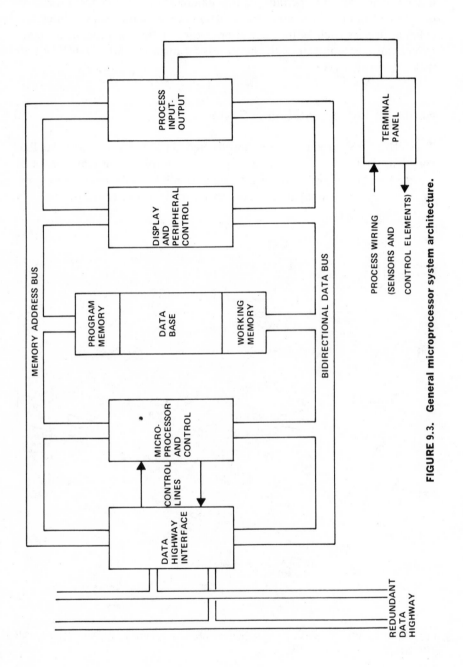

FIGURE 9.3. General microprocessor system architecture.

For any specific subsystem, the program memory contents (ROM) are unique. The data bus permits intercommunication among the processor, data base, local displays, and process data. Via the data highway interface, external devices such as the central operator's station or supervisory computers can communicate with the processor memory directly (DMA) or with the process I/O.

Hardware Implementation of System

The TDC 2000 architecture is constructed on a modular basis, so that complete implementation of a large process control system may consist of a large number of parts which may include 60 or more microprocessors, as shown by the overall schematic drawing in Fig. 9.4, or may have only

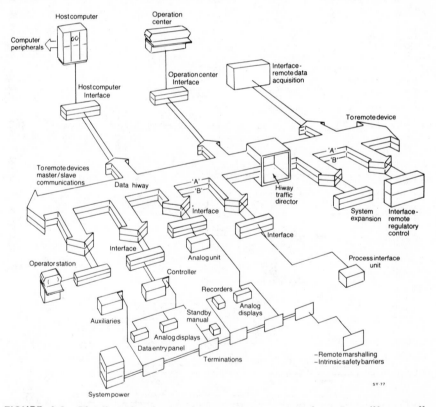

FIGURE 9.4. Distributed microprocessor process control system (Honeywell TDC 2000).

the few basic units needed to control small systems. In this section we describe briefly the technical features of the basic controller, the major piece of hardware implementing the guidelines just enunciated. Other hardware units necessary for the entire system are more briefly described, emphasizing those utilizing separate microprocessors.

The basic modules are:

1. Controller file
2. Operator station
3. Highway traffic director (HTD)
4. Analog unit
5. Process interface unit

Before examining the details, let us first obtain an overview of the system to see how these modules function together.

As generally discussed above, the system architecture is that of multi-processor units linked by a data highway (or "hiway," as it is frequently spelled in control systems practice). Each processor is a bus-oriented microprocessor (the General Instrument CP 1600 discussed in a previous chapter) linked to the data highway through interface units that permit DMA data transfer between units.

Referring to Fig. 9.4, the flow of data on the highway is directed by the HTD, which repeats messages on the various branches, assigns priority access to units competing for the serial channel, and conducts the polling of modules acquiring change-of-status data. The HTD does not check messages for accuracy; this is accomplished by the individual interface units.

The highway connects to the individual controller files (microprocessors) which are each wired to process transducers (I/O devices) and can acquire PV and SP data from or control up to eight individual loops. Conventional appearing panel meters or recorders, displaying PV and SP data, can be wired to the controllers using plug-in cords. (Analog signals can also be modified with electronic analog computing units or signal conditioners (auxiliaries) but these are also direct-wired and do not affect the digital operation of the system.) PV-SP data can be displayed digitally by means of a data entry panel (DEP) which also permits configurations of up to 16 controllers, or manual control of any loop, via a pushbutton operator interface. All this data exchange is carried on external to the data highway and is independent of it. Therefore the controller file and its peripherals can be used in a stand-alone mode to provide conventional regulatory control of eight loops.

Each controller, however, interfaces with the highway, permitting any part of its data base to be communicated to another module (Fig. 9.3).

A specific receiver is a central operations' location utilizing a micropro-cessor-based CRT data display and control keyboard, called an *operator station*. These units have a function similar to the "intelligent" terminals used in data processing computer systems, in that the display and the key-board operation are controlled by the microprocessor using its own ROM program and data base (up to 40K words of memory) without reference to a central computer. The keyboard permits the choice of various fixed program displays showing the status of the overall system or process, or that of individual controllers and loops. It also allows the operator to in-tervene directly in the configuration of controllers and in the automatic or manual control of loops. The operator stations, as suggested in Fig. 9.4, can be used individually or combined in an *operation center* console so several displays can be presented simultaneously to the operator.

The data highway also provides essentially the same service for host computers interfaced with it for supervisory or data processing purposes. That is, the host computer may have access to each controller's data base and can manipulate it or the output to the process, or operate on and display the data, in the same manner as the operator. The host computer of course can be of any size and power so long as it obeys the highway protocol, or it can be omitted entirely, leaving the full functioning multi-processor system.

Figure 9.4 also shows modules called *analog units* connected to the highway and process similarly to the controllers. These perform the same function as far as the highway system is concerned but do not have the instructions for process control algorithms that allow independent oper-ation of the controller. They are thus primarily I/O devices, permitting data acquisition and manual control of loops via the operator station (in manual mode) or a host computer in DDC mode. Because they lack inde-pendent regulatory loop control, their program memory structure is much simpler, and they can service 16 loops (16 analog inputs and 16 analog outputs) rather than the controller's 8 loops. Also, because the analog units are not controllers, they need not be configured and have no need of the DEP.

Another significant module appearing in Fig. 9.4 is the *process interface unit* (PIU). This device is unique in that it can be polled by the HTD. Its major function is to interface the process and acquire large quantities of data, either digital (status of closure contacts, for example) or analog, such as thermocouple millivoltages. A change in digital status is recognized as a response to the regular polling inquiries of the HTD, after which the unit is requested to transmit its new data. When this capability is not used (and it is useful mainly with a sequence or digital logic system controlled by a specifically programmed host computer), the PIU is employed as an analog data acquisition unit (A/D and D/A) and responds on the highway only to requests from the operator station or the host computer, in the same way the analog unit and controller file respond.

The Microprocessor Controller File

The controller file provides eight computing blocks or "slots" which can be linked with each other or with external process variables to achieve multiloop control strategies (see Fig. 9.5). Each slot can be configured to

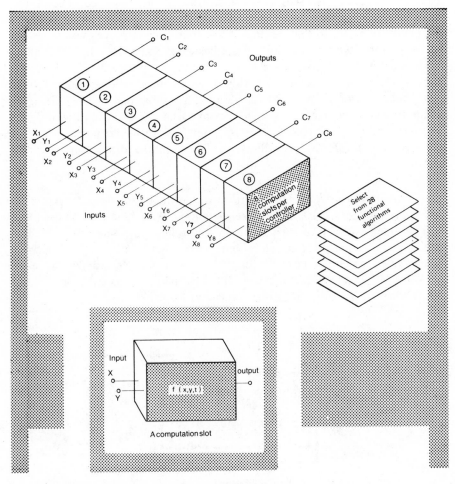

FIGURE 9.5. Microprocessor controller time-shared computing "slots."

perform any of 28 algorithms encompassing both control and algebraic (auxiliary) functions.

Physically, the controller file consists of three parts: the microprocessor-driven controller itself, including its I/O function and an optional highway interface; a terminal panel for wiring to the process transducers; and the DEP digital operator interface (Fig. 9.6).

Control Functions.[8]   A standard file contains eight printed circuit boards: power regulator, solid state memory, processor, core memory, DEP interface, A/D multiplexer, and two output cards. For connection to priority access devices (the operator station or the control computer) a coaxial cable data highway is used, and interface boards are supplied. The A/D scan rate is $\frac{1}{3}$ sec, the controller file cycle is $\frac{1}{3}$ sec, and the D/A update occurs every $\frac{1}{3}$ sec, so that the file's basic frequency is 3 cycles/sec.

Of the three types of memory in the basic controller, ROM, RAM, and core backup, ROM contains the basic controller program as well as a library of operator-selectable algorithms. ROM information is nonvolatile and cannot be lost. The RAM functions as a scratch pad or work area, a temporary storage area, and a point record variable storage area (the data base pertaining to a particular control point). Core memory can be used as a backup for RAM, as will be explained in the discussion of card details.

Operator Interface.   Operator interface within the basic controller module is achieved with the DEP and slot selector (Fig. 9.6). The DEP is used to display data, enter set points, manually control output, enter parameters, and configure; that is, select algorithms and assign inputs. There are two four-digit-plus-sign displays. One is dedicated to the selected slot process variable (PV). The other indicates other variables, constants, or limits. Either display indicates diagnostic fault and error codes.

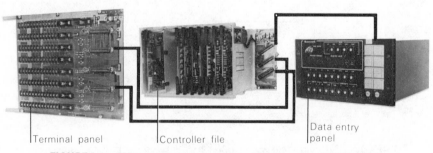

Terminal panel   Controller file   Data entry panel

FIGURE 9.6.   Microprocessor controller file (Honeywell TDC 2000).

Process Interface. The terminal panel (Fig. 9.6) provides a process interface through connections to process transmitters and final control elements.

Range resistors transform 1 to 5, 10 to 50, and 4 to 20 mA input signals to 1 to 5 V dc for A/D multiplexing into the controller. Figure 9.7 graphically illustrates the role of the terminal panel as a process interface. The terminal panel can accommodate up to 16 analog inputs representing measured process or remote variables, plus 8 analog outputs to final control elements.

Computational Card and Central Processing Functions. The controller file contains the computational card and central processing functions (in a bus-organized microprocessor). The basic controller block diagram (Fig. 9.8) shows how process information enters and leaves the terminal panel and interacts with data bus–connected controller file cards. The signals used to communicate on the bus are the same for all devices. The processor reads and writes into the I/O devices in exactly the same way it reads and writes into memory. Likewise, the highway interface can control the bus exactly as the processor does and can write or read into all devices, using a bus sharing technique.

The memory blocks mentioned in Fig. 9.8 are reserved areas of memory used for data storage and transfer. They contain information in addition to process I/O data, but useful in controller operation, for example, the local set point.

Discrete process information can enter any one of eight memory blocks, since each block has its own corresponding terminal strip. Controller configuration selects process I/O data from any memory block combination. These groupings of data are input for up to 8 selected algorithms. The algorithms are selected from a preprogrammed set of 28 residing as a library in the basic controller's memory. These eight computational assemblies are those we have referred to as computational slots. They are the source of the process control outputs available at the appropriate terminal strip for connection to final control elements in the field.

Card Details. The power regulator board takes the +24 V dc bulk supply voltage and provides +5 V dc switching regulation, +12 V dc linear reg-

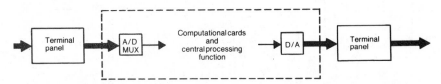

FIGURE 9.7. Terminal panels for microprocessor controller-process interface.

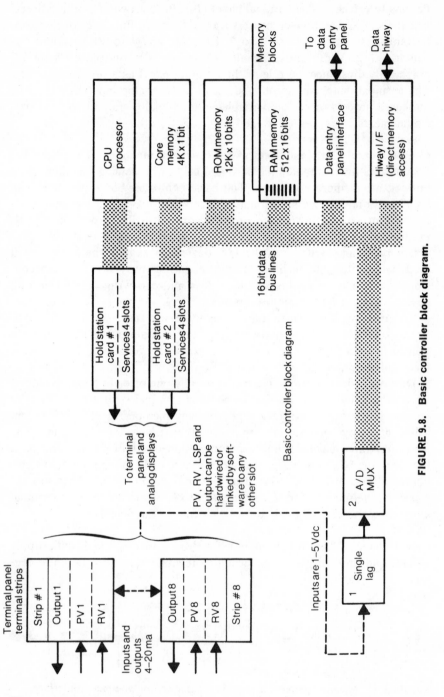

FIGURE 9.8. Basic controller block diagram.

268

ulation, and -12 V dc inverter regulation for controller file power requirements. It also incorporates a power-down monitor which provides early detection of power outages and signals the CPU to execute power-down commands. The regulator card also contains circuit fuses and status lights.

The solid state memory card contains decoding and auxiliary logic necessary to operate the 0.5K of RAM and 12K of ROM, which are resident on the board. The ROM contains the program for the basic controller as well as the algorithms selectable for slot configuration.

The CPU (processor board) contains the microprocessor control logic, a micro-ROM, a bus address register (BAR), an ALU, an H multiplexer, a shift multiplexer, status flip-flops, various control registers including working registers, and internal control flip-flops essential to microprocessor operation (see Fig. 7.9).

The core memory contains 4K of one bit word mass storage and is wired through a switch for use as a backup for the RAM. With the core switch enabled, part of the contents of the RAM will be copied periodically into the core. In the event of power loss, the core will have the point record variables for the eight slots, since the core will not be erased; on power recovery, restarting the processor will restore the RAM from the core.

The DEP interface board (Fig. 9.8) has a 64 bit RAM which stores data to be DEP-displayed and data received from DEP switches. It provides communication between the microprocessor and the DEP, under program control.

The A/D multiplexer functions as the information buffer between the process and the controller. Under CPU control, the A/D selectively converts each of its 16 analog inputs (8 process variables and 8 remote variables) into 12 bit digital words. These data are transferred to the rest of the system by means of data bus lines. The A/D conversion technique utilized is the dual slope integration method. The dc input signal is integrated for a fixed time. At the end of this time, the output of the integrator linearly decreases at a fixed rate to a voltage reference level. The magnitude of the input voltage is directly proportional to the integration time required to decrease to this reference level.

The controller file contains two output boards. An output board interfaces the controller with its appropriate control elements and analog displays. It contains four identical circuits ("hold stations" in Fig. 9.9) which generate four 4 to 20 mA output currents and drive four analog displays. Data are stored within the hold station and converted to appropriate output signals for valve actuation, set point word, mode indication, and alarm status. The hold station has two modes of operation. One is loop manual

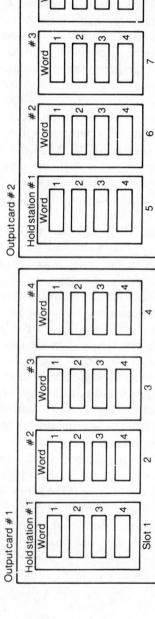

FIGURE 9.9. Output hold stations.

in which the valve signal is manually adjusted from a separate analog display and the processor is inhibited from writing into the valve location. The other is automatic, in which the valve signal is controlled by the processor. These modes are selected at the analog display and DEP, respectively.

The highway interface boards (Fig. 9.8) provide access employing DMA of the basic controller memory to the data highway and its devices. They perform highway message error checking and word format conversion, that is, serial to parallel.

Controller Program Flow

The controller file sampling interval is $\frac{1}{3}$ sec. This coincides with the A/D scan rate. Under normal operating conditions, every $\frac{1}{3}$ sec the DEP interface transmits, the A/D multiplexer card is serviced, the core memory card is serviced, the status word is generated, periodic checks are performed, and a diagnostic exercises all CPU instructions and registers. The controller program flowchart (Fig. 9.10) illustrates the file timing cycle.

Clear Routine.   A reset button at the DEP unit is used to start the controller on initial start-up, after a power interruption, after a function called a *watchdog timer* times out, or after a self-test failure. It has no effect on controller operation during normal running conditions. When the "reset" button is pressed, the controller starts a clear routine that clears various registers, initializes the A/D converter, and copies configuration information into the RAM from the core.

Periodic Checks.   Once every $\frac{1}{3}$ sec during normal operation, or if the "reset" button is pressed, the controller performs periodic software checks. Each A/D conversion is checked for completion within 30 msec. The zero and full scale voltages of 1 and 5 V dc are checked to 1% tolerance. A sense line from each hold station card indicating the presence of regulated power is checked. Also a read-after-write check is made after each write to a set point location in the hold station. A diagnostic exercises all instructions and registers. If this check fails, the CPU will stall and the watchdog timer will time out.

Slot Service.   During the time allotted to slot service, the machine services slots 1 to 8 in the following sequence:

1.   Convert *PV* or *RV* from analog to digital in A/D converter (*RV* is a remote analog variable such as the input to a cascaded controller).

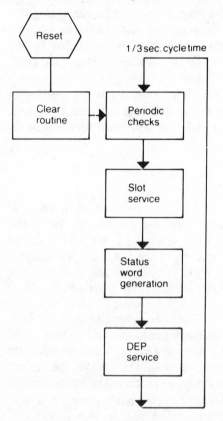

FIGURE 9.10. Controller program flow chart.

2. Store conversion result in the RAM *PV* location for this slot.
3. Execute algorithms for this slot.
4. Store result of algorithm in the RAM and in proper hold station.
5. Repeat steps 1 through 4 for the next slot in sequence.

DEP Service. During the time allotted for DEP service, the machine sends and receives data from the DEP.

Fault Indication. As a result of any hardware fault detected by the software, the processor will perform the following sequence:

1. Update the DMA-accessible status word.
2. Attempt to update the DEP display.
3. Stall until the watchdog timer times out.

Controller Signal Flow

Controller signal flow details can be summarized as follows (refer to Fig. 9.8):

The PV and RV input signals are wired to appropriate terminals at the terminal panel. The signals are multiplexed and converted to digital form. The converted values are square-rooted (if desired), filtered, and stored in the RAM.

The CPU performs selected mathematical computations on the process variables and produces a digital output signal which is transmitted to the proper hold station.

Programs for the CPU are stored in the ROM. The user selects the control equation and configures a loop via the DEP or over the data highway from an operator station. These process and configuration details are stored in the RAM.

The sections of the controller file memory containing process and configuration information are addressable by other units in a complex system over the data highway via the DMA port, which provides the necessary interface.

Communication between the internal components of the basic controller file is via a single, bidirectional bus. The bus consists of 40 wires on the back plane of the controller file which connects all the plug-in cards. They are divided into three categories: 16 data lines, 16 address lines, and 8 control lines. They are terminated at both ends to allow high speed signal transmission without distortions or echoes. Thirty-nine of the forty lines are bidirectional to permit signal flow in either direction, from any device to any other device. The unidirectional line is used to grant control of the bus to the highest priority device requesting it.

The DEP and Configuration

The DEP is essentially an operator interface with the basic controller and can be shared with as many as 16 controllers. It has two functions: configuration, and process parameter observation and control. The latter is the easiest to explain. The data are displayed on two four-digit-plus-sign light emitting diode (LED) indicators (with decimal point) built into the face of the unit (Fig. 9.11). The type of information and its range are shown in Table 9.1. Note that it includes control algorithm constants as well as I/O data. The display is chosen by means of the labeled keys. Since there are eight computing slots (loops) for each processor, an eight

TABLE 9.1. Operating Parameters of the DEP

Parameter Description	Selection Keys	Display Range	Display Resolution
Process variable, X input to algorithm in engineering units	None	Engineering units	Up to 1 in 10,000
or percent	%	-6.86 to $+99.99$ to $+106.9$	0.01
Remote variable analog input in engineering units	RV	Engineering units as process variable	Up to 1 in 10,000
or percent	RV-%	Range as process variable	0.01
Set point, Y input to algorithm in engineering units	SP	Engineering units as process variable	Up to 1 in 10,000
or percent	SP-%	Range as process variable	0.01
Valve signal or algorithm output in percent	VAL	-6.9 to $+106.9$	0.1
Deviation $(X - Y)$ in engineering units	DEV	Engineering units as process variable	Up to 1 in 10,000
or percent	DEV-%	-113.7 to 0.00 to $+113.7$	0.01
PV alarm limits in engineering units	SP-HI/ SP-LO	Engineering units as process variable	Up to 1 in 10,000
or percent	SP-HI-%/ SP-LO-%	Range as process variable	0.01
Deviation alarm limits in percent	DEV-HI DEV-LO	$+0.00$ to $+106.9$ $+0.00$ to -113.7	0.01 0.01
Ratio coefficient of PID ratio algorithm	RATIO	$+0.100$ to $+9.999$	0.001
Bias coefficient of PID ratio algorithm and automatic-manual station in percent	BIAS	-99.99 to $+99.99$	0.01

Description	Mnemonic	Range	Resolution
K, controller gain; 0.00 indicates no gain action	GAIN	$+0.10$ to $+99.99$	0.01
K_A, auxiliary scaling coefficient on Y input	GAIN	-9.999 to $+9.999$	0.001
T_1, reset in minutes for PID algorithms; 0.0 (infinity) indicates no action	T1	$+0.01$ to $+91.02$	Permitted values computed by $182.03/N$ $N = 2, 3, \ldots$
T_2, rate in minutes for PID algorithm; 0.00 indicates no action	T2	$+0.04$ to $+97.04$	Permitted values computed by $1456.4/N -$ 0.04; $N = 15, 16, \ldots$
T_D, digital filter time constant in minutes	TD	$+0.00$ to $+91.02$	Permitted values computed by $182.03/N -$ 0.0056; $N = 2, 3, \ldots$
0%, zero scale engineering units	0%	Engineering units	Up to 1 in 10,000 (or 1 DEG for T/C)
100%, full scale engineering units	100%	Engineering units	Up to 1 in 10,000 (or 1 DEG for T/C)
Valve output limits in percent	VAL-HI/ VAL-LO	-5.0 to $+105.0$	0.1
Reset limits in percent output	TI-HI/ TI-LO	-6.9 to $+106.9$	0.1

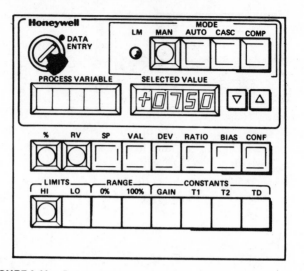

FIGURE 9.11.   Data entry panel (Honeywell TDC 2000 controller).

point selector switch unit (shown at the right in Fig. 9.6) is needed to choose which slot is to be displayed. Sixteen of these switch units can be combined with one DEP for a total of 128 slots.

Direct control of the controller mode by the operator through the DEP is possible. Four modes can be selected by pushbutton. These are automatic (normal controller action), cascade (see Fig. 9.13), manual, and computer. In the computer mode an, external processor can either place the output value in the hold station or insert a set point into the microprocessor algorithm. When the manual mode is selected, the operator can raise or lower the slot output to the valve by means of two incrementing "raise" and "lower" buttons. This output is shown by one of the LED displays.

Configuration requires somewhat more complex manipulation but need only be done at infrequent intervals, such as when changing the control strategy or starting up the plant. Basically, configuration is the selection of one of 28 control or calculation algorithms for every slot, and the interconnection of slots and wired analog inputs.

Configuration is accomplished by using the same keyboard and LED display to insert a *configuration word* into the processor memory. The word consists of 16 octal numbers displayed in four 4-number segments (Fig. 9.12). For example, the first two numbers of the first segment represent the choice of control algorithms, from 00 to 37 (octal). The fifth

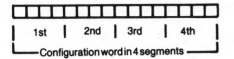

FIGURE 9.12.   Controller configuration word.

digit (in the second segment) determines the address of the X (process variable) input in terms of memory blocks (Fig. 9.8) 1 through 8.

Likewise, the sixth digit determines the type of X input, whether an output, a process variable, a remote variable, or a local set point derived from the DEP. In a similar manner, the seventh and eighth digits specify the Y (set point) input. Alarms, limits, and other parameters are inserted in the same way until the complete word is built up.

The advantage of this form of configuration is that any block input or output can be connected to any other (within the same controller file) with no change in external wiring. Consequently, a multicontroller interconnected control strategy such as a cascade (Fig. 9.13) is easily put together or changed to another arrangement. Since cascade controllers are difficult to start into operation, it is convenient with this arrangement to initiate each loop separately and connect them together after they reach equilibrium.

Initialization and *PV* Tracking Configuration Options.   The capability of electronically switching all the data belonging to several control loops or computing blocks under the control of a single microprocessor yields additional advantages. One of these is the ability to automate the above-mentioned and sometimes delicate problem of starting a cascade system without introducing a sudden command change or bump in the process while switching modes. The cascade pictured in Fig. 9.13 consists of two controllers; the output of the primary or outer loop is the input (*SP*) to the secondary or minor loop.

To make the example concrete, consider the outer loop the automatic temperature control for a chemical reactor and the minor loop the control for cooling water in the jacket surrounding the reactor. In other words, the reactor temperature is controlled indirectly by adjusting the flow of cooling water, which flow is protected from external disturbances, such as water pressure fluctuations, by its own control loop. Since the inner loop reacts much faster to these disturbances than the unaided outer loop (which must wait for a pressure fluctuation to be reflected in terms of temperature change before sensing an error), the two-loop cascade system is a very valuable control strategy.

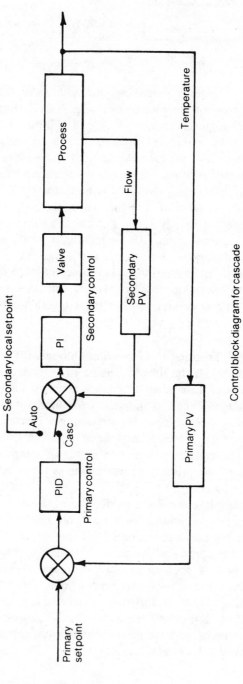

Control block diagram for cascade

FIGURE 9.13. Control block diagram for cascade.

Returning to the initialization problem, let us assume that the two loops are decoupled (not in cascade) and under manual or open loop control, and also that the reactor temperature is observed to be approximately correct when the cooling water valve has been manually set to some point. In order to put the system into fully automatic operation, the following steps must be taken by the operator:

1.   The input (*SP*) of the secondary loop is adjusted to equal the actual flow measured (*PV*).

2.   The secondary loop is closed by switching the controller to "auto." Since the error, the difference between *SP* and *PV*, is now zero, the flow output will remain steady.

3.   The primary output is balanced to equal the secondary *SP*.

4.   The cascade is readied by switching the secondary to cascade.

5.   The primary loop is closed by switching to "auto." The system is now in the automatic and cascade modes.

As can be seen, there are numerous places for error in balancing, which may cause switching transients and upset the process. Initialization automatically balances the slot outputs and permits a transfer from the manual, automatic, or computer mode to the cascade mode without bumping the process. The method of accomplishing this within the eight slots controlled by one microprocessor is seen in Fig. 9.14. First, the microprocessor initialization program must be selected for the secondary slot, using the fourth digit of the configuration word, which gives a choice of initialization, *PV* tracking, both, or neither for every slot.

When initialization is configured for the secondary slot and it is in the manual, automatic, or computer mode, the set point value of the secondary is automatically stored in the output location of the primary (i.e., the primary's output is back-calculated by the processor program to equal the secondary's set point). Transferring the secondary to the cascade mode, then, is bumpless and balance-free. This accomplishes steps 3 and 4 above.

The *PV* tracking option completes automatic balancing of the system. In this mode, the set point automatically tracks the process variable when the slot mode is manual or when the back-calculation process of initialization is taking place. *PV* tracking permits the slot to be switched from manual to automatic without bumping. This eliminates the need for operator adjustment of *SP* in step 1. The start-up is now completely automatic except for the transfer to the cascade mode.

With the automated system, the primary and secondary loops are set in the automatic and manual modes, respectively. The secondary output is

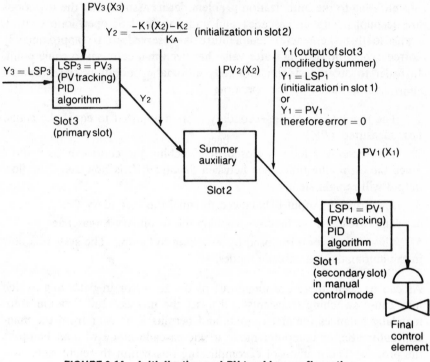

FIGURE 9.14.   Initialization and PV tracking configuration.

again manipulated by the operator until the primary *PV* has reached the desired value. The following steps take place:

1.   The secondary *SP* automatically equals the secondary *PV*, because of *PV* tracking.

2.   The secondary is switched to the cascade mode.

3.   The primary output automatically equals the secondary *SP*, because of initialization.

4.   The primary *SP* automatically equals the primary *PV*, because of *PV* tracking in the intialization manual mode.

Algorithms.   The control algorithms available by configuration of the TDC 2000 controller are listed in Table 9.2. Note that several more can be added (octal 15 through 17 and 27) without altering the configuration scheme, however, at the cost of more memory. Also, the listed algorithms can be changed to any others at the price of requiring new ROM programming.

The algorithms are divided into two classes: *control* or *floating* algorithms, which contain dynamic terms and are responsive to an error signal, and *auxiliary* or *computing* algorithms, which are purely algebraic in nature. In addition, there is a data acquisition choice (00) which merely stores and displays the value of the two inputs (PV and RV) and provides manual control and alarms. Many of the algorithm functions are obvious from their names, and others have been discussed earlier in this text, however, special features are explained below.

The PID algorithm (Fig. 9.15) was discussed in earlier chapters, except for the A/B equation choice, which is selected during configuration. The B equation limits action to integral only on Y or SP inputs, and thus produces a smoother output transition when the SP command is suddenly changed (as in batch operations). In this equation, PV changes continue to elicit proportional and derivative action.

Figure 9.16 shows the PID ratio algorithm which multiplies the normal Y input by a constant R and adds a bias to produce the SP:

$$SP = YR + B$$

Automatic ratio and automatic bias are variations which differ in their initialization requirements.

Computer-manual-automatic (CMA) and computer-manual (CM) modes permit an external computer to enter a calculated valve output directly through the DMA (via the data highway) into the controller output memory. They differ in their response to a "shed" signal (given on computer failure)—CMA reverts to the automatic (or cascade) mode, and CM returns to the manual mode. PID SPC allows the external (supervisory) computer to insert an SP command into the controller, which behaves like a normal PID controller otherwise.

Code 10 (error square on gain) is a variation in which the overall gain constant of the PID equation is multiplied by a normalized absolute value of error. This results in a nonlinear response in which the effective gain is greater with large errors and less with small ones. Algorithm 11 is similar, except that the normalized absolute error factor operates only on the integral term.

PID gap introduces a dead band (gap) in the PID algorithm, such that a new output is computed only if the error is outside the gap limits (Fig. 9.17). The computed error E_{cn} remains constant between limits and equals the true error otherwise.

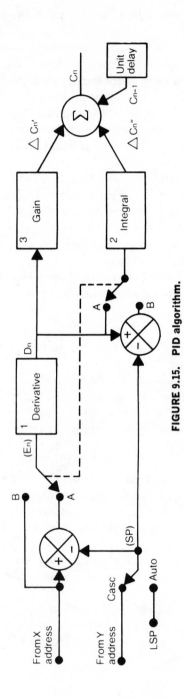

FIGURE 9.15. PID algorithm.

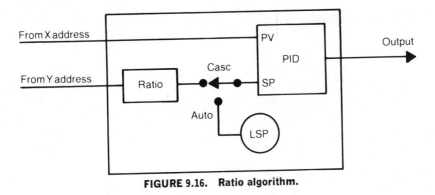

FIGURE 9.16.   Ratio algorithm.

The derivation of the lead-lag function code 20 in Table 9.2 has been discussed in Chapter 6. It provides lead-lag dynamic compensation of the form

$$\frac{\text{Output}}{\text{Input}} = K \left(\frac{T_2 S + 1}{T_1 S + 1} \right)$$

where K = gain constant
$\quad T_1$ = lag time constant (min)
$\quad T_2$ = lead time constant (min)
$\quad T_s$ = sampling time (see below)
$\quad S$ = Laplace variable

This algorithm has only one input, namely, X (Fig. 9.18).
The equivalent difference equation is

$$D_n = D_{n-1} + \frac{T_s}{T_1 + T_s} (X \text{ signal} - D_{n-1})$$

$$C_n' = \frac{T_2}{T_s} (D_n - D_{n-1}) + D_n$$

$$C_n = K C_n'$$

The override selectors codes 21 and 22 will choose the highest (or lowest) of eight possible inputs, which may be:

1.   The output of any slot
2.   Remote set points of any slot

The low and high selectors perform the same service for two (X and Y) inputs; that is, they will output the highest (or lowest) of the two.

TABLE 9.2. Controller Algorithms (TDC 2000)

Algorithm Configuration Code	Algorithm
00	Data acquisition
01	PID normal
02	PID ratio
03	PID automatic ratio
04	PID automatic bias
05	PID CMA
06	PID CM
07	PID SPC
10	PID error square on gain
11	PID error square on integral
12	PID gap
13	PD with 50% bias
14	PD with 50% bias (CMA)
20	Lead-lag
	Auxiliary with free manual access (FMA)
21	Override high selector
22	Override low selector
23	Summer
24	Multiplier
25	Automatic-manual station
26	Switch
	Auxiliary with restricted manual access (RMA)
30	Summer
31	Multiplier
32	Divider
33	Square root
34	Square root of the XY product
35	Sum of square roots
36	High selector
37	Low selector

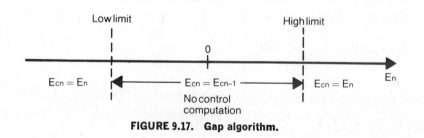

FIGURE 9.17. Gap algorithm.

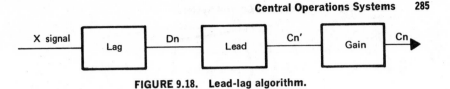

FIGURE 9.18. Lead-lag algorithm.

The function of the other algebraic algorithms—summer, multiplier, divider, square root—are more or less as they appear to be. Some of these may be secured with a key lock switch so that they are protected against unauthorized change.

Central Operations Systems

A more advanced distributed microprocessor system can perform all the basic functions described for the controller but possesses, in addition, the capability for central operation—all loop variables can be displayed and manipulated from a single console. It is oriented toward unit and plant control through enhancement of the operator's capability. It includes the following additional modules

> Operator station
> Data highway and traffic director
> Process interface or analog units

The central operations concept revolves around the operator station, a desk-sized CRT console bringing to the seated operator selective displays of the plant state under control of operator keyboard pushbuttons (Fig. 9.19). The same keyboard permits the operator to examine the detail of any loop or group of process variables, to alter set points, outputs, controller algorithms and parameters, operating modes, or to reconfigure cascades and interacting loops. Operator stations can connect to one or more data highways and communicate with the devices on each one. The operator station has a standard set of selective displays which include the following (see Fig. 9.20):

Overview   A "patterned" analog display showing the deviation from the target of up to 288 variables, arranged in addressable groups of eight loops.

Group   Any group can be examined in detail at the same or another CRT, in a display that provides an analog (bar graph) pic-

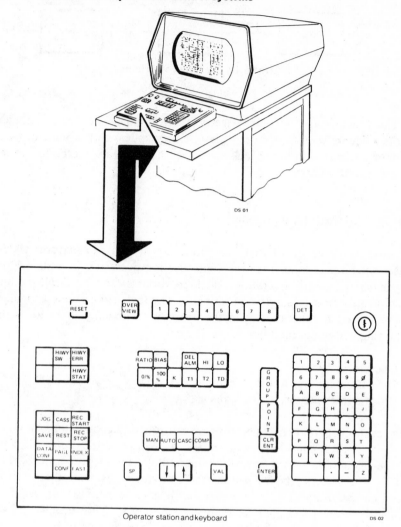

Operator station and keyboard

FIGURE 9.19.   Operator station and keyboard.

ture of the *PV,* set point, and output (if a control loop), plus alphanumeric data identifying and digitizing the variables of each loop. Set point control modes can be altered by the operator with this display.

Detail   Detail parameters and configuration of each loop can be monitored and manipulated for a single loop from this analog and alphanumeric display.

The operator station module is an "intelligent" CRT terminal driven by its own ROM-programmed microprocessor. It is therefore a stand-alone device not dependent on a host computer. It brings together all the perceptual and manipulative requirements required to recognize plant state changes, fine-tune units, and respond to upsets or emergencies.

From the overview display of 36 groups (or any other configured group of eight loops), the operator can select one by name, using the keyboard for group display (Fig. 9.20b); this puts alphanumeric information (such as the *SP* or *PV* in engineering units) on the screen, as well as expanded bar graphs. Using one of eight dedicated pushbuttons, he can further select a display showing detail and configuration parameters for a single loop (Fig. 9.20c).

Operator Keyboard. The keyboard (see Fig. 9.19) allows the operator to react to the process information so displayed. Its alphanumeric keyboard and dedicated pushbuttons are arranged to facilitate its basic functions: display call-up, loop parameter control, configuration, and special functions associated with the data highway and peripheral equipment. As in the controller, he can display any data, but certain functions, such as controller configuration, are protected by a key lock switch. Control modes, such as automatic, cascade, and computer, can be selected from the keyboard. If the manual mode is selected, valves can be remotely controlled by "raise" and "lower" buttons and the degree of valve opening observed on the detail or group bar graphs. The "raise" and "lower" pair can also be used to alter the set point, or a completely new value can be entered through the numeric keys.

Essentially, the operator station duplicates remotely the local functions of the DEP, but with the addition of an alphanumeric CRT presentation. Although the operator station function is a very interesting microprocessor application, its program details are too advanced to detail in this volume.

Security and Control of Data Highway Traffic. Since the operator station and control operations are dependent on the functioning of the data highway, design features must be incorporated to reduce the probability of failure to a negligibly small amount.

The data highway employs serial digital data transmission rather than parallel, as it is more simply and reliably isolated from the noisy industrial environment encountered when transmitting process data over long distances. Dual (backup) cables are used for redundancy and security. Each cable has separate electronic interfaces with each connected device for greater reliability. A highway subsystem can consist of three branches, each up to 5000 ft long, and may connect 63 controllers or other devices, limited to 28 to a branch.

Highways may include more than one operator station; thus a large amount of redundancy and reliability can be built into the system. Each unit is merely "hung on" to the highway (via a standard interface), and every message is transmitted to all units on the highway—only those that are addressed responding. Thus failure of any unit does not affect any

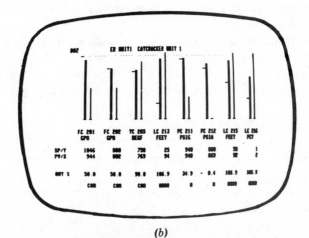

FIGURE 9.20.   Microprocessor-controlled displays for process control central operation (Honeywell TDC 2000). (a) Overview. (b) Group display. (c) Loop detail.

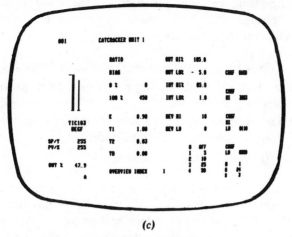

(c)

FIGURE 9.20. *(Continued).*

other unit. Certain units, including the operator station, have preferred access to the highway through the HTD. Preferred access gives the favored unit immediate use of the communication channel over the claims of other devices, for example, in the event the operator wishes to switch to manual control. The HTD has other important functions. These include:

Repeats. Repeating a message originated by one device on all branches of the highway.

Polls and call-ups. Querying process interface units as to messages at intervals not preempted by preferred devices.

Priority. Assigning message priority to each device.

Redundancy. Each HTD has two functional directors which are connected to single or redundant cables for each branch.

Switchover. Directors and cables are switched automatically at the command of a preferred device (operator station), or manually at the HTD.

The bits traveling on the highway are alternate polarity 0.6 V signals transmitted at a 250K Hz bit rate or 124 μsec for a 31 bit word. Interface with each device on the highway is through special boards carrying the necessary counters, registers, and logic to recognize addresses, check parity codes, and convert between serial and parallel memory words (which is necessary since processors use parallel data input to memory).

Devices originating and receiving messages, including the operator station, basic controller, PIU, and computers, perform numerous checks to test the accuracy of the data. These include:

Bit logic.   Each bit must contain one positive and one negative pulse.

BCH code.   Five extra bits are appended to each word to detect and reject noise or other errors.

Echo.   Each message written by one device into another's memory must be repeated by the receiving device.

Bit count.   A count is made on each word.

In the event that an error is found, an indication will show on the operator station keyboard. Pushing a lighted button will then produce a diagnostic display on the CRT (Fig. 9.21), which will reveal the type of error and its location and sequence on the highway. (A display also permits the operator to configure the highway, assigning each device to a six bit "box" number in the station data base, which determines its sequence within its priority class.)

Systems with Higher Level Computers

At still higher levels of automation, such as supervisory or DDC control for unit and plant optimization, or for special logs, displays, computations, and peripherals, it is necessary to incorporate computers possessing more power and memory and a more global data base than that of a microprocessor.

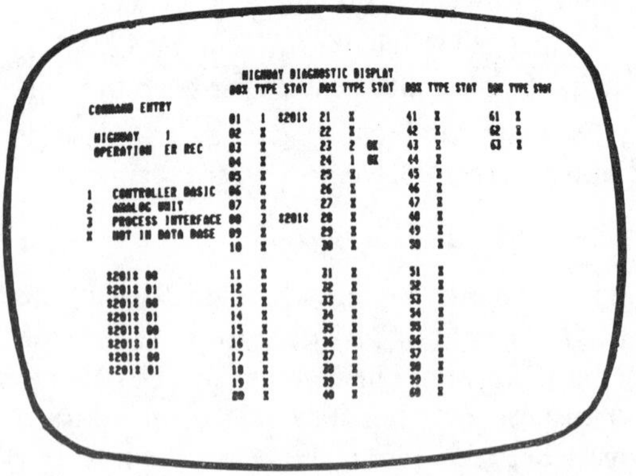

FIGURE 9.21.   Data highway error diagnostic display.

A higher level computer communicates with the microprocessor modules through the data highway. It thereby can access and alter the distributed data base of the controllers to ascertain the status of each loop for data acquisition or directly to control the set points or outputs for supervisory and DDC operation. Thus optimization routines available with the computers can be applied to the controller units or plant. Control can be monitored and modes altered through an operations center utilizing various forms of computer video displays. The process I/O function is accomplished by the controllers or the process interface units.

Ideally, the process control computer acting through the microprocessor system is able to make all necessary reports and decisions anticipated by the designers; the operator, through an operating center console, observes, monitors, and intervenes only when unforseeable inputs are required.

Higher level computers require a highway interface. This serves to tie the data highway into the computer I/O bus lines and to convert the serial 31-bit highway data format to the parallel bit word structure and driver voltage levels of the computer.

Figure 9.22 illustrates a typical computer–TDC 2000 system. This system is capable of an expanded range of control tasks, including:

Data acquisition
Data base building and maintenance
Configuration and reconfiguration of the data highway and controllers
  from the console
Control—DDC and supervisory
Digital and sequencing control
Optimizing and model calculations
Overview, group, detail CRT displays
Maintenance and status displays
Plant graphics and flowcharts
Operator mode switching and manual control from the console
On-line computed variables
Monitoring TDC parameter changes made by the operator
Alarms (CRT, audible, annunicator)
Routine logs
Histories (alarm and log)
Special formatted logs
Background calculation
Laboratory data, using on-line data
Program development
Engineers' interface

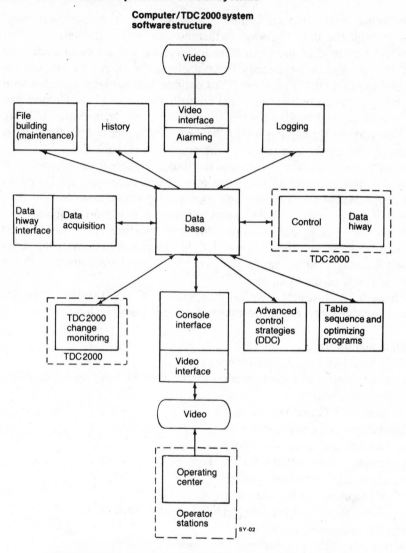

FIGURE 9.22.   Computer/TDC 2000 system software structure.

In this type of system, the synergy promoted by the distributed multi-micro-processor combined with its larger counterpart ensure that the necessary computing and data handling effectiveness is available at minimum overall cost. This scheme, then, points the way to the solution of many problems of the "automatic factory" that have proved so intractible to brute force, high powered computers in the past.

References

1. W. B. Barket, "A Multiprocessor Design," Doctoral Thesis, Harvard University, Report 2136, Bolt, Beranek, and Newman, Boston, Mass., Oct. 1975. Published as AD/A-018 341 under ARPA/DOD contracts DAHC15-69-C-0147 and others.

2. C. A. Wiatrowski and C. R. Teeple, *Instrum. Control Syst.* **49**(3) 37–41 (Mar. 1976).

3. J. M. Watson, *Chem. Eng.* (London) **54** 167–170 (March 1976).

4. *Guidelines for the Design of Man/Machine Interfaces for Process Control*, International Purdue Workshop on Industrial Computer Systems, Purdue University, Lafayette, Ind., Oct. 1975.

5. W. W. Peterson, *Error Correcting Codes*, John Wiley, New York, 1961.

6. IEEE Standard 472-1974 (ANSI C37.90a-1974), IEEE Standards Office, New York, N. Y. (1974).

7. R. J. Bibbero, "Analysis of Data Highway Loading by Simulation," Paper no. 540, Proceedings of the ISA International Conference, Houston, Texas, Oct. 10–14, 1976.

8. Extracted from Technical Data Sheets, TDC 2000, Honeywell Inc., Ft. Washington, Pa., by permission of Honeywell Inc.

9. L. B. Evans, *Science* **195**(4283) 1146–1151 (1977).

10. R. Dallimonti, "New Designs for Process Control Consoles," paper presented at ISA International Conference, Houston, Texas (1973).

Index